SMITH'S REVIEW
LEGAL GEM SERIES
LABOR LAW
AND
EMPLOYMENT DISCRIMINATION

For LAW SCHOOL, BAR and COLLEGE
EXAMINATIONS

Second Edition

By

MYRON G. HILL, Jr.
Member of District of Columbia, Ohio
and U. S. Supreme Court Bars

HOWARD M. ROSSEN
Director, Ohio Bar Review and Writing Seminar
Member of Ohio, District of Columbia, Florida, Pennsylvania
and U. S. Supreme Court Bars

and

WILTON S. SOGG
Adjunct Professor of Law, Cleveland-Marshall
College of Law, Cleveland State University
Lecturer on Law, Harvard Law School
Member of Ohio, District of Columbia, Florida
U. S. Tax Court and U. S. Supreme Court Bars

WEST PUBLISHING CO.
ST. PAUL, MINN.
1980

COPYRIGHT © 1971 By WEST PUBLISHING CO.
COPYRIGHT © 1980 By WEST PUBLISHING CO.
All rights reserved
Printed in the United States of America

Library of Congress Cataloging in Publication Data

Smith, Chester Howard, 1893–1964.
    Smith's Review of labor law and employment discrimination.
    (Legal gem series)
    Includes index.
    1. Labor laws and legislation—United States—Outlines, syllabi, etc. I. Hill, Myron G., 1936– II. Rossen, Howard M., 1936– III. Sogg, Wilton S., 1935– IV. Title. V. Title: Review of labor law and employment discrimination.
KF3369.5.S57   1980   344'.73'01   79–23934

ISBN 0-8299-2069-2

Smith's Review of Labor Law 2d Ed.

TO
MY PARENTS
Myron and Marian Hill

*

PREFACE

Since the last edition of this Review was published, Labor Law has undergone many additional significant changes and important developments. The authors have broadened the scope of this review to include most aspects of employment discrimination. In this revised volume the authors have attempted to organize and put into perspective the basic materials for the course in Labor Law as it is taught in law schools today. In addition, the authors have attempted to structure the material with an eye to the pragmatic, so that practitioners as well as students will find the volume useful.

The authors have made use of the CAVEAT and NOTE throughout, to alert the reader to important areas of difficulty, change and development.

This Review contains several CHARTS, which are designed to put the entire subject matter of this volume into perspective.

The Index contains Tables of References to federal statutory labor law. The Table of Cases lists cases under both the name of the employer and of the union.

The authors express their most sincere appreciation to F. D. Motil, Attorney, Cleveland, Ohio and Frank J. Tuk, Esquire, Lecturer at Law, Temple University School of Law for their many significant and helpful suggestions in the revision and editing of the text of this volume.

Apart from the cases cited, the citations in this Review are as follows: "CCH" refers to Commerce Clearing House, Inc. Labor Law Course, 24th Edition, 1979; "Cox" refers to Archibald Cox, Derek Curtis Bok and Robert A. Gorman, Cases and Materials on Labor Law, Eighth Edition, by The Foundation Press, Inc., 1977; "Smith" refers to Russell A. Smith, Leroy S. Merrifield and Theodore J. St. Antoine, Labor Relations Law, Cases and Materials, Fifth Edition, 1974; The Bobbs-Merrill Company; and "Gorman" refers to Robert A. Gorman's Labor Law, Unionization and Collective Bargaining, 1976 by West Publishing Company.

MYRON G. HILL, JR.

HOWARD M. ROSSEN

WILTON S. SOGG

Washington, D.C.,
Cleveland, Ohio
November, 1979

SUMMARY OF CONTENTS

		Page
Outline		XVII
I.	INTRODUCTION AND ANALYSIS	1
II.	TERMINOLOGY USED IN LABOR RELATIONS	7
III.	THE DEVELOPMENT OF LABOR LEGISLATION	14
IV.	PROCEDURE AND REMEDIES	29
V.	EMPLOYER UNFAIR LABOR PRACTICES	32
VI.	GOOD FAITH BARGAINING	59
VII.	THE COLLECTIVE BARGAINING AGREEMENT	80
VIII.	PUBLIC SECTOR BARGAINING	97
IX.	UNION UNFAIR LABOR PRACTICES	104
X.	PICKETING AND BOYCOTTS	125
XI.	OTHER RIGHTS OF EMPLOYEES	153
XII.	REPRESENTATION PROCEEDINGS	170
XIII.	OTHER LAWS GOVERNING LABOR RELATIONS	187
Table of Cases		217
Table of Federal Statutes		223
Table of Statutory References		225
Index		227

*

TABLE OF CONTENTS

		Page
	OUTLINE	XVII
I.	INTRODUCTION AND ANALYSIS	1
	Legal Gems—Labor Law—Introduction	1
	Legal Gems—Analysis of a Labor Law Problem	5
II.	TERMINOLOGY USED IN LABOR RELATIONS	7
III.	THE DEVELOPMENT OF LABOR LEGISLATION	14
	Legal Gems—Development of Labor Legislation—Introduction	14
	Legal Gems—Common Law Decisions Unfavorable to Labor	14
	Legal Gems—Antitrust Acts Used Against Labor	16
	Legal Gems—The Railway Labor Act of 1926 Protects Right to Organize	18
	Legal Gems—Norris-LaGuardia Act of 1932 Favors Organized Labor	19
	Case 1—strike not a criminal conspiracy—antitrust acts interpreted	21
	Case 2—injunction proper for breach of no-strike clause where grievance subject to arbitration	21
	Case 3—union agreement restraining competition without futhering federal labor policy subject to antitrust laws	22
	Legal Gems—The National Labor Relations Act of 1935 (Wagner Act)	24
	Case 4—Wagner Act Constitutional under Interstate Commerce Clause	25
	Legal Gems—The Labor-Management Relations Act of 1947 (Taft-Hartley Act)	27
	Legal Gems—Labor-Management Reporting and Disclosure Act of 1959 (Landrum-Griffin Act)	28
IV.	PROCEDURE AND REMEDIES	29
	Legal Gems—Procedure and Remedies—Introduction	29
	Legal Gems—Procedure Before NLRB in Unfair Labor Practice Cases	29
	Legal Gems—The Board and Its Remedies	30
	Legal Gems—Remedies—Computation of Back Pay	31
V.	EMPLOYER UNFAIR LABOR PRACTICES	32
	Legal Gems—Employer Unfair Labor Practices—Introduction	32
	Legal Gems—Rights of Employees—Section 8(a)(1) Violations	33
	Case 5—section 8(a)(1) prohibits benefits to influence union activity	36

Smith's Review of Labor Law 2d Ed.

TABLE OF CONTENTS

V. **EMPLOYER UNFAIR LABOR PRACTICES**—Continued   Page
    Legal Gems—Discharge for Concerted Activities _____ 36
        Case 6—discharge without anti-union motivation held unlawful _____ 39
        Case 7—employee entitled to union representation at investigative interview _____ 40
    Legal Gems—Communications Among Employees—No-Solicitation and No-Distribution Rules _____ 41
        Case 8—prohibitions of union activities in the plant—the rules and exceptions _____ 44
    Legal Gems—Discrimination Based on Race, Color, Religion, Sex or National Origin _____ 44
    Legal Gems—Domination or Assistance of Union _____ 45
    Legal Gems—Remedies for Domination or Assistance _____ 46
        Case 9—competing unions—employer recognition prohibited _____ 47
        Case 10—recognition of minority union violates Section 8(a)(2)—good faith no defense _____ 47
    Legal Gems—Discrimination for Union Activities—Section 8(a)(3) and (4) _____ 48
        Case 11—discharge for union activities unlawful _____ 49
        Case 12—discrimination regarding the hiring of employees unlawful _____ 49
    Legal Gems—Rights of Strikers _____ 50
        Case 13—withholding of benefits to striking employees to which they were entitled held unlawful _____ 53
        Case 14—replacement of economic strikers—may not discriminate against union supporters _____ 54
        Case 15—limitation on strikes in contract and Act not applicable to unfair labor practice strikes _____ 55
    Legal Gems—Temporary or Permanent Plant Closing _____ 56
        Case 16—employer may lockout employees after impasse _____ 56
        Case 17—discriminatory closing of entire business lawful _____ 58

VI. **GOOD FAITH BARGAINING** _____ 59
    Legal Gems—Good Faith Bargaining—Introduction _____ 59
    Legal Gems—The Concept of Good Faith Bargaining _____ 59
        Case 18—insisting on clause giving employer great control over employment terms not unlawful per se _____ 61
        Case 19—bad faith bargaining shown by course of conduct _____ 62
    Legal Gems—Obligations Arising During Collective Bargaining _____ 64
        Case 20—employer required to show financial records if ability to pay at issue _____ 64
        Case 21—employer not required to show financial records if ability to pay is not at issue _____ 65
        Case 22—unilateral change in employment terms of employer during negotiations held unlawful _____ 66

TABLE OF CONTENTS

VI. GOOD FAITH BARGAINING—Continued
Page

Legal Gems—Obtaining Bargaining Rights 66
    Case 23—obtaining bargaining rights without an election after substantial employer violations 67
    Case 24—employer's right to insist on NLRB election under the Act 69

Legal Gems—The Employer's Bargaining Obligation 70
    Case 25—individual employee privileges subservient to collective interests under Act's scheme of collective bargaining 71
    Case 26—duration of a bargaining order 71
    Case 27—board cannot require parties to agree to a specific contract clause 72

Legal Gems—Subjects for Bargaining 73
    Case 28—party may not insist permissive bargaining subjects be included in contract 77
    Case 29—subcontracting as a mandatory subject of bargaining 77

Legal Gems—Collective Bargaining—Rights of Individual Employees 78
    Case 30—no duty to bargain with subgroup of employees who are represented by union 79

VII. THE COLLECTIVE BARGAINING AGREEMENT 80

Legal Gems—The Collective Bargaining Agreement—Introduction 80

Legal Gems—The Collective Bargaining Agreement—Typical Clauses 80

Legal Gems—Duties During Contract Period of the Agreement 83
    Case 31—wage re-opening clause limits employer's duty to bargain 84
    Case 32—bargaining required when jobs are eliminated 84

Legal Gems—Enforcement of a Collective Bargaining Agreement 85
    Case 33—court may compel arbitration of grievance 86
    Case 34—court favors arbitration of disputes 86
    Case 35—court will not review arbitrator's decision on merits 87
    Case 36—federal law prevails over state law in resolving dispute under collective bargaining agreement 87

Legal Gems—Obligations of Successor Employers 88
    Case 37—duty to arbitrate may survive merger and bind successor 89
    Case 38—successor has duty to recognize union if majority of work force unchanged 90
    Case 39—successor has no duty to recognize union if work force substantially changed 92

TABLE OF CONTENTS

VII. THE COLLECTIVE BARGAINING AGREEMENT—Continued

	Page
Legal Gems—The NLRB and Arbitration Proceedings	94
Case 40—arbitration award binding on parties	96

VIII. PUBLIC SECTOR BARGAINING ... 97

Legal Gems—Public Sector Bargaining—Introduction	97
Legal Gems—Collective Bargaining in the Federal Government	98
Legal Gems—Labor Relations Under State Laws	100
Legal Gems—Representation Elections in the States	101
Legal Gems—Collective Bargaining Agreements for State Employees	101
Legal Gems—State Labor Relations—Unfair Labor Practices	102

IX. UNION UNFAIR LABOR PRACTICES ... 104

Legal Gems—Union Unfair Labor Practices—Introduction	104
Legal Gems—Section 8(b)(1)(A)—Restraint or Coercion of Employees	105
Case 41—union responsible for picket line misconduct	106
Legal Gems—Union's Duty to Represent Employees in the Bargaining Unit	107
Case 42—duty to represent all employees in bargaining unit fairly	108
Case 43—union's duty to bargaining unit employees—differing views of court and Board	108
Case 44—failure to process grievance in good faith violates Section 8(b)(1)(A)	109
Legal Gems—Section 8(b)(1)(A)—Union's Right to Govern Its Internal Affairs	110
Case 45—union may fine members for crossing picket line	112
Case 46—NLRB lacks authority to determine reasonableness of otherwise valid union discipline	113
Case 47—union may not limit employees' right to utilize Board's processes	114
Case 48—union may expel member to protect itself	114
Legal Gems—Section 8(b)(1)(B)—Restraint or Coercion of Employer by Union	115
Case 49—supervisor-members subject to discipline by union for crossing picket line	116
Legal Gems—Section 8(b)(2)—Discharges Caused by Unions	117
Case 50—exclusive hiring hall requires employer to hire all employees through hall	117
Legal Gems—Remedies for Union Unfair Labor Practices	119
Legal Gems—Section 8(b)(3)—Union's Duty to Bargain	119
Case 51—unlawful conduct during negotiations does not mean that union bargained in bad faith	120

TABLE OF CONTENTS

IX. UNION UNFAIR LABOR PRACTICES—Continued

Page

Legal Gems—Section 8(b)(5)—Discriminatory or Excessive Union Initiation Fees 121

Legal Gems—Section 8(b)(6)—Featherbedding—Payment for Work Not Performed 122

    Case 52—full payment for minor services is not featherbedding 123

Legal Gems—Section 8(g)—Strikes Against Health Care Institutions 123

X. PICKETING AND BOYCOTTS 125

Legal Gems—Picketing and Boycotts—Introduction 125

Legal Gems—Constitutionality of State Laws Regulating Picketing 127

    Case 53—broad statute prohibiting all picketing unconstitutional 128

    Case 54—right to picket on private property in shopping mall explained 128

Legal Gems—Circumstances Where Recognition Picketing is Prohibited 129

    Case 55—publicity picketing permitted even if the ultimate object is recognition 131

    Case 56—failure to file petition within thirty days is not excused by filing an unfair labor practice charge 132

Legal Gems—Legal Restrictions on Secondary Boycotts 133

    Case 57—strike against general contractor to force him to stop doing business with subcontractor is secondary boycott 136

    Case 58—picketing prohibited at gate reserved for neutral employers 137

    Case 59—picketing of neutral employer permitted when primary employer is working there 138

Legal Gems—Secondary Boycotts—Ally Doctrine 139

Legal Gems—Other Elements of Secondary Boycott 140

    Case 60—request to neutral employers not to handle certain goods is lawful 141

    Case 61—peaceful publicity picketing which specifies struck product permitted at business of a neutral employer 142

    Case 62—defenses to charge of unlawful secondary activity analyzed 143

Legal Gems—Section 8(e)—Hot Cargo Clauses Unlawful 146

    Case 63—union may recapture lost work 148

Legal Gems—Sections 8(b)(4)(D) and 10(k)—Jurisdictional Disputes 149

    Case 64—board must consider all relevant factors in resolving jurisdictional disputes 151

TABLE OF CONTENTS

		Page
XI.	**OTHER RIGHTS OF EMPLOYEES**	153
	Legal Gems—Other Rights of Employees—Introduction	153
	Legal Gems—Employee's Right to Sue on His Own Behalf	153
	Case 65—bargaining agent must represent all employees fairly	155
	Case 66—employees may sue union under section 301 for a violation of duty under contract	156
	Case 67—no federal preemption of employee's right to sue union for arbitrary and capricious conduct under contract	157
	Legal Gems—Rights Under Landrum-Griffin Act	158
	Case 68—union officers may be summarily removed from office	162
	Case 69—member may not sue for Title IV violation	163
	Case 70—no absolute duty to exhaust internal union remedies prior to suit	163
	Legal Gems—Responsibility of Union Officers	164
	Legal Gems—Rights of Union Members under State Law	165
	Case 71—state court jurisdiction preempted by federal labor law	167
	Case 72—expenditure of union funds for political purposes limited	168
XII.	**REPRESENTATION PROCEEDINGS**	170
	Legal Gems—Representation Proceedings—Introduction	170
	Legal Gems—NLRB Election Procedure	172
	Legal Gems—Showing of Interest	174
	Legal Gems—Questions Concerning Representation—Contract Bar	175
	Legal Gems—The Appropriate Bargaining Unit	175
	Case 73—company wide units—extent of organization considered	177
	Case 74—severance of a craft unit—factors considered	178
	Legal Gems—Judicial Review of Representation Cases	179
	Case 75—original court review when board violates statute	179
	Legal Gems—Setting Aside an Election	180
	Case 76—influencing employees by unfair means invalidates election	182
	Case 77—false election campaign statements may cause election to be set aside	183
	Legal Gems—Rule Making Authority of the NLRB	183
	Case 78—failure to follow APA rule making requirements invalidates rule	184
	Case 79—agency has discretion to make rules either through adjudication or rule making procedures	186

TABLE OF CONTENTS

		Page
XIII.	OTHER LAWS GOVERNING LABOR RELATIONS	187
	Legal Gems—Other Laws Governing Labor Relations	187
	Legal Gems—Civil Rights Act—Equal Employment Opportunity Act—Introduction	188
	Legal Gems—Title VII—General Types of Discrimination Prohibited	190
	Legal Gems—Title VII—Specific Discriminatory Acts Prohibited	192
	Case 80—only job related tests permissible for employees	196
	Legal Gems—Title VII—Procedure for Instituting Suit	198
	Case 81—Title VII suit—plaintiff has burden of proof	200
	Legal Gems—Class Actions Under Title VII	203
	Legal Gems—Preliminary Injunctive Relief	203
	Legal Gems—EEOC Reporting Requirements	205
	Legal Gems—Fair Labor Standards Act	205
	Legal Gems—Equal Pay Act	207
	Case 82—unequal base rates for the same work on different shifts unlawful	208
	Legal Gems—Age Discrimination in Employment Act	208
	Legal Gems—Walsh-Healey Public Contracts Act	209
	Legal Gems—Davis-Bacon Act	210
	Legal Gems—Service Contract Act	210
	Legal Gems—Executive Order No. 11246—Office of Federal Contract Compliance	211
	Case 83—seniority system carrying forward effects of former, discriminatory system found unlawful	213
	Legal Gems—Occupational Safety and Health Act	214
	Legal Gems—Consumer Credit Protection Act	216

Table of Cases 217

Table of Federal Statutes 223

Table of Statutory References 225

Index 227

*

LABOR LAW AND EMPLOYMENT DISCRIMINATION—OUTLINE

I. **INTRODUCTION**
   A. Based primarily on federal statutes
   B. Most of course concerns study of National Labor Relations Board
      1. rights of employees
      2. rights of unions
      3. rights of employers

II. **TERMINOLOGY**
   A. Some terms are defined in Section 2 of the National Labor Relations Act
   B. Other terms with specialized meanings came into use with the development of labor law

III. **DEVELOPMENT OF LABOR LEGISLATION**
   A. Early decisions unfavorable to labor
      1. early court decisions considered employee organization as unlawful criminal conspiracy
      2. by the mid-nineteenth century courts began to abandon the criminal conspiracy doctrine
      3. courts then prohibited strikes and picketing by injunction
      4. employers used "Yellow Dog" contracts to prevent unionization
      5. Sherman Antitrust Act used against labor to prohibit strikes
   B. Legislation favorable to labor
      1. Railway Labor Act of 1926 prohibited railroads from interfering with the right of their employees to organize and bargain collectively
      2. Norris-LaGuardia Act of 1932
         a. declared right to organize and bargain collectively to be public policy
         b. prohibited injunctions in most labor disputes to conform to public policy
      3. Wagner Act (National Labor Relations Act) of 1935
         a. regulated conduct of employers by protecting right of employees to organize and bargain (See V, below)
         b. provided for secret ballot elections to determine union representation (See XII, below)
         c. created the NLRB to administer the Act
   C. Legislation to balance rights of labor, management and employees
      1. Taft-Hartley Act (Labor-Management Relations Act) of 1947
         a. attempted to redress balance between labor and management by prohibiting certain union conduct (See IX and X, below)
         b. gave employees the right to refrain from union activities
         c. revived the use of the injunction to prevent unfair labor practices
         d. reorganize the NLRB

LABOR LAW—OUTLINE

III. DEVELOPMENT OF LABOR LEGISLATION—Continued
C. Legislation to balance rights of labor, management and employees —Continued
   2. Landrum-Griffin Act (Labor-Management Reporting and Disclosure Act) of 1959
      a. designed to protect rights of employees by regulating internal union conduct (See XI, below)
      b. expanded Taft-Hartley provisions on picketing and boycotts (See X, below)

IV. PROCEDURE AND REMEDIES
A. Charge filed with NLRB within six months
B. Charge investigated
C. Complaint issued if charge meritorious
D. Hearing before administrative law judge who makes decisions
E. Appeal to NLRB
F. Court review of board decision
G. Usual remedy
   1. post notice for sixty days
   2. reinstate employee with back pay if wrongful discharge
   3. take other appropriate action to remedy unfair labor practice

V. EMPLOYER UNFAIR LABOR PRACTICES
A. Section 7 guarantees employees their rights:
   1. to self-organization
   2. to join or assist unions
   3. to bargain collectively
   4. to engage in other concerted activities
   5. to refrain from any or all such activities
B. Section 8(a)(1)—interfere with, restrain or coerce employees in the exercise of Section 7 rights; prohibited activities include:
   1. question employees about their union sympathies
   2. promise or grant benefits to discourage union activity
   3. threaten employees with loss of benefits or other reprisals because of their union activity
   4. surveillance of union activities or giving employees impression that their union activities are being watched
   5. discharge for concerted activity protected by Section 7, but which does not encourage or discourage union activity, violates only Section 8(a)(1)

   NOTE—Discharge which encourages or discourages union activity violates Section 8(a)(3), and is an 8(a)(1) violation only by derivation

   6. rebuttable presumptions governing no-solicitation and no-distribution rules:
      a. forbidding oral solicitation during working time is presumptively valid
      b. forbidding oral solicitation on company premises during nonworking time (e. g. breaks) is presumptively invalid, violating Section 8(a)(1)
      c. forbidding distribution of literature in working areas is presumptively valid

LABOR LAW—OUTLINE

V. EMPLOYER UNFAIR LABOR PRACTICES—Continued

B. Section 8(a)(1)—interfere with, restrain or coerce employees in the exercise of Section 7 rights; prohibited activities include:—Continued
   6. rebuttable presumptions governing no-solicitation and no-distribution rules—Continued
      d. forbidding distribution of literature in nonworking areas on nonworking time presumptively invalid, violating Section 8(a)(1)
   NOTE—No-solicitation and no-distribution rules must be applied uniformly. Rules applicable only to union solicitation or union literature violates Section 8(a)(1)

C. Section 8(a)(2)—domination or assistance of union prohibited
   1. union representing employees must be independent of company
   2. company assistance of union prohibited

D. Section 8(a)(3)—discrimination regarding hire or tenure of employment or terms or conditions of employment to encourage or discourage union membership is prohibited
   1. violation depends on effect of activity—anti-union motivation not required
   2. discharge under valid union security clause does not violate Act
   3. discipline or discharge for engaging in lawful strike violates Section 8(a)(3)
   4. partial closing of a business to chill unionism violates Section 8(a)(3)
   5. closing entire business is permitted regardless of motivation
   6. lockout of employees after bargaining to an impasse is permitted

E. Section 8(a)(4)—discharge or other discrimination against employee for filing charges or giving testimony under Act is prohibited

F. Section 8(a)(5)—refusing to bargain in good faith with union representing employees is an unfair labor practice, see VII, below

VI. GOOD FAITH BARGAINING

A. Section 8(a)(5)—requires employer to bargain in good faith with majority representative of employees in appropriate bargaining unit
   1. good faith bargaining under Section 8(d) is mutual obligation of employer and union to:
      a. meet at reasonable times
      b. confer in good faith with respect to wages, hours and other terms and conditions of employment, and
      c. execute written contract of agreement
   NOTE—Section 8(d) does not require either party to make concessions
   2. Section 9(a) provides that the bargaining representative of employees shall be:
      a. selected by a majority of employees
      b. in an appropriate unit
      c. as the exclusive representative of employees, and
      d. for the purposes of collective bargaining regarding wages, hours and other conditions of employment

LABOR LAW—OUTLINE

VI. GOOD FAITH BARGAINING—Continued
  B. Obligations during bargaining
    1. party must make "relevant and necessary" information to support position available during bargaining
    2. employer may not change any term or condition of employment before bargaining to impasse on the matter
  C. Bargaining rights obtained by
    1. voluntary recognition
    2. certification after NLRB election
    3. to remedy substantial unfair labor practices which prevent a fair election where union represented majority of employees in appropriate unit
  D. Subjects for bargaining
    1. mandatory or compulsory subjects—anything covered by "wages, hours and other terms and conditions of employment"—bargaining required
    2. permissive subjects—bargaining permitted but not required e. g. performance bond
    3. non-bargainable subject—no bargaining permitted e. g. a closed shop because illegal
    4. bargaining *may* be required where the employer:
      a. subcontracts work done by bargaining unit employees
      b. closes part of business

VII. COLLECTIVE BARGAINING AGREEMENT
  A. Contract between employer and union covering wages, hours and other terms of employment is called a collective bargaining agreement
  B. Duty to bargain continues after contract is executed
    1. bargaining may be required as to matters not covered by contract during its term
    2. section 8(d) limits right to modify or terminate contract
    3. section 301 provides for enforcement of contract in any federal district court
      a. state courts may enforce if federal law applied
    4. collective bargaining agreements interpreted in light of federal labor policy
      a. courts favor arbitrability of grievances unless arbitration specifically prohibited
      b. courts do not review arbitrator's decision on merits—it is binding on parties
  C. Duties of successor employers
    1. normally need not assume existing contract
    2. may be required to recognize and bargain with union if work force substantially unchanged
    3. may be required to remedy unfair labor practices of predecessor if business purchased with knowledge of them
  D. NLRB may honor arbitration award and dismiss subsequent charge where
    1. proceedings fair and regular
    2. all parties agreed to be bound, and
    3. decision not repugnant to policies of Act

LABOR LAW—OUTLINE

VII. COLLECTIVE BARGAINING AGREEMENT—Continued
E. NLRB may defer action on refusal to bargain charge where parties could arbitrate under contract where
   1. history of collective bargaining
   2. no minor animus
   3. employer desires to submit matter to arbitration
   4. contract provides for arbitration of dispute
   5. resolution of charge depends on interpretation of contract, and
   6. the decision of arbitrator will probably resolve issue presented to Board

VIII. PUBLIC SECTOR BARGAINING—INCLUDES EMPLOYEES OF FEDERAL, STATE AND LOCAL GOVERNMENTS
A. No constitutional right to strike by federal or state employees
B. Federal employees governed by Federal Service Labor Management and Employee Relations Law of 1978
   1. established Federal Labor Relations Authority
   2. gives employees right to join or assist unions
   3. enumerates matters subject to collective bargaining
   4. makes government and union responsible for unfair labor practices
C. State laws vary
   1. generally agency similar to NLRB established, which
      a. determines appropriate unit
      b. conducts elections
      c. investigates and prosecutes unfair labor practices by state agency and unions
   2. statute lists subjects for bargaining

IX. UNION UNFAIR LABOR PRACTICES
A. Section 8(b)(1)(A)—restraint or coercion of employees in exercise of their Section 7 rights
   1. union may not threaten, intimidate or assault employees
   2. union may not prevent employees from entering or leaving plant during strike
   3. union responsibility for acts of strikers determined by usual rules of agency
   4. union required to represent all employees in bargaining unit fairly
   5. unions may regulate own internal affairs
      a. members may be fined or disciplined for violation of valid union rules
      b. union may not limit right of members to Board's processes
B. Section 8(b)(1)(B)—restraint or coercion of employer
   1. union may not refuse to bargain with employer representative or strike with that object
   2. union may not discipline a supervisor-member for collective bargaining activities

IX. UNION UNFAIR LABOR PRACTICES—Continued
C. Section 8(b)(2)—discharges caused by union
1. union may not attempt or cause employer to discharge or discipline employee except
   a. under valid union security clause
   b. under valid hiring hall
2. union may not discriminate in operation of hiring hall
D. Section 8(b)(3)—duty to bargain
1. union must bargain in good faith with employer
2. union must comply with Section 8(d)
E. Section 8(b)(5)—discriminatory or excessive initiation fees prohibited
F. Section 8(b)(6)—featherbedding prohibited
1. strictly construed
2. payments when no work performed prohibited
G. Section 8(g)—strikes against health care institutions restricted

X. SECTIONS 8(b)(4) AND (7)—PICKETING AND BOYCOTTS
A. Section 8(b)(4) prohibits strikes and boycotts with certain objects
1. prohibited objects
   a. compel employer to join any labor or employer association or sign hot cargo agreement
   b. secondary boycotts
   c. requiring employer to recognize union unless presently certified
   d. force assignment of certain work to a particular union
2. prohibited objects may not be accomplished by
   a. inducing employees to strike
   b. threatening, coercing or restraining employer
3. publicity other than picketing permitted to advise public that products of primary employer are distributed by another employer
   a. such publicity may not have effect of inducing neutral employees to strike
B. Section 8(b)(7)—prohibits recognition picketing where
1. employer has lawfully recognized another union
2. valid NLRB election held within one year
3. picketing continues for unreasonable time (not exceeding 30 days) without petition for election being filed
C. Ally doctrine
1. employer who performs struck work is ally
2. "ally" is considered a primary employer because no longer neutral
D. Section 8(e)—hot cargo clauses unlawful
1. hot cargo refers to goods produced or handled by "unfair" employer
2. agreement not to handle "hot cargo" is unlawful
3. construction industry exception—work performed at job site
4. clause to recapture, preserve or fairly expand bargaining unit work is permitted

XI. OTHER RIGHTS OF EMPLOYEES
  A. Right to sue
   1. employee must exhaust contract remedies
   2. employee may then enforce individual rights under collective bargaining agreement
  B. Landrum-Griffin Act
   1. establishes Bill of Rights for union members
   2. provides for financial reports by unions
   3. regulates election of union officers
   4. deals with fiduciary responsibility of union officers

XII. REPRESENTATION PROCEEDINGS
  A. Representation by NLRB election
   1. petition filed
      a. jurisdiction
      b. showing of interest
      c. question concerning representation exists
         i. no present contract
         ii. 90-60 days before existing contract expires—otherwise contract bar to election
   2. appropriate unit determined based on community of interest of employees
      a. by agreement of parties
      b. by Regional Director after hearing, or
      c. by Board if Director's decision appealed
   3. secret ballot election conducted by Board
   4. five days to file objections
      a. investigation of objections
      b. hearing, if necessary
      c. ruling on objections
   5. certification of union if it receives a majority of valid votes.
  B. Types of election petitions
   1. certification of Representative—union seeks certification for specific group (unit) of employees
   2. decertification—employer or employee claims union no longer represents employees
   3. Employer Representation Petition—filed by employer which wants determination of union representation claim
   4. withdrawal of Union Shop Authority—filed by employees who want union security clause in contract rescinded
      a. may be filed at any time there is an existing contract with a union security clause
  C. Judicial Review of representation cases
   1. no direct review
   2. ULP method of review
      a. refusal to bargain
      b. ULP charge filed
      c. Board finds violation
      d. respondent seeks court review of Board decision and court determines
         i. if unit appropriate
         ii. if election was fair

XII. REPRESENTATION PROCEEDINGS—Continued
D. Conduct warranting setting aside election
1. ULP which could have affected outcome
2. Peerless Plywood or 24 Hour Rule—captive audience speech within 24 hours of election
3. employer's failure to provide union with names and address of all voters
4. misrepresentation by party if
   a. it concerns an important matter
   b. it is a substantial departure from truth
   c. there is no opportunity for reply
   d. misrepresentations, innocent or intentional, had impact on election
5. other conduct interfering with free choice of employees

E. Rule making authority
1. under APA by
   a. publication in Federal Register
   b. opportunity for public to present views on rule
   c. publication of final rule
2. in adjudication of cases

XIII. OTHER LAWS GOVERNING LABOR RELATIONS
A. Title VII of Civil Rights Act, as amended by Equal Employment Opportunity Act
1. prohibits discrimination based on
   a. race
   b. color
   c. religion
   d. sex
   e. national origin
2. coverage
   a. employers with 15 or more employees
   b. employment agencies
   c. unions with 15 or more members

B. Fair Labor Standards Act
1. regulates
   a. minimum wage
   b. overtime for work over 40 hours in a work week
   c. child labor prohibited

C. Equal Pay Act
1. sex discrimination in payment of wages prohibited
2. wage differential permitted if pursuant to
   a. seniority system
   b. merit system
   c. system which measures earnings by quantity or quality of work
   d. differential based on factor other than sex

D. Age discrimination in Employment Act
1. prohibits discrimination against persons 40 to 70 in
   a. hiring
   b. discharge
   c. compensation
   d. other terms and conditions of employment

LABOR LAW—OUTLINE

XIII. OTHER LAWS GOVERNING LABOR RELATIONS—Continued
  D. Age discrimination in Employment Act—Continued
     2. Does not apply where
        a. age is reasonably necessary bona fide occupational qualification
        b. different treatment based on factor other than age
        c. employee discharged for cause
  E. Walsh-Healey Public Contracts Act
     1. applies to government contracts and subcontractors
     2. requires employees to be paid prevailing wage rates in locality as determined by Secretary of Labor
  F. Davis-Bacon Act
     1. applies to public construction work
     2. requires employees to be paid prevailing wage rates in locality as determined by Secretary of Labor
  G. Service Contract Act
     1. applies to service employees working under a service contract with the federal government
     2. requires the contractor to pay its employees the prevailing wage rate in the locality
  H. Executive Order No. 11246
     1. prohibits discrimination by government contractors because of
        a. race
        b. color
        c. religion
        d. sex
        e. national origin
     2. administered by OFCC, in Department of Labor
  I. Occupational Safety and Health Act
     1. requires employers to provide "safe and healthful working conditions"
     2. premises may be inspected and fines imposed for violations
  J. Consumer Credit Protection Act
     1. regulates wage garnishments
     2. prohibits discharge for garnishment for any one indebtedness

*

LABOR LAW
EMPLOYMENT DISCRIMINATION

I. INTRODUCTION AND ANALYSIS

LEGAL GEMS—Labor Law—Introduction

1. Labor law is essentially a body of statutory law, based primarily upon federal labor statutes.

2. The great bulk of the reported cases in labor law is the product of decisions of the National Labor Relations Board and their review by the federal courts of appeal and the U. S. Supreme Court.

3. The NLRB is the federal administrative agency which administers the National Labor Relations Act.

4. Because the make-up of the five man NLRB is appointed by the President, and is thus subject to regular change, and because new issues are constantly coming before the Board, the study of any labor law problem is not complete without reference to the most recent cases and decisions. These are reported in loose-leaf services, principal among which are those published by CCH and BNA.

5. The student must be aware of the entire fabric of labor law and must understand where any given fact situation fits into it. For this reason, this Review contains a CHART which summarizes and organizes unfair labor practices and directs the student to the applicable section of the Act together with the relevant portions and the illustrative CASES in this Review. See CHART I on pages 2 and 3.

6. Traditionally, a course in Labor Law considered only the National Labor Relations Act, as amended. With the trend to broaden the course in law schools, all of the other important laws governing labor relations are analyzed in this Review.

LABOR LAW—EMPLOYMENT DISCRIMINATION

CHART I
TYPES OF CHARGES UNDER THE NATIONAL LABOR RELATIONS ACT
UNFAIR LABOR PRACTICE CHARGES

Charges Against Employer	Charges Against Labor Organizations
Section of the Act	Section of the Act
8(a)(1) Interfere with, restrain or coerce employees in exercise of their rights under Section 7 (to join or assist a labor organization or to refrain). pages 36-44 CASES 5-8	8(b)(1)(A) Restrain or coerce employees in exercise of their rights under Section 7 (to join or assist a labor organization or to refrain). pages 106-115 CASES 41-48
8(a)(2) Dominate or interfere with the formation or administration of a labor organization or contribute financial or other support to it. pages 47-48 CASE 10	8(b)(1)(B) Restrain or coerce an employer in the selection of his representatives for collective bargaining or adjustment of grievances. pages 116-117 CASE 49
8(a)(3) Encourage or discourage membership in a labor organization by discrimination in regard to employment or working conditions. pages 49-50 CASES 11-12	8(b)(2) Cause or attempt to cause an employer to discriminate against an employee. pages 117-118 CASE 50
8(a)(4) Discharge or otherwise discriminate against an employee because he has filed charges or given testimony under the Act. pages 48-49	8(b)(3) Refuse to bargain collectively with employer. pages 120-121 CASE 51
8(a)(5) Refuse to bargain collectively with employees' representative. Duties *Prior* to Agreement pages 61-70 CASES 18-24 Duties *During* Term of Agreement pages 71-96 CASES 25-40	8(b)(5) Require employees covered by a union security clause to pay excessive or discriminatory fees for membership. pages 121-122
	8(b)(6) Cause or attempt to cause an employer to pay or agree to pay money or other thing of value for services which are not performed or not to be performed. page 122 CASE 52
	8(b)(4) (i) TO ENGAGE IN, OR INDUCE OR ENCOURAGE ANY INDIVIDUAL EMPLOYED BY ANY PERSON ENGAGED IN COMMERCE OR IN AN INDUSTRY AFFECTING COMMERCE TO ENGAGE IN, A STRIKE OR A REFUSAL IN THE COURSE OF HIS EMPLOYMENT TO USE, MANUFACTURE, PROCESS, TRANSPORT, OR OTHERWISE HANDLE OR WORK ON ANY GOODS OR TO PERFORM ANY SERVICES; OR (ii) TO THREATEN, COERCE OR RESTRAIN ANY PERSON ENGAGED IN COMMERCE OR IN AN INDUSTRY AFFECTING COMMERCE, WHERE IN EITHER CASE AN OBJECT THEREOF IS: (A) To force or require any employer or self-employed person to join any labor or employer organization or to enter into any agreement prohibited by Sec. 8(e). (B) To force or require any person to cease using, selling, handling, transporting, or otherwise dealing in the products of any other producer, processor, or manufacturer, or cease doing business with any other person, or force or require any other employer to recognize or bargain with a labor organization as the representative of his employees unless such labor organization has been so certified. (C) To force or require any employer to recognize or bargain with a particular labor organization as the representative of his employees if another labor organization has been certified as the representative. As to Subsections (A), (B) and (C) pages 136-145 CASES 57-62 (D) To force or require any employer to assign particular work to employees in a particular labor organization or in a particular trade, craft, or class rather than to employees in another trade, craft, or class, unless such employer is failing to conform to an appropriate Board order or certification. pages 151-152 CASE 64

[C483]

INTRODUCTION AND ANALYSIS

Section of the Act	Section of the Act	Charge Against Labor Organizations and Employer — Section of the Act
8(g) To strike, picket, or otherwise concertedly refuse to work at any health care institution without notifying the institution and the Federal Mediation and Conciliation Service in writing 10 days prior to such action. pages 123-124	8(b)(7) To picket, cause, or threaten the picketing of any employer where an object is to force or require an employer to recognize or bargain with a labor organization as the representative of his employees, or to force or require the employees of an employer to select such labor organization as their collective bargaining representative, unless such labor organization is currently certified as the representative of such employees: (A) where the employer has lawfully recognized any other labor organization, and a question concerning representation may not appropriately be raised under Section 9(c), (B) where within the preceding 12 months a valid election under 9(c) has been conducted, or (C) where picketing has been conducted without a petition under 9(c) being filed within a reasonable period of time not to exceed 30 days from the commencement of such picketing; except where the picketing is for the purpose of truthfully advising the public (including consumers) that an employer does not employ members of, or have a contract with, a labor organization, and it does not have an effect of interference with deliveries or services. As to Subsections (A), (B) and (C) pages 131-133 CASES 55-56	8(e) To enter into any contract or agreement (any labor organization and any employer) whereby such employer ceases or refrains or agrees to cease or refrain from handling or dealing in any product of any other employer, or to cease doing business with any other person. pages 148-149 CASE 63

CHART II

TYPES OF PETITIONS WHICH MAY BE FILED UNDER THE NATIONAL LABOR RELATIONS ACT

Section of the Act	Section of the Act	Section of the Act
9(c) (1) (A) (i) REPRESENTATION FOR CERTIFICATION—RC	9(c) (1) (A) (ii) DECERTIFICATION—RD	9(b) AMENDMENT TO CERTIFICATION—AC
Alleges that a substantial number of employees wish to be represented for collective bargaining and their employer declines to recognize their representative.	Alleges that a substantial number of employees assert that the certified or currently recognized bargaining representative is no longer their representative.	The petitioner seeks to amend the certification which has been issued.
9(c) (1) (B) REPRESENTATION FILED BY MANAGEMENT—RM	9(e) (1) UNION SHOP DEAUTHORIZATION—UD	9(b) UNIT CLARIFICATION—UC The petitioner seeks to clarify the bargaining unit for which a union has been recognized.
Alleges that one or more claims for recognition as exclusive bargaining agent have been received by employer.	Alleges that employees wish to rescind a union security clause.	

NOTE—The National Labor Relations Act, as amended, permits unions, employers or individual employees to file one or more types of petitions to resolve a variety of matters relating to union representation.

CHART II, above, sets forth the six types of petitions which may be filed, together with the Section of the Act upon which each is based, the shorthand designation of each, and the purpose of each.

As to RC, RM, RD and UD Petitions a secret ballot election is held. As to AC and UC Petitions the Board makes the requested determination after an investigation or hearing.

See Chapter XII, Representation Proceedings, pp. 151-162, below, which discusses the procedures followed and the legal rights and obligations of the parties after a petition is filed. See also NLRB Rules and Regulations, Sections 101.17-101.21.

[50-Z]

4

INTRODUCTION AND ANALYSIS

LEGAL GEMS—Analysis of a Labor Law Problem

1. The initial step in analyzing any labor law fact situation is to recognize that labor law problems involve:

    (a) employers,

    (b) employees, and

    (c) unions.

    Fact patterns should be carefully sorted to establish the relationships of the parties and issues in each case.

2. The student should be aware that labor law has a terminology all of its own. It is imperative that the student familiarize himself with the meaning and significance of all labor law terms involved in each case. See Chapters II and VII.

3. The development of labor legislation may be traced through the following stages:

    (a) common law decisions,

    (b) Sherman and Clayton Anti-Trust Acts (1890 and 1914),

    (c) Railway Labor Act (1926),

    (d) Norris-LaGuardia Act (1932),

    (e) Wagner Act (The National Labor Relations Act) (1935),

    (f) Taft-Hartley Act (amending the National Labor Relations Act) (1947), and

    (g) Landrum-Griffin Act (1959).

4. Federal labor legislation is designed to protect employee rights vis-à-vis the employer and vis-à-vis the union. It also prescribes the rules of fair play for employer and union dealings with each other. This is principally provided for in the acts listed under GEM 3(e), (f) and (g) above.

5. The basic federal legislation in the labor law area is called the National Labor Relations Act, which is the Wagner Act, as amended by the Taft-Hartley Act, as further amended by a portion of the Landrum-Griffin Act. See Chapter III.

6. The National Labor Relations Board is a wholly independent administrative agency created by Congress. It has two primary functions:

    (a) To prevent and remedy unfair labor practices. See Chapter IV, and

    (b) To conduct secret ballot elections to determine whether employees must be represented by a union. See CHART II, on page 4, above, and Chapter XII.

7. The National Labor Relations Act is designed to prevent and remedy unfair labor practices. If the fact situation involves an unfair labor practice, the student must determine the appropriate

LABOR LAW—EMPLOYMENT DISCRIMINATION

procedure of the Board and the remedy for its redress. See Chapter IV.

8. The Board has also been given the responsibility for conducting representation elections. The student must consider whether the fact situation involves the specialized procedures and remedies applicable to such elections. See Chapters IV and XII.

9. *The essence of the course in labor law is a thorough study and understanding of all types of unfair labor practices.* If the fact situation involves an unfair labor practice, the student must refer to the specific bodies of law that have been established with respect to:

   (a) *employer* unfair labor practices, See Chapters V and VI, and

   (b) *union* unfair labor practices, See Chapter IX.

10. Typical *employer* unfair labor practices generally involve interference with or discrimination because of the union activities of its employees. See Chapter V.

11. Typical *union* unfair labor practices involve restraint of employees in their rights to engage in or refrain from engaging in activities. See Chapter VII.

12. *Union* unfair labor practices also include restraint or coercion directed against employers, such as secondary boycotts and picketing. See Chapter X.

13. Both the *union* and the *employer* have a duty to bargain with one another in good faith, and violation of that duty is an unfair labor practice. See Chapter VI.

14. The end product of the collective bargaining process is the collective bargaining agreement. The student should understand the basic terms of any collective bargaining agreement which is applicable to the fact situation, and the law relating to the administration and enforcement of the agreement. See Chapter VII.

15. Employees of federal, state and local governments may also be covered by collective bargaining agreements under laws other than the National Labor Relations Act. See Chapter VIII.

16. The student should also consider whether the fact situation involves a violation of the employee's rights under the Landrum-Griffin Act, which deals with the regulation of internal union affairs. It is administered by the Labor-Management Services Administration of the United States Department of Labor. See Chapter XI.

17. Employees have rights under many other laws to protect them from discrimination or other unfair treatment. See Chapter XIII.

II. TERMINOLOGY USED IN LABOR RELATIONS

The development of labor relations law has brought with it a specialized vocabulary. Legal and business terms as well as descriptive colloquialisms of "rank and file" employees are used, and they have special significance or connotations. Some of the more frequently used terms are defined below. Page references are also provided to enable the student to easily locate the principal use of key terms in this Review.

Page

Administrative Law Judge—An administrative official of the National Labor Relations Board, formerly known as a Trial Examiner, who conducts unfair labor practice hearings. He is comparable to a judge who hears a case without a jury. He functions independently from the Board, which reviews his decision on appeal, and the General Counsel, who investigates and prosecutes cases. See Section 11 of the Administrative Procedure Act and Sections 4(a) and 10(c) of the NLRA for the status, authority and limitations of administrative law judges.

Affirmative Order—A written order requiring specific action which must be taken by the charged party (respondent) in an unfair labor practice case to remedy the violation, such as reinstatement of an unlawfully discharged employee with back pay.

AFL–CIO—American Federation of Labor—Congress of Industrial Organizations—a national federation of labor unions. The initials are used after the name of individual affiliated unions.

Authorization Card—A card which designates a union to represent the employee who signs it for purposes of collective bargaining. These cards are used during union organizational campaigns to support a petition filed with the NLRB and/or to demand recognition from the employer _____ 174

Bargaining Unit—A particular group of employees with a similar community of interest appropriate for bargaining _____ 176

Bid (for a job)—Application for another job by an employee.

Board—See National Labor Relations Board.

Boycott—Concerted refusal to work for, purchase from, or handle the products of an employer. Where the action is directed against the employer directly involved in the labor dispute, it is termed a *primary* boycott. Where the action is directed against other, neutral employers in an attempt to have them cease doing business with the employer with which the union has a dispute, it is known as a *secondary* boycott _____ 125

LABOR LAW—EMPLOYMENT DISCRIMINATION

Cease and Desist Order—Ruling issued in an unfair labor practice case requiring the charged party (respondent) to stop the conduct found illegal and take specified affirmative action designed to remedy the unfair labor practice 29–31

Certification—Formal designation by NLRB that a labor organization represents a majority of employees in a particular bargaining unit 172

Charge—A written document, signed by the charging party, and filed with an administrative agency. The charge alleges the unlawful conduct of the party charged and initiates action by the administrative agency. Compare Complaint 2

Check-off—Written authorization by an employee to his employer to have his union dues deducted from his wages and paid directly to the union 81

Civil Rights Act—See Title VII.

Closed Shop—Requirement that an employee be a member of a union before he is hired. This practice was made unlawful by the Taft-Hartley Act 27

Collective Bargaining—The process of negotiation between a company and union concerning wages, hours, and other terms and conditions of employment in order to arrive at a collective bargaining agreement or settle some dispute 78

Collective Bargaining Agreement—An enforceable contract between a company and a union setting forth the terms and conditions of employment for a group of employees, usually for a specific period of time. See Chapter VII for an outline of typical contract terms 80

Complaint—A formal document specifically alleging the unlawful conduct charged and issued prior to a hearing on the merits. A complaint issued by the NLRB must be based on a charge filed with that agency and sets the matter for an administrative hearing. Where a Title VII violation is alleged, the complaint is filed with the appropriate United States District Court.

Contract Bar—The period of a valid collective bargaining agreement during which no question concerning representation may be raised. The petition raising a question concerning representation must be filed from ninety to sixty days before the expiration of the contract or after it expires. A contract may bar a representation election for up to three years. Compare Insulated Period 175

Craft—A trade requiring special skills, manual ability and a fixed training period, e. g., carpenters, painters, custom tailors, meat cutters, tool and die makers, or photoengravers are craftsmen 178

TERMINOLOGY IN LABOR RELATIONS

	Page

Dovetail Seniority—Combining two or more seniority lists (usually of different companies being merged) into a master seniority list, with each employee keeping the seniority he had previously acquired even though he may thereafter be employed by a new employer. Compare Endtail Seniority 156

Economic Strike—A work stoppage by employees seeking some economic benefit 50

Endtail Seniority—Combining two or more seniority lists (usually from a merger of different companies) into a single seniority list with the group of employees from one company being placed at the bottom of the new seniority list. Compare Dovetail Seniority.

Equal Employment Opportunity Commission (EEOC)—The administrative agency which administers Title VII of the Civil Rights Act. It is headed by five commissioners appointed by the President. See Title VII 188

Featherbedding—Receiving payment for work which has not been performed and which will not be performed 122

Globe Election—Special election to determine whether a particular group of employees desires to become part of a larger bargaining unit. The smaller unit to be "globed" must constitute an appropriate unit by itself 176

Hearing Officer—An administrative official who conducts a hearing to develop evidence concerning a representation matter or jurisdictional dispute. He differs from an administrative law judge principally in that he does not make recommendations or findings of fact or issue a decision, except in a post-election hearing on objections or challenges, when he makes recommendations of fact and law which are served on the parties who may file exceptions thereto 173

Hiring Hall—The union's place of business where it receives employer requests for employees and refers workers to jobs 117

Hot Cargo—Designates goods produced or handled by an employer with whom the union has a dispute 146

Impasse—A stalemate in bargaining negotiations; employer and union representatives have bargained to a point where neither is willing to make any concessions 64

Insulated Period—The sixty days immediately preceding the expiration of a collective bargaining agreement when no representation petition may be filed. This is to give the employer and the incumbent union the opportunity to negotiate a new contract without rival claims for recognition. Compare Contract Bar 175

LABOR LAW—EMPLOYMENT DISCRIMINATION

Page

Jurisdictional Dispute—Competing claims made to an employer by different unions that their members are entitled to be assigned certain work by the employer. There must be evidence of a threat of coercive action for the Board to conduct a hearing and make an assignment of the work ———————————————————————— 149

Lockout—The temporary shutdown of a plant by an employer to gain some bargaining concession or discourage union activity ———— 56

Maintenance of Membership—Contract clause requiring employees who are members of a union to continue their membership as a condition of employment ———————————————————————— 49

Mass Picketing—Consists of a large number of employees at entrances to a plant making it difficult or impossible for anyone to enter or leave. See Chapter X for a discussion of picketing ————127–128

Most Favored Nation Clause—A clause in a collective bargaining agreement whereby the union agrees that if it signs a contract with another employer containing more favorable terms such terms will automatically apply to the present contract. Sometimes the term is applied where the union only agrees that it will not execute a contract with more favorable terms with another employer, or that the contract is reopened for negotiation if a more favorable clause is granted to another employer. See CASE 3.

National Labor Relations Board—An independent administrative agency responsible directly to the President which administers most of the provisions of the National Labor Relations Act. It is subdivided into two branches: the General Counsel, who investigates and prosecutes cases, and the Board which is the decision making body ———————————————————————— 5

Peerless Plywood Rule—A prohibition of captive audience speeches before NLRB elections derived from the Board's holding in Peerless Plywood Co., 107 NLRB 427 (1953). See Twenty-Four Hour Rule ———————————————————————————————— 180

Petition—A formal paper filed with the NLRB seeking a secret ballot election among a certain group of employees (bargaining unit). See Chapter XII, Representation Proceedings, for a description of various types of petitions, the requirements to file them, and the procedure followed after filing. See also Chart II ————— 172

Picketing—The presence at an employer's business by one or more persons to publicize a labor dispute, influence employees or customers to withhold their business, or show the union's desire to represent the employees. This is usually accomplished by patroling with signs, but neither is required. Merely sitting in a car

TERMINOLOGY IN LABOR RELATIONS

with a sign stuck in the ground is sufficient to constitute picketing. It has also been held that employees congregated around, or in, their parked cars without any signs were picketing. See Chapter X, Picketing and Boycotts 125

Primary Activity—Concerted action such as a strike or picketing directed against the employer with which the union has a dispute. Compare, Secondary Activity 133

Primary Boycott—Action against an employer with which the union has a dispute with the object of preventing the use, purchase or handling of the products or services of such employer. See Boycott.

Primary Employer—The employer with which the union has a labor dispute. Compare Secondary Employer 133

Protected Activity—Conduct of employees which neither an employer nor a union may interfere with. Section 7 of the Act lists protected employee rights. See also Unprotected Activity.

Question Concerning Representation (QCR)—A question exists whether one or more unions represents a majority of employees in a bargaining unit 175

Red Circle Rate—A wage rate for a particular job which is higher than the rate assigned to that job. This can occur after a re-evaluation of the job. Present employees on the job continue to receive their higher "red circle" rate, but when new employees are assigned to that job they receive the normal rate and not the "red circle" rate. The purpose is to effectuate a reduction in a job rate without causing any employee to have his or her wages reduced. See CASE 82.

Runaway Shop—Closing a plant and reopening it somewhere else in order to avoid dealing with a union 56

Scab—Colloquialism for any person who crosses a picket line to work.

Schism—A division of a union into two factions resulting in one group leaving the union 175

Secondary Activity—Actions such as a strike, picketing, or boycott against an employer with which the union does not have a dispute (secondary employer) with an object of forcing that employer to stop doing business with the employer with which the union has a dispute (primary employer). See Boycott. Compare Primary Activity 133

Secondary Boycott—Refusal to work for, purchase from or handle products of an employer with whom the union has no dispute with an object of forcing that employer to stop doing business with the employer with which the union has a dispute 125

LABOR LAW—EMPLOYMENT DISCRIMINATION

Page

Secondary Employer—An employer who has no dispute with the union, a neutral, or an employer who cannot take the action which the union wants to accomplish its objective. Compare Primary Employer 133

Seniority—The length of service of an employee. There are no seniority rights as such under the law, but a collective bargaining agreement may provide that seniority be used in determining layoffs, recalls, job assignments and transfers 81

Steelworkers Trilogy—Three Supreme Court decisions which emphasized the importance of arbitration as an instrument of federal policy for resolving disputes between labor and management and cautioned the lower courts against usurping the functions of the arbitrator. See CASES 33, 34 and 35 86

Strike—A concerted refusal of employees to perform work which they have been assigned. See Economic Strike, Sympathy Strike, Unfair Labor Practice Strike, Whipsaw Strike, and Wildcat Strike .. 50

Sympathy Strike—A concerted work stoppage by employees to support the objective of another organization when the resolution of such dispute will not directly benefit the sympathy strikers.

Title VII—Part of the Civil Rights Act of 1964 which established the EEOC. Title VII, as amended by the Equal Employment Opportunity Act of 1972, prohibits discrimination based on race, color, religion, sex and national origin 188

Trial Examiner—See Administrative Law Judge.

Twenty-Four Hour Rule—Prohibits election speeches by anyone on company time to massed assemblies of employees within 24 hours of a scheduled NLRB election. This is also known as the Peerless Plywood Rule 180

Unfair Labor Practice Strike—A work stoppage by employees caused or prolonged, at least in part, by the unfair labor practices of the employer 50

Unilateral Action—Action taken by an employer or union without bargaining with the other party to the collective bargaining relation ... 74

Union—An organization in which employees participate and existing, in whole or in part, to deal with employers concerning terms and conditions of employment. See Section 2(5) of the Act. No formal organization is required for a union to be a labor organization under the Act.

    A. **International Union**—A parent union which is composed of affiliated unions called "locals" in the United States and in foreign countries.

TERMINOLOGY IN LABOR RELATIONS

Page

B. **Local Union**—Consists of employees in one or more bargaining units at a single plant or in a limited geographical area. It is chartered by a national or international union with which it is affiliated. A local union is the basic unit of labor organization.

C. **Independent Union**—In a broad sense, any union which is not affiliated with the AFL–CIO. Usually it is a group of employees at a single plant or company which is not affiliated with a national or international union.

Union Security—Any contract clause requiring some or all employees represented by a union to become or remain members of the union as a condition of employment, e. g., maintenance or membership or union shop _____ 81

Union Shop—A clause in a collective bargaining agreement in which membership in the union is required as a condition of employment on or after the thirtieth day following the beginning of employment or the effective date of the agreement, whichever is later ___ 81

Unit—See Bargaining Unit.

Unprotected Activity—Any conduct for which employees may be discharged or disciplined by an employer. For example, a "sit-down" strike is not protected because it consists of taking over the employer's property and preventing him from running his business; a partial strike is the refusal to do some but not all assigned work, such as the refusal to work overtime. An employee must either perform the work assigned or strike. Performance of only some of the work assigned is a partial strike and is unprotected _____ 32–35

Whipsaw Strike—A work stoppage against some, but not all employers in a multiemployer bargaining group. The purpose is to apply pressure to one or more employers in the group and obtain bargaining concessions from them. That agreement is then used by the union as a pattern to obtain similar terms from the other employers, one by one, by threatening to strike them.

Wildcat Strike—A work stoppage by employees which has not been authorized by their union. The term may also refer to a strike in violation of a collective bargaining agreement.

Yellow Dog Contract—Agreement by an employee not to join a union or remain in a union. This was made unlawful by the Wagner Act _____ 20

III. THE DEVELOPMENT OF LABOR LEGISLATION

LEGAL GEMS—Development of Labor Legislation—Introduction

1. Early decisions in the United States were unfavorable to labor. Unions were regarded by the courts as criminal conspiracies to deprive the employer of property.

2. With the industralization of the economy in the United States from 1865 to 1914 employees attempted to organize.

3. Although the criminal conspiracy doctrine was gradually rejected, antitrust laws were used against unions and their concerted activities, such as strikes and boycotts, were enjoined.

4. Federal legislation in the 1930's encouraged the growth of unions.

    (a) The Norris-LaGuardia Act prohibited most injunctions against unions.

    (b) The Wagner Act protected the right of employees to organize and bargain collectively.

5. In 1947 the Taft-Hartley Act imposed duties on unions to prevent abuses of union power.

6. Further experience with labor laws resulted in passage of the Landrum-Griffin Act in 1959. This Act regulated internal union affairs and gave union members a "bill of rights."

7. Today the entire field of labor-management relations is governed by statutes.

LEGAL GEMS—Common Law Decisions Unfavorable to Labor

1. English Courts in the early Eighteenth Century considered concerted activities by employees to be criminal conspiracies.

2. The first decision of a labor case in America held that a strike for higher wages constituted a criminal conspiracy. The court said that an individual employee, by himself, may refuse to work, but the agreement among employees to refuse to work constituted an unlawful criminal conspiracy. See Commonwealth v. Pullis (Philadelphia Cordwainers' case), 3 Doc.Hist. of Am.Ind.Soc. 59 (2nd ed. Commons, 1910), Philadelphia Mayor's Court (1806). See also Nelles, "The First American Labor Case", 41 Yale L.J. 165 (1931).

3. By the middle of the Nineteenth Century courts began to abandon the criminal conspiracy doctrine.

    e.g. Employees of X demanded that Z be discharged for violation of union rules. X discharged Z to prevent a strike. The state prosecuted the union officers for causing Z's discharge. The officers were convicted and, on appeal, the Massachusetts

DEVELOPMENT OF LABOR LEGISLATION

Supreme Court refused to apply the criminal conspiracy doctrine and reversed the conviction. The court said that only if the act was accomplished "by falsehood or force" would it constitute a criminal conspiracy. This decision was the beginning of judicial recognition of a union's right to strike. See Commonwealth v. Hunt, 45 Mass. (4 Metc.) 111, 38 Am. Dec. 346 (1842). See also Smith, p. 7.

4. After the criminal conspiracy theory had been rejected, courts then began to issue injunctions to prohibit strikes and picketing.

    e.g. P's employees went on strike and picketed in front of P's business. The pickets threatened prospective replacements for the striking employees, preventing P from hiring new employees. P sought to enjoin the picketing. The Massachusetts Supreme Court enjoined the picketing because it interfered with the employer's business by attempting "with social pressure, threats of personal injury or unlawful harm and persuasion to break existing (employment) contracts". The court concluded that the United States Constitution gave an employer the right to employ persons at agreed upon wages and also gave employees the right to enter the employer's premises and to work there. The court enjoined *all* picketing reasoning that the concerted action of the striking employees was a "combination to do injurious acts expressly directed to another, by way of intimidation or restraint" and was, therefore, unlawful.

    Justice Holmes dissented. He reasoned that *mere* picketing to publicize a dispute did not carry with it the threat of bodily harm, and only force, or the threats of force, should be enjoined. He concluded that working men should be permitted to combine to obtain higher wages just as businesses may combine to increase their return on invested capital. See Vegelahn v. Guntner, 167 Mass. 92, 44 N.E. 1077 (1896).

    NOTE—The view of Justice Holmes that it should not be unlawful for a combination of persons to do what any one of them might do lawfully by himself was finally recognized nationally about forty years later in the Norris-LaGuardia and Wagner Acts.

5. Employers attempted to stifle the growth of the labor movement through the use of "Yellow Dog" contracts. Under the terms of such a contract an employee agreed not to join a union.

    (a) In 1887 states began to enact laws to outlaw "Yellow Dog" contracts.

    (b) In 1888 Congress passed the Erdman Act which prohibited discharging, or threatening to discharge, an employee because of his union membership.

    CAVEAT—The Supreme Court held that the Erdman Act violated the Fifth Amendment because it deprived an employer of his personal liberty and property right by requiring him to retain a person in his employ against his will. The Court stated that the power of Congress to regulate interstate commerce could not be used to deprive a person of other rights guaranteed by the constitution. See Adair v. United States, 208 U.S. 161, 28 S.Ct. 277, 52 L.Ed. 436 (1908). See also Gorman, pp. 4, 209; Smith, pp. 8–22.

LEGAL GEMS—Antitrust Acts Used Against Labor

1. There is a conflict between the basic philosophies underlying antitrust laws and labor laws.

    (a) The theory of *antitrust* laws is the prevention of combinations of competitors, whether they are employers or employees, because they reduce competition and will injure the consumer.

    (b) The purpose of *labor* laws is to foster the development of combinations of employees, who form a union, and thus to promote collective bargaining, which is often a combination of competing employers and unions, to establish wages and conditions of employment.

2. The Sherman Act (1890) outlawed "Every contract, combination in the form of a trust or otherwise, or conspiracy, in restraint of trade or commerce among the several states. . . ." Section 1.

3. Courts interpreted the Sherman Act to prohibit strikes which affected interstate commerce and enjoined such strikes. They also permitted employers to sue for treble damages under the Act.

    e.g. The union called a strike for recognition against the employer and instituted a nationwide boycott of the employer's products handled by wholesalers and retailers. The employer sued the union for treble damages under the Sherman Act. In overruling the union's demurrer the court held: "If the purposes of the combination were, as alleged, to prevent any interstate transportation at all, the fact that the means operated at one end before physical transportation commenced and at the other end after the physical transportation ended was immaterial." The Court held that the Act applied to combinations of employees and permitted a suit for damages. See Loewe v. Lawlor (Danbury Hatters case), 208 U.S. 274, 28 S.Ct. 301, 52 L.Ed. 488 (1908).

4. In an effort to limit the courts' interpretation of the Sherman Act, the Clayton Act (1914) provided:

    (a) "That the labor of a human being is not a commodity or article of commerce. Nothing contained in the anti-trust laws shall be construed to forbid the existence and operation of labor, agricultural, or horticultural organizations, instituted for the purposes of mutual help, and not having capital stock or conduct-

DEVELOPMENT OF LABOR LEGISLATION

ed for profit, or to forbid or restrain individual members of such organizations from lawfully carrying out the legitimate objects thereof; nor shall such organizations, or the members thereof, be held or construed to be illegal combinations or conspiracies in restraint of trade, under the anti-trust laws." Section 6.

* * *

(b) "That no restraining order or injunction shall be granted by any court of the United States, or a judge or the judges thereof, in any case between an employer and employees . . . growing out of a dispute concerning terms or conditions of employment, unless necessary to prevent irreparable injury to property, or to a property right. . . ." Section 20.

* * *

(c) "And no such restraining order or injunction shall prohibit any person or persons, whether singly or in concert, from terminating any relation of employment, or from ceasing to perform any work or labor, or from recommending, advising, or persuading others by peaceful means to do so; . . . or from peacefully persuading any person to work or to abstain from working; or from ceasing to patronize or to employ any parties to such dispute. . . ." Section 20.

5. The Clayton Act was not effective in protecting employees who engaged in a strike or picketing.

   e.g. The union struck for recognition and higher wages and instituted a nationwide boycott of the employer's products. The union also threatened to take action against persons doing business with the employer in other states to make them stop doing business with the struck employer. The Court considered the effect of the Clayton Act on the Sherman Act, and concluded:

   (a) Section 6 assumed that the normal objects of a union were legitimate, but the Act was not intended to legalize activities which were otherwise unlawful under the Sherman Act,

   (b) Section 20 applied only to employees directly affected by the labor dispute and not to unions or employees of other employers, and

   (c) Congress did not intend to restrict the issuance of injunctions where a secondary boycott was threatened.

   Although the Clayton Act declared that antitrust laws did not prohibit a union from carrying out its legitimate objectives, in this case the union was not carrying out a legitimate object because the boycott of the employer's customers and sympathetic strikes were not lawful. The limitation of a court's power to issue injunctions in a labor dispute applies only where there is an employer-employee relationship, and no such relation existed in the present case. Thus, the injunction was issued against the union. See Duplex Printing Press Co. v. Deering, 254 U.S. 443, 41 S.Ct. 172, 65 L.Ed. 349 (1921). See also *Boudin*, "The Sherman Act and Labor Disputes", 39 Colum.L.Rev. 1283 (1939), 40 Colum.L.Rev. 14 (1940).

6. In the 1930's federal statutes were enacted which effectively prevented the use of the injunction against labor and encouraged collective bargaining. Court interpretation of these statutes has attempted to reconcile the differing philosophies of antitrust and labor legislation.

LEGAL GEMS—The Railway Labor Act of 1926 Protects Right to Organize

1. The Railway Labor Act prohibited railroads from interfering with the right of their employees to organize and bargain collectively.

2. Other provisions of the Act included:

    (a) establishment of a National Mediation Board to assist the parties in collective bargaining,

    (b) creation of the National Railroad Adjustment Board which could render binding decisions in disputes over working conditions and require compulsory arbitration of disputes involving an existing contract, and

    (c) authorization of the President to appoint an investigative board if a labor dispute threatened to halt essential rail service.

NOTE—The Act was held constitutional under Congress' power to regulate interstate commerce. The Supreme Court held that such power included the authority to pass legislation in order to facilitate the amicable settlement of disputes which threatened interstate commerce. The Act covered only the operations of railroads because they directly affected interstate commerce. The Act also safeguarded the right of employees to engage in collective action regarding grievances and working conditions, which right had already been recognized by the courts. Since railroads had no constitutional right to interfere with those employee rights, the Act did not take away any rights of the carriers and the Act was held constitutional. See Texas & New Orleans Railroad Co. v. Brotherhood of Railway Clerks, 281 U.S. 548, 50 S.Ct. 427, 74 L.Ed. 1034 (1930).

3. The Act originally covered only employees of railroads. In 1936, however, the Act was amended to cover airline employees as well.

4. The Act remains in effect today and is the basis for collective bargaining in the railroad and airline industries.

DEVELOPMENT OF LABOR LEGISLATION

See generally Cox, pp. 75-78; Gorman, pp. 209-210; Smith, pp. 26-29.

LEGAL GEMS—Norris-LaGuardia Act of 1932 Favors Organized Labor

1. The Norris-LaGuardia Act declared it to be public policy that each employee shall have "full freedom of association, self-organization, and designation of representatives of his own choosing to negotiate the terms and conditions of his employment," free from employer interference in the exercise of these rights or other concerted activities for mutual aid or protection.

2. The Act, also known as the Anti-Injunction Act, defined and limited the powers of federal courts to issue injunctions in labor disputes to conform with the Act's policy. See CASE 1, below.

3. The effect of the Act was summarized by one authority as follows:

    (a) "the act rejected the injunction as a remedy in labor disputes,"

    (b) "it declared that federal courts were not the proper agency of the government to formulate substantive labor policy," and

    (c) "it repudiated the federal common law of labor relations and established a policy of governmental neutrality in labor disputes as a means of aiding the growth of organized labor. Although the act's policy of governmental neutrality has given way to pervasive federal regulation, its remedial proscriptions and strictures on the role of the judiciary remain fundamental to the scheme of federal labor law."

    See Winter, "Labor Injunctions and Judge-made Labor Law: The Contemporary Role of Norris-LaGuardia," 70 Yale L.J. 70 (1960); Meltzer, p. 394.

4. The Act prohibited federal courts from enjoining any labor dispute unless there was violence or other legislation authorizing an injunction. See CASE 2, below.

5. The Act also provided in Section 7 that an injunction could only be issued after notice to all parties and a hearing in which the court found:

    (a) unlawful acts had been threatened or committed and will be committed in the future unless restrained,

    (b) substantial and irreparable property damage will follow,

    (c) greater injury will result to the complainant from denying the injunction than to the defendant from granting it,

    (d) the complainant has no adequate remedy at law,

    (e) public officers are unable or unwilling to furnish adequate protection, and

LABOR LAW—EMPLOYMENT DISCRIMINATION

    (f) the complainant has complied with every legal obligation involved in the dispute and has made every reasonable effort to settle the dispute by negotiation.

6. The Act, in Section 3, provided that employment contracts whereby a worker agreed not to join a union, or to resign if he was a union member, were declared contrary to public policy and unenforceable in federal courts. Such contracts are known as "Yellow Dog" Contracts.

7. Congressional policy reflected in the Norris-LaGuardia Act and subsequent labor legislation fostering collective bargaining has conflicted at times with national policy expressed in antitrust legislation favoring free competition in business markets. The courts have had to accommodate the two policies.

    (a) Concerted action or an agreement between a union and a non-labor party are not exempt from antitrust laws.

        (i) The United Mine Workers negotiated an agreement with large coal companies in which the union agreed to permit mechanization of mines which would substantially reduce mine employment, in return for higher wages and royalty payments for miners. The union also agreed to impose the same high wages on smaller companies regardless of whether they were mechanized. The purpose was to drive smaller companies out of business thereby reducing the overproduction of coal. Did the union violate antitrust laws by the agreement? Ans. Yes. A union forfeits its exemption from antitrust laws when it agrees with one group of employers to impose certain wage scales on other employers. Some employers could not lawfully conspire to eliminate competitors from the industry, and a union is liable if it joins the conspiracy. The fact that the union's part in the conspiracy was to impose certain wage rates on other employers is not a valid defense because the rates were to be imposed on employers outside the bargaining unit for which the union was negotiating. See United Mine Workers of America v. Pennington, 381 U.S. 657, 85 S.Ct. 1585, 14 L.Ed.2d 626 (1965).

        (ii) In negotiating a collective bargaining agreement the union insisted that marketing hours at stores in the bargaining unit be 9:00 a. m. to 6:00 p. m. An employer which was threatened with a strike signed the contract containing that clause, and brought suit against the union contending that the union's demand violated antitrust laws by restricting the employer's marketing hours. Is the union exempt from antitrust regulation in these circumstances? Ans. Yes. There is no proof that the union conspired with other employers against the employer bringing suit. The union acted to further its own policies. The hours and days which employees work are proper subjects of bargaining because they are intimately related to wages, hours and working conditions. Thus, there was no violation of antitrust laws. See Local 189, Amalgamated Meat Cutters v. Jewel Tea Co., 381 U.S. 676, 85 S.Ct. 1596, 14 L.Ed.2d 640 (1965).

(b) Secondary activities which directly restrain competition are not exempt from antitrust laws where the agreement does not promote an objective favored by national labor policy. See CASE 3, below.

See generally Cox, pp. 60–68, 702–715; Gorman, pp. 624–627; Meltzer, pp. 392–395, 510–546.

CASE 1—*strike not a criminal conspiracy—antitrust acts interpreted*

Union A claimed that certain work should be assigned to its members, but the employer assigned the work to members of Union B. Union A struck and refused to submit the matter to arbitration as provided in its contract with the employer. Was the strike a criminal conspiracy in violation of the Sherman Anti-Trust Act?

Ans. No. The strike was not a crime under the Sherman Act. The court reasoned that Section 20 of the Clayton Act provided that the normal object of a union, such as securing work for its members, did not violate any antitrust law. Further, the Norris-LaGuardia Act prohibited federal courts from enjoining such a strike. Congress would not have intended to make an act a criminal offense and then not permit it to be enjoined. The effect of the Sherman Act can only be determined by reading it in conjunction with Section 20 of the Clayton Act and the Norris-LaGuardia Act. Under the Norris-LaGuardia Act a labor dispute may exist regardless of whether there is an employer-employee relation, thus eliminating the distinction made by the courts under antitrust laws. Therefore, the union's strike was not a criminal offense under the Sherman Act. This decision is the basis for exempting union activities from antitrust laws and is, therefore, important even today.

See United States v. Hutcheson, 312 U.S. 219, 61 S.Ct. 463, 85 L.Ed. 788 (1941).

NOTE—Compare CASE 1 above, with CASE 2, below, in which the Supreme Court "accommodates" the Norris-LaGuardia Act to the Taft-Hartley Act and federal labor policy as it is recognized today.

CASE 2—*injunction proper for breach of no-strike clause where grievance subject to arbitration*

The employer and the union were parties to a collective bargaining agreement which provided that all controversies concerning the interpretation and application of the agreement would be resolved through a specified grievance procedure which provided for arbitration. The contract also contained a no-strike clause. A dispute arose over work which the union claimed should be assigned to bargaining unit employees. When the employer refused to assign the work to the union employees, they began a strike. Does the Norris-LaGuardia Act preclude federal courts from issuing injunctions to stop the breach of a no-strike clause in a collective bargaining agreement?

Ans. No. The Norris-LaGuardia Act was passed to limit the power of federal courts to issue injunctions in any case growing out of a labor dispute. Later the Wagner and Taft-Hartley Acts were passed with the purpose of encouraging collective bargaining and the peaceful settlement of labor disputes. Since the Norris-LaGuardia Act was not amended, it is for the courts to accommodate the older statute to the more recent ones. In the present case, unless federal courts were permitted to grant injunctive relief, Congressional policy favoring the voluntary establishment of a peaceful resolution of labor disputes would be thwarted. Therefore, a federal district court may enjoin a strike if it finds: (1) that the collective bargaining agreement provides for arbitration of the grievance which caused the strike; (2) that the employer must be willing to arbitrate the matter; and (3) that the injunction is warranted under ordinary principles of equity (e. g., is the employer suffering irreparable injury?).

See Boys Markets, Inc. v. Retail Clerk's Union, Local 770, 398 U.S. 235, 90 S.Ct. 1583, 26 L.Ed.2d 199 (1970).

NOTE—An injunctive remedy in a state court proceeding in the above situation would only theoretically be possible. 28 U.S.C.A. § 1441 permits all Section 301(a) suits to be removed to federal courts in order to insure the protection of federal rights and a more accurate development of federal law. See Avco Corp. v. Aero Lodge No. 735, Int'l Ass'n of Machinists and Aerospace Workers, 390 U.S. 557, 88 S.Ct. 1235, 20 L.Ed.2d 126 (1968), rehearing denied 391 U.S. 929, 88 S.Ct. 1801, 20 L.Ed.2d 670 (1968).

CASE 3—*union agreement restraining competition without furthering federal labor policy subject to antitrust laws*

Connell Construction Co. was the general contractor for a large construction project. The Plumbers Union had a collective bargaining agreement with a multiemployer association of mechanical contractors. That contract contained a "most favored nation" clause which provided that if the Plumbers granted a more favorable contract to another employer the more favorable clause or clauses would apply to employers in the association. The Plumbers asked Connell to agree that all plumbing and mechanical work at the construction site would be performed only by subcontractors with a contract with the Plumbers Union. Connell refused and a picket was posted at the entrance to the site. Other unions refused to work while the picket was present, and the job was shut down. The union's object was not to organize Connell's employees, but to exclude nonunion subcontractors from the market. That would exert pressure on those employers to execute collective bargaining agreements with the union. Connell signed the agreement with the Plumbers "under protest" and brought the present suit against the union for treble damages under the Sherman Antitrust Act and state antitrust laws. The Plumbers defended in part on the ground that the union was exempt from antitrust regulation. Is that defense valid?

Ans. No. Federal antitrust laws and the Norris-LaGuardia Act "declare that labor unions are not combinations or conspiracies in restraint of trade, and exempt specific union activities, including secondary picketing and boycotts, from the operation of the antitrust laws." However, that exception does not apply to agreements between a union and a nonlabor party where business competition is restrained. Such agreements are lawful only to the extent necessary to eliminate competition over wages and working conditions. The contract which the union forced Connell to sign by picketing "indiscriminately excluded nonunion subcontractors from a portion of the market, even if their competitive advantages were not derived from substandard wages and working conditions but rather from more efficient operating methods. Curtailment of competition based on efficiency is neither a goal of federal labor policy nor a necessary effect of the elimination of competition among workers. Moreover, competition based on efficiency is a positive value that the antitrust laws strive to protect." The effect of the challenged agreement was to eliminate competition among mechanical subcontractors on all subjects covered by the Plumbers' contract with the employer association even where the terms were not related to wages and working conditions. "The federal policy favoring collective bargaining therefore can offer no shelter for the union's coercive action against Connell or its campaign to exclude nonunion firms from the subcontracting market." With respect to the alleged violations of state antitrust laws, the Court held that they were preempted by federal law because they may conflict with federal labor policy. The Court held that the contract was subject to federal antitrust laws, but since the lower courts did not decide whether the contract restrains trade within the meaning of such laws, the case was remanded for that determination.

 See Connell Constr. Co. v. Plumbers and Steamfitters, Local 100, 421 U.S. 616, 95 S.Ct. 1830, 44 L.Ed.2d 418 (1975).

NOTE 1—Although the goal of the Plumbers, to organize subcontractors, was legal, that goal did not automatically exempt the method they used in an attempt to achieve it from the antitrust statutes. The Court concluded that the agreement which the Plumbers demanded Connell sign was unlawful in three respects: (a) Nonunion employers which might obtain subcontracts because of efficiency rather than substandard wages were prevented from obtaining subcontracts, and that did not advance any goal of national labor policy. (b) The "most favored nation" clause was not limited to terms or conditions of employment, thereby reducing competition among employers on unrelated matters. That is contrary to the Court's decision in Local 189, Amalgamated Meat Cutters v. Jewel Tea Co., 381 U.S. 676, 85 S.Ct. 1596, 14 L.Ed.2d 640 (1965) in which Justice White stated that federal labor policy only requires tolerance of labor agreements which lessen competition among employers on wages, hours and working conditions. (c) If the agreement between Connell and the Plumbers were valid, the union could arbitrarily exclude subcontractors from the market by refusing to sign a contract with them. These factors constituted a "direct restraint" on the construction market in the area.

NOTE 2—In CASE 3 above, the union also contended that Section 8(e) of the National Labor Relations Act, as amended, authorized agreements of the type sought. Section 8(e) prohibits, inter alia, agreements between an employer and a union whereby the employer agrees not to do business with any other person. However, a proviso to Section 8(e) exempts agreements in the construction industry relating to subcontracting of work to be performed at the construction site. The Court reviewed the legislative history of Section 8(e) and concluded that Congress only intended to exempt agreements arising from collective bargaining relationships. Since there was no such relationship between Connell and the Plumbers, the agreement sought was not protected by the proviso. The Court said that a contrary construction "would give construction unions an almost unlimited organizational weapon. The unions would be free to enlist any general contractor to bring economic pressure on nonunion subcontractors, as long as the agreement recited that it only covered work to be performed on some jobsite somewhere." The Court said that NLRB jurisdiction over Section 8(e) violations was not exclusive where, as in the present CASE, the question arose as a collateral issue in a suit based upon other federal laws. See Chapter X, LEGAL GEMS—Section 8(e)—Hot Cargo Clauses Unlawful, below.

LEGAL GEMS—The National Labor Relations Act of 1935 (Wagner Act)

1. Section 1 of the National Labor Relations Act states the Congressional purpose which is "to eliminate the causes of certain substantial obstructions to the free-flow of commerce . . . by encouraging the practice and procedure of collective bargaining and by protecting the exercise by workers of full freedom of association, self-organization, and designation of representatives of their own choosing, for the purpose of negotiating the terms and conditions of their employment or other mutual aid or protection."

2. The Act was held a valid exercise of Congress' power to regulate interstate commerce. See CASE 4, below.

3. The Act regulated the conduct of employers only, by creating five unfair labor practices which protected the organizational rights of employees and their right to bargain collectively. It was made an unfair labor practice for an employer to:
    (a) interfere with employees in the exercise of their right to join or assist unions,
    (b) dominate or interfere with the administration of a union,
    (c) discriminate against or discharge employees because of their union activities,
    (d) discriminate or discharge employees for assisting the National Labor Relations Board, and
    (e) refusing to bargain with the employees' representative.
    See Chapter V, Employer Unfair Labor Practices, and Chapter VI, Good Faith Bargaining, below.

DEVELOPMENT OF LABOR LEGISLATION

4. The Act created the National Labor Relations Board to:

    (a) conduct secret ballot elections among employees to determine whether they desired to be represented by a union, and

    (b) investigate, determine, and remedy unfair labor practices.

5. The Act covers all employees of employers in interstate commerce, except agricultural employees and supervisors.

NOTE 1—Retired employees are not included in the definition of "employee" in Section 2(3) of the Act. The Act "is concerned with the disruption to commerce that arises from interference with the organization and collective-bargaining rights of 'workers'—not those who have retired from the work force." Therefore, an employer is not required under the Act to bargain with the union concerning changes in benefits offered to retired employees. See Allied Chem. Workers v. Pittsburgh Plate Glass Co., 404 U.S. 157, 92 S.Ct. 383, 30 L.Ed.2d 341 (1971).

NOTE 2—A supervisor, as defined in Section 2(11) of the Act, may be protected under Section 8(a)(1) of the Act if he is discharged for the failure to commit unfair labor practices or as part of the employer's anti-union campaign. See N. L. R. B. v. Thermo-Rite Manufacturing Co., 406 F.2d 1033 (6th Cir. 1969). See also Chapter V, Employer Unfair Labor Practices, below.

CASE 4—*Wagner Act constitutional under Interstate Commerce Clause*

The Jones & Laughlin Steel Corporation was the fourth largest producer of steel in the United States. Its internal operations included mines, quarries and raw materials in many states and the means of transporting such materials to its main plant in Pennsylvania which plant the National Labor Relations Board said might be "likened to the heart of a self-contained, highly integrated body. They draw in the raw materials from Michigan, Minnesota, West Virginia, Pennsylvania in part through arteries and by means controlled by the respondent; they transform the materials and then pump them out to all parts of the nation through the vast mechanism which the respondent has elaborated." The corporation discharged certain employees for engaging in union activities, which discharges constituted an unfair labor practice under the National Labor Relations Act of 1935 (Wagner Act). It was alleged that the corporation was attempting by intimidation and coercion to prevent its employees from freely organizing themselves in a union. The corporation contended that the Act was in fact attempting to regulate labor relations between employers and employees and not interstate commerce, and that the Act was unconstitutional because the subject matter of labor relations, that is, problems of hiring, firing and organizing personnel, was wholly an *intra*-state matter. Is the contention correct?

Ans. No. The Act is constitutional on the ground that the corporation's vast transportation system constituted interstate commerce. Thus any strike, lockout or disruption of peaceful relations between the corporation and its employees

LABOR LAW—EMPLOYMENT DISCRIMINATION

was bound to AFFECT interstate commerce. The court took judicial notice of the fact that steel strikes have not only affected interstate commerce, but they have also been devastating in their economic effect. Under the Commerce Clause, Congress can regulate internal affairs of a company, such as the discharge of an employee, where the business affects interstate commerce. Thus, the employer was subject to the Act.

>See NLRB v. Jones & Laughlin Steel Corp., 301 U.S. 1, 57 S.Ct. 615, 81 L.Ed. 893 (1937). See also, Smith's Review, Constitutional Law, Chapter II, LEGAL GEMS—Federal Regulation of Interstate Commerce.

NOTE 1—CASE 4 above, illustrates the current definitional approach to interstate commerce utilizing the "Affectation Doctrine." The doctrine is the result of the Court's reasoning that the framers of the Constitution intended that Congress should have power to regulate an activity if it could be found as a fact that it "AFFECTS" interstate commerce. See Smith's Review, Constitutional Law, Chapter II, LEGAL GEMS —Federal Regulation of Interstate Commerce.

NOTE 2—Although the National Labor Relations Board could assert jurisdiction over all businesses that "affect" interstate commerce, the Board has voluntarily limited its jurisdiction with respect to different kinds of employers. The following are examples of the various standards applied to various kinds of business:

(a) The Board asserts jurisdiction over all nonretail businesses which have an annual outflow or inflow across state lines of at least $50,000, whether such outflow or inflow is regarded as direct or indirect. For the purposes of applying that standard, direct outflow is defined as goods shipped or services furnished by the employer outside his home state. Indirect outflow is defined as the sale of goods or services to users meeting any of the Board's jurisdictional standards excepting the indirect outflow or indirect inflow standard. Direct inflow is defined as goods or services furnished the employer directly from outside the state. Indirect inflow is defined as goods which originated outside the state, but which the employer purchased from a seller or supplier within the state. See Siemons Mailing Service, 122 NLRB 81 (1958).

(b) The Board asserts jurisdiction over all retail enterprises which have a gross volume of business of at least $500,000 annually. See Carolina Supplies and Cement Co., 122 NLRB 88 (1958).

(c) The Board has asserted jurisdiction over professional baseball teams. See The American League of Professional Baseball Clubs, 180 NLRB 190 (1969).

(d) The Board asserts jurisdiction over private universities and colleges and symphony orchestras which have at least $1,000,000 gross annual revenue from all sources, excluding contributions not available for operating expenses because of limitations imposed by the grantor.

DEVELOPMENT OF LABOR LEGISLATION

LEGAL GEMS—The Labor-Management Relations Act of 1947 (Taft-Hartley Act)

1. Union membership grew from three million in 1935 to almost fifteen million in 1947. This growth was made possible by:

    (a) the Norris-LaGuardia Act which prevented courts from enjoining most strikes, boycotts and picketing,

    (b) the Wagner Act which protected employees in organizing and required employers to bargain in good faith with the union selected by the employees, and

    (c) the Smith-Connally Act, sometimes called the War Labor Disputes Act, which gave statutory recognition to the National War Labor Board. This Board resolved management-union disputes during World War II to prevent strikes, and its policies assisted labor organizational efforts.

2. In 1947 the general public was concerned over many strikes, secondary boycotts and the abuse of power by union officials.

3. This public concern led to passage of the Taft-Hartley Act in 1947 to balance some of the advantages given to unions under prior legislation by imposing corresponding duties on unions.

4. The Taft-Hartley Act retained the employer unfair labor practices of the Wagner Act, but made certain union conduct an unfair labor practice. See Chapter IX, Union Unfair Labor Practices, and Chapter X, Picketing and Boycotts, below.

5. The principal changes in the Act may be summarized as follows:

    (a) "It abolishes the closed shop, but permits the union shop under conditions specified in the Act;"

    (b) "It exempts supervisors from its coverage;"

    (c) "It requires the Board to accord equal treatment to both independent and affiliated unions;"

    (d) "It permits the employer to file a representation petition even though only one union seeks to represent the employees;"

    (e) "It reorganizes the National Labor Relations Board and establishes guideposts to assist the Board in establishing the appropriate unit;"

    (f) "It grants employees the right not only to organize and bargain collectively but also to refrain from such activities;"

    (g) "It permits employees to file decertification petitions for elections to determine whether or not employees desire to revoke a union's designation as their bargaining agent;"

    (h) "It declares certain activities engaged in by unions to be unfair labor practices;"

LABOR LAW—EMPLOYMENT DISCRIMINATION

(i) "It gives to employers, employees, and unions new guarantees of the right of free speech;"

(j) "It provides for settlement by the Board of certain jurisdictional disputes;"

(k) "It vests in the General Counsel, rather than in the Board, the authority to investigate and prosecute unfair labor practices. This permits the Board to serve in a judicial capacity." CCH ¶ 1012.

NOTE—By an amendment to Section 7 of the Act, employees were given the right to refrain from union activities. See Chapter V, LEGAL GEMS—Rights of Employees—Section 8(a)(1) Violations, below.

6. The Taft-Hartley Act also revived use of the injunction in certain situations to prevent or stop unfair labor practices.

e.g. Jurisdictional strikes by unions over the assignment of work by the employer could be enjoined.

See generally Cox, pp. 88–94; Gorman, pp. 5–6; Smith, pp. 44–45.

LEGAL GEMS—Labor-Management Reporting and Disclosure Act of 1959 (Landrum-Griffin Act)

1. Further experience with labor laws brought to light corruption in some unions and the conduct of internal affairs of some unions in an undemocratic manner. This led to passage of the Landrum-Griffin Act.

2. The Act was passed to protect the rights and interests of employees and the public generally as they related to the activities of labor organizations, employers and labor relations consultants. See Section 2 of the Act.

3. The Act sought to eliminate or prevent certain improper or unethical practices by:

(a) giving union members a Bill of Rights, Title I, see Chapter XI, Other Rights of Employees, below,

(b) reporting to the Office of Labor-Management and Welfare-Pension Reports various union affairs, including Trusteeships and transactions between employers and unions, Titles II & III, see Chapter XI, Other Rights of Employees below, and

(c) amending the Taft-Hartley Act to strengthen the secondary boycott sections which limited picketing in certain circumstances and Section 8(e), "hot cargo" section, see Chapter X, Picketing and Boycotts, below.

See generally Cox, pp. 95–96; Gorman, p. 6; Smith, pp. 47–49.

IV. PROCEDURE AND REMEDIES

LEGAL GEMS—Procedure and Remedies—Introduction

1. The procedure by which a right granted by statute is vindicated depends on the statute which grants that right.
2. The administration of rights guaranteed by the NLRA, as amended, rests with the NLRB.
3. Where the Act has been violated a charge must be filed with the NLRB, which has exclusive original jurisdiction over the matter. A party may not file suit directly in federal court alleging a violation of the NLRA.

NOTE—The procedure for remedying violations of the NLRA, as amended, should be contrasted to the procedure which must be followed under other labor laws whereby the aggrieved party may:

    (a) bring suit in federal court originally, or

    (b) bring suit in federal court after filing a charge with the appropriate administrative agency.

See Chapter XIII, Other Laws Governing Labor Relations, below.

4. The NLRB investigates charges and adjudicates disputes arising under the Act in administrative proceedings.

LEGAL GEMS—Procedure Before NLRB in Unfair Labor Practice Cases

1. Within six months of the alleged unfair labor practice, a charge must be filed with the NLRB and served on the charged employer or union. The charge must state the nature of the alleged unfair labor practice.
2. Any individual, company or union may file a charge; there are no restrictions.
3. The charge is then investigated:

    (a) If it has no merit, it is dismissed.

    (b) If a prima facie case is presented by the charging party which is not rebutted by the charged party, a formal complaint is issued by the General Counsel of the Board.

4. There are three parties to an NLRB proceeding:

    (a) the charging party,

    (b) the General Counsel, and

(c) the respondent.

5. If a complaint is issued, the matter is heard in an administrative proceeding before an administrative law judge who makes findings of fact and conclusions of law in a written decision.

6. The decision of the administrative law judge may be appealed by any party to the five man National Labor Relations Board (hereinafter NLRB or the Board).

7. The Board reviews the trial examiner's decision and issues a decision of its own. *That decision is not self-enforcing.*

8. If the respondent does not comply with the Board's decision, the Board must seek enforcement in a federal court of appeals.

9. In addition, any aggrieved party may petition a federal court of appeals to review the Board's decision.

NOTE—On review the court must find that the evidence supporting the decision is substantial when viewed in the light of the entire record, including whatever evidence fairly detracts from its weight. The evidence is substantial if a reasonable mind might accept it as adequate to support a conclusion. See Universal Camera Corp. v. NLRB, 340 U.S. 474, 71 S.Ct. 456, 95 L.Ed. 456 (1951). See also Smith's Review Administrative Law, Chapter X, Scope of Judicial Review.

10. The decision of a federal court of appeals may be appealed to the United States Supreme Court.

LEGAL GEMS—The Board and Its Remedies

1. The National Labor Relations Act is administered by the National Labor Relations Board.

2. There are two principal functions of the Board:

    (a) to prevent and remedy unfair labor practices, and

    (b) to conduct secret ballot elections to determine whether employees want to be represented by a union for collective bargaining. See Chapter XII, Representation Proceedings, below.

3. Section 3 of the Act divides the Board into two separate entities:

    (a) the General Counsel, who investigates and prosecutes unfair labor practices, and

    (b) the Board, which decides cases arising under the Act.

4. When a court of appeals refuses to enforce a Board decision, the Board is not bound to follow that court decision in subsequent cases. The Board has stated: "It has been the Board's consistent policy for itself to determine whether to acquiesce in the contrary views of a circuit court of appeals or whether, with due deference to the court's opinion, to adhere to its previous holding until the Supreme Court of the United States has ruled otherwise." Insurance Agents' Int'l Union, AFL–CIO, 119 NLRB 768 (1957).

PROCEDURE AND REMEDIES

5. The remedies for employer or union unfair labor practices include:
   (a) Posting a signed notice for sixty (60) days which states:
   - (1) that the offending party will not engage in those violations which it has committed (negative provisions),
   - (2) the affirmative action which will be done to remedy the unfair labor practices (affirmative provisions), and
   - (3) a summary of the rights of employees under the Act.

   (b) An employer must offer reinstatement with back pay to any unlawfully discharged employee.

   (c) A union must notify the employer and the employee in writing that it has no objection to the employment of the employee whom it has caused to be discharged and give him back pay.

6. If a union engages in mass picketing or other unlawful conduct and prevents employees from working, the union is not required to give back pay to those workers. See United Furniture Workers of America, CIO, 84 NLRB 563 (1949); Local 983, United Bhd. of Carpenters and Joiners of America, AFL-CIO, 115 NLRB 1123 (1956).

CAVEAT—Section 303 of the Act authorizes private suits by an employer for damages resulting from unlawful secondary activity by a union. See Chapter X, LEGAL GEMS—Legal Restrictions on Secondary Boycotts, above.

LEGAL GEMS—Remedies—Computation of Back Pay

1. Back pay is the amount of money which the discriminatee would have earned absent the discrimination against him.
2. In addition to the usual wages of the employee, back pay includes:
   (a) lost overtime,
   (b) paid holidays,
   (c) vacation pay, and
   (d) other fringe benefits such as bonuses and insurance benefits.
3. The discriminatee has the duty to mitigate the amount of damages (back pay) by seeking other employment.
4. Money earned during the back pay period is deducted from back pay.
5. Back pay is computed by calendar quarter. If a discriminatee obtains a higher paying job in one quarter, this will not affect the back pay due in any other quarter.
6. Interest at the rate of 6% is added to back pay. See Isis Plumbing and Heating Co., 138 NLRB 716 (1962).

V. EMPLOYER UNFAIR LABOR PRACTICES

LEGAL GEMS—Employer Unfair Labor Practices—Introduction

1. There are five employer unfair labor practices listed in Section 8(a) of the National Labor Relations Act, as amended. It is an unfair labor practice:

    8(a)(1) "to interfere with, restrain, or coerce employees in the exercise of the rights guaranteed in Section 7;"

    8(a)(2) "to dominate or interfere with the formation or administration of any labor organization or contribute financial or other support to it . . . ;"

    8(a)(3) "by discrimination in regard to hire or tenure of employment or any term or condition of employment to encourage or discourage membership in any labor organization . . . ;"

    8(a)(4) "to discharge or otherwise discriminate against an employee because he has filed charges or given testimony under this Act;"

    8(a)(5) "to refuse to bargain collectively with the representatives of his employees . . . ."

    Section 8(a)(5) violations are analyzed in Chapter VI, Good Faith Bargaining, and Chapter VII, The Collective Bargaining Agreement, below. The other employer unfair labor practices are analyzed in this Chapter.

2. Section 7 provides that: "Employees shall have the right to self-organization, to form, join, or assist labor organizations, to bargain collectively through representatives of their own choosing, and to engage in other concerted activities for the purpose of collective bargaining or other mutual aid or protection, and shall also have the right to refrain from any or all of such activities . . . ."

3. An employer is responsible for the actions of its supervisors and also for employees and non-employees if they are authorized to act as agents of the employer, or if the employer fails to repudiate their conduct when known to him. Thus, upon the agency principle of ratification an employer may be responsible for interference by non-employees with employee rights guaranteed in Section 7.

4. A violation of Section 8(a)(2), (3), (4), or (5), is also a DERIVATIVE violation of Section 8(a)(1).

5. A violation of Section 8(a)(1) which does *not* also violate some other section of the Act is an INDEPENDENT violation.

6. A discharge for concerted activities alone, as distinguished from a discharge to encourage or discourage union membership, violates

EMPLOYER UNFAIR LABOR PRACTICES

only Section 8(a)(1). However, the remedy, reinstatement with back pay, is the same for both violations.

LEGAL GEMS—Rights of Employees—Section 8(a)(1) Violations

1. The interference, restraint or coercion which are proscribed by Section 8(a)(1) may be summarized by the key word "FIBS":

   Futility of Unionization—telling employees that selecting a union will not benefit them because the employer will not bargain with the union, or will not give the employees any more benefits than they now receive.

   Interrogation—questioning employees regarding their union activities or sympathies. See GEMS 5-8, below.

   Benefits—promising benefits or threatening employees with the loss of present privileges. See CASE 5, below.

   Surveillance—watching a union meeting or giving employees the impression that their union activities are being watched.

      e.g. Statements such as "I know all about the union meeting last night" or "I know who signed union cards" violate the Act.

2. In analyzing whether certain statements of an employer violate Section 8(a)(1) reference must be made to Section 8(c) of the Act which provides: "The expressing of any views, argument, or opinion . . . shall not constitute or be evidence of an unfair labor practice . . . if such expression contains no threat of reprisal or force or promise of benefit."

3. Section 8(c) means that speech, which by its own terms is not coercive, cannot violate the Act unless it is intertwined with unlawful conduct. The employer's statements must be considered against the entire labor relations background to determine whether they constitute a threat of reprisal or are a mere prediction of what might occur.

   (a) The employer made several speeches to employees during an organizational campaign by a union. In those speeches the employer listed present benefits and asked whether they wanted "to gamble all these things." He explained that if required to bargain he would do so on "a cold-blooded business basis" so that employees "may come out with a lot less than you have now." The employer emphasized his own control over wages, and that he could not be forced to sign a contract in the absence of agreement, "so what will probably happen is the union will call a strike." The employer then told employees how they could be replaced if they went on strike. Furthermore, the idea that union representation would be futile was conveyed. The employer said that he would not change his wage policy and would only sign a contract he wanted and agreed to. The court noted that during the campaign some employees were unlawfully discharge or demoted. It had no difficulty in finding that the employer's statements were not protected by Section 8(c). There was a threat that the employer would bargain "from scratch" as though no economic benefits had been given, and the employees would suffer economic loss if they selected the union. Other statements showed the futility of selecting a union. Thus, the statements constituted a violation of Section 8(a)(1). See Dal-Tex Optical Co., 137 NLRB 1782 (1962).

(b) During a union organizing campaign the employer sent letters to employees saying that similar businesses which have been organized have had to increase the work load of employees by reducing the number of employees to offset higher costs and remain competitive. In a speech employees were reminded of favors given to them such as time off for special reasons. The employer then said: "We will always give you reasonable consideration. Under a contract we would be subject to the rules of that contract. If we did these things, we could be charged with favoritism, we would be violating our contract. These things could well go by the board as a result." The NLRB concluded that the employer's remarks were calculated to create a fear of loss of benefits and economic suffering if they supported the union and found that they violated Section 8(a)(1). On appeal the Board was reversed. The court noted that it was not alleged that the employer committed any other unfair labor practices. A fair reading of the employer's letters showed that the employer would increase the work load or reduce employment only for economic necessity. The withdrawal of special privileges would not be in retaliation for union activities, but the contract with the union might forbid giving a benefit to one employee unless it were given to all. Thus, the employer's statements were not threats of reprisal and there was no violation of Section 8(a)(1). See NLRB v. Golub Corp., 388 F.2d 921 (2nd Cir. 1967).

4. Where there is only an isolated instance of conduct violative of Section 8(a)(1), the Board may decline to proceed with a charge against the employer because it would not effectuate the purposes of the Act.

e.g. Foreman X, a supervisor, and employee Y are good friends and always travel to and from work together in X's car. During a union organizational campaign, while they were riding in the car, X asked Y, "What do you think about the union?" This question is unlawful interrogation, but if no other unfair labor practices were committed by other supervisors, the Board would not issue an unfair labor practice complaint based on that single incident.

NOTE—In deciding whether unlawful statements are isolated the Board considers, inter alia:

  (a) the number of incidents compared to the number of employees in the unit,

  (b) whether the person making the statement is a high management official or a low echelon supervisor, and

  (c) whether the unlawful statement is likely to be spread among employees.

   e.g. A foreman tells one employee that the employer will close the plant rather than bargain with a union. This is a threat which the employee is likely to communicate to other employees. Where there is interrogation in the course of a casual conversation, such as in the example after **GEM 4**, above, it is not likely that the employee will tell others that the employer is trying to learn the identity of union supporters. Thus, the nature of the statement made may determine in some cases whether the Board will proceed against the employer for violation of the Act.

5. Interrogation concerning union sympathies is a violation "because of its natural tendency to instill in the minds of employees fear of discrimination on the basis of the information the employer has obtained." NLRB v. West Coast Gasket Co., 205 F.2d 902, 904 (9th Cir. 1953).

6. If an employee *freely* volunteers information about a union to a supervisor, it is not an unfair labor practice for the supervisor to listen to what the employee says.

7. If the union has demanded recognition the employer may poll, as distinguished from interrogate, employees concerning their union sympathies to decide whether to recognize the union under the following conditions:

  (a) the purpose of the poll is to determine the truth of a union's claim of majority,

  (b) that purpose is communicated to the employees,

  (c) assurances against reprisal are given,

  (d) the employees are polled by secret ballot, and

  (e) the employer has not engaged in unfair labor practices or otherwise created a coercive atmosphere.

   See Struksnes Constr. Co., 165 NLRB 1062 (1967), which revised the criteria for polling employees formerly governed by Blue Flash Express, Inc., 109 NLRB 591 (1954).

8. A poll of employees may not be taken while a petition for a Board election is pending because it would not serve any legitimate in-

terest of the employer that would not be better served by the forthcoming Board election.

9. If the employer's unfair labor practices outlined above make it impossible to conduct a fair election to determine whether a majority of employees want to be represented by a union, and a union has valid authorization cards signed by a majority of employees, the Board will order the employer to bargain with the union in order to remedy its unfair labor practice. See **CASE 23**, below.

NOTE—A union may also violate the Act by restraining or coercing employees in the exercise of their Section 7 rights. For union violations see the analysis under Section 8(b)(1)(A) in Chapter VIII, Union Unfair Labor Practices, below.

CASE 5—*section 8(a)(1) prohibits benefits to influence union activity*

During an organizational drive the employer granted employees an extra holiday and additional overtime and vacation benefits. These benefits were placed into effect unconditionally on a permanent basis and no other unlawful conduct was alleged. May an employer confer benefits on employees while a petition for a representation election is pending?

Ans. No. Section 8(a)(1) gives employees the right to organize without employer interference. Benefits conferred on employees prior to an election interfere with this right just as threats or promises of benefit. It must be presumed that the benefits were given to influence the outcome of the election. Therefore, the granting of benefits interfered with the employees' exercise of their Section 7 rights and violated Section 8(a)(1) of the Act.

See NLRB v. Exchange Parts Co., 375 U.S. 405, 84 S.Ct. 457, 11 L.Ed.2d 435 (1964).

NOTE—Withholding a benefit because of the union organizing would likewise be an unfair labor practice.

> *e.g.* An employer has announced that certain benefits will be effective on a specific date in the future. If a union organizing drive is in progress on that date NOT placing the benefits into effect violates the Act because it interferes with employee rights. Employees might believe that the benefit was postponed or lost because they engaged in union activity. This would discourage the activity which the Act was designed to protect. The same principle would apply to any annual benefit given to employees, such as a Christmas bonus.

LEGAL GEMS—Discharge for Concerted Activities

1. The discharge of an employee for engaging in activity protected by Section 7, but which does not encourage or discourage union activity violates ONLY Section 8(a)(1). A discharge which encourages or discourages union activity violates Section 8(a)(3) and is an 8(a)(1) violation only by derivation. See **CASE 6**, below.

(a) If two employees approach their supervisor and together complain that the plant is too cold, or if one employee asks for a raise on behalf of the other employees, there is *concerted activity for mutual aid* and the employees cannot be discriminated against because of this. However, if one employee asks for a wage increase only for himself, he is not acting in concert with anyone and could be discharged for that request without violating the Act.

(b) The coats of several female employees were slashed with a knife by an unknown person while they were working at the plant. Four girls approached their foreman to complain about this. Their spokesman said, "Some son-of-a-bitch cut my coat," and she wanted to know "What kind of goddam shit is this?" They proceeded to the company offices and she asked the vice president "what the hell was going on" and told the company president that she was "mad, goddammed good and mad." The employees asked to be reimbursed for the damage to their coats, but the president refused. However, he said that he would consider buying a large locker to keep the coats in until quitting time. When the girls' spokesman reported for work the next day she was suspended for "her foul and abusive language when coming into the main office." When she reported back to work after her suspension she was discharged. The Board found that the employees were engaged in protected activity when they protested the lack of protection for their wearing apparel. The vulgarities used were not so reprehensible as to have removed the employee from the protection of the Act. The reason given for the suspension and discharge was a pretext and the employee was actually suspended and discharged for her participation in the presentation of employee grievances, a right guaranteed by Section 7 of the Act. Therefore, the suspension and discharge violated Section 8(a)(1) and the employee was ordered reinstated with back pay. See G & S Metal Products Co., Inc., 182 NLRB 111 (1970).

2. Discussion among employees of the appointment of an inexperienced foreman is protected activity because it affects their working conditions.

   e.g. The employees did not choose a spokesman, but went individually to the employer and complained about the new foreman, because his inexperience made their work more difficult in the field. Each employee was protected in making his complaints because their activity was also concerted because of their previous discussion of the matter together and the fact that the complaints were designed to assist all employees. Therefore, discharges because of the complaints violated Section 8(a)(1). See NLRB v. Guernsey-Muskingum Electric Co-op, 285 F.2d 8 (6th Cir. 1960).

LABOR LAW—EMPLOYMENT DISCRIMINATION

3. If an employer investigates a matter which may result in disciplinary action being taken against an employee, the employer must permit a union representative to be present when the employee is questioned if the employee so requests. The refusal of the employer to honor such a request violates Section 8(a)(1) because it denies to the employee the right to engage in concerted activities for mutual aid or protection. See CASE 7, below.

4. Not all concerted activity of employees is protected. The purpose of the activity must be lawful and the means used must be consistent with national labor policy.

   (a) E employed carloaders who were paid on an incentive basis, averaging $2.71 an hour. E installed new equipment which changed the method of loading and made it easier. At the same time wages were reduced to $1.52½ an hour. The carloaders, who were not represented by a union, decided to load only one car a day to protest E's actions although they could have loaded more than one car. A spokesman for the carloaders told E that they would not increase their work unless their wages were increased. E discharged five carloaders who filed a charge with the NLRB. They contended that they were discharged for engaging in concerted activity protected by the Act. The Board concluded that although the carloaders acted with the lawful object of increasing their wages, their plan of decreasing production to what they considered adequate was not protected. "In effect, this constituted a refusal on their part to accept the terms of employment set by their employer without engaging in a stoppage, but to continue rather to work on their own terms." This conduct justified their discharges. The carloaders had the legal right to strike, but they did not have the right to report to work, accept the wages E paid, and perform only so much work as they chose. Since the slowdown was not protected activity the discharges were lawful. See Elk Lumber Co., 91 NLRB 333 (1950).

   (b) The union representing television technicians at station WBTV was not able to agree on the renewal of their collective bargaining agreement. The technicians continued to work without a contract, but peacefully picketed the station while they were not on duty to publicize their labor dispute. In addition, some of the technicians had 5,000 handbills printed which disparaged their employer's programs, service and business policies. It suggested the reason was that the station considered the city a "second-class city." The handbill was signed "WBT Technicians." It did not mention the labor dispute. The handbills were widely distributed throughout the city in an attempt to harm the station's reputation and reduce its advertising income. The station discharged ten employees for distributing the handbills. The employees filed a charge with the Board alleging that their discharges were unlawful because the distribution of the handbills was protected concerted activity. The discharge of one employee was found unlawful because he had not in fact distributed the handbill. However, the discharge of the other nine employees was upheld. Insubordination, disobedience or disloyalty are adequate grounds for discharge. The handbill attacked interests of WBTV that employees were being paid to conserve and develop. That a labor dispute existed when the attack was made does not protect the activity. Even if the technicians were acting in furtherance of their Section 7 rights, the means used deprived them of the protection of the Act. The discharge of the technicians who distributed the handbills was upheld. See NLRB v. Local 1229, IBEW (Jefferson Standard Broadcasting Co.), 346 U.S. 464, 74 S.Ct. 172, 98 L.Ed. 195 (1953).

CASE 6—*discharge without anti-union motivation held unlawful*

Employee X tells his employer that Y and Z, while soliciting membership in a union, said that if they did not get enough employees to join, the union would get into the plant by dynamite. Based on this evidence the employer discharged Y and Z. The accusations of X were later found to be false. Did the discharge violate the Act?

Ans. Yes. Interference with the rights guaranteed in Section 7 of the Act does not necessarily depend on the existence of anti-union bias by the employer. Section 8(a)(1) is violated if it is shown that: (a) the discharged employee was at the time engaged in a protected activity; (b) the employer knew it was such; (c) the basis of the discharge was an alleged act of misconduct in the course of that activity; (d) the employee was not, in fact, guilty of that misconduct. On these facts the discharges are unlawful. Otherwise, protected activity would lose some of its immunity since employees could be discharged on false charges.

See NLRB v. Burnup & Sims, Inc., 379 U.S. 21, 85 S.Ct. 171, 13 L.Ed.2d 1 (1964).

NOTE—The rule in CASE 6 above, is broad enough to cover the following situation: For many years a house near the employer's plant was operated as a brothel. This fact was known to everyone in the town. The employer, a deeply religious man, warned employees many times that any employee seen entering that house would be summarily discharged. Unknown to the employer the house went out of business and was sold to a union which used it as an office for organizational activity. The employer saw an employee entering the house and, thinking it was still a house of ill repute, summarily discharged him. Did this violate the Act? Ans. Yes. The discharge violates Section 8(a)(1) because the employee was engaged in protected activity—seeking to meet with union representatives. That the employer did not know this and thought the employee intended to engage in some immoral activity does not excuse the employer's action. The employer acted at his own peril. However, if the house had been converted into a school instead of a Union Hall the discharge would not violate the Act since going to school is not a protected activity under the Act.

CASE 7—*employee entitled to union representation at investigative interview*

An employer was investigating losses from shoplifting and employee dishonesty at one of its retail stores. Based upon the report of another employee the store manager called an employee into his office. She was questioned by the store manager and an undercover security person. The employee requested several times that her union shop steward be called into the meeting, but her requests were denied. The employee was cleared of any wrongdoing and permitted to return to work. Subsequently, the employee reported the details of the interview to her union and an unfair labor practice charge was filed with the NLRB. The Board concluded that the denial of union representation to the employee after it was requested interfered with the employee's right to engage in concerted activities for mutual aid or protection. Since this right is guaranteed by Section 7 of the Act, the employer was found to have violated Section 8(a)(1) of the Act. On appeal the employer contended that the Board's construction of the Act was improper. Should the Board's decision be enforced?

Ans. Yes. The Board's holding is a permissible construction of the Act. The Court approved the Board's deliniation of the employee's right, which is as follows: (a) The right of employees to act in concert for mutual aid or protection is guaranteed in Section 7 of the Act. To require an employee to appear unassisted at an interview which may result in disciplinary action against him dilutes the right to act collectively rather than rely on individual self protection. (b) The right to union representation arises only when the employee requests it. The employee can waive that right by failing to ask for a union representative. (c) The employee's right to representation is limited to situations in which the employee reasonably believes that the investigation will result in disciplinary action. The rule does not apply where an employee is merely being instructed in his work. (d) The exercise of the right may not interfere with legitimate employer prerogatives. Thus, an employer may decline to interview an employee if the employee insists that a union representative be present. The employer may also continue the investigation without any information which the employee might furnish. (e) If a union representative attends the investigative interview, the employer is not obligated to bargain with the representative. It is only after discipline has been taken that the duty to bargain arises. The union representative is present only to assist the employee. He may clarify facts and suggest other employees who may have knowledge of pertinent facts. The Court concluded that the Board's construction of "concerted activities . . . for mutual aid or protection" was a reasonable construction of Section 7 and within the special expertise of the agency. It found that the Board fully explained its interpretation which attempted to balance the conflicting interests of labor and management. Therefore, the Board's finding that the denial of union representation to the employee violated Section 8(a)(1) was enforced.

See NLRB v. J. Weingarten, Inc., 420 U.S. 251, 95 S.Ct. 959, 43 L.Ed.2d 171 (1975). See also International Ladies' Garment Workers Union

v. Quality Mfg. Co., 420 U.S. 276, 95 S.Ct. 972, 43 L.Ed.2d 189 (1975).

LEGAL GEMS—Communications Among Employees—No-solicitation and No-distribution Rules

1. There have been numerous cases involving communications among employees at their employer's place of business, and this is a changing area of the law. The legal problem arises from a balancing of the employer's right to maintain production and discipline on its own property, and the right of employees to self-organization guaranteed in Section 7 of the Act.

2. A distinction is made between oral solicitation and the distribution of literature because these two organizational techniques are inherently different.

    (a) Oral solicitation, which includes signing union authorization cards, can impinge upon the employer's interests only if it occurs on working time.

    (b) Distribution of literature, since it might litter the premises and create a hazard to production, can impinge on the employer's interests whether it occurs on working time or nonworking time.

3. In balancing the right of employees to self-organization and the right of employers to maintain discipline in their establishments, the Board has established *rebuttable presumptions* to determine the legality of any particular rule.

    (a) A rule forbidding solicitation by employees during working time is presumptively valid.

    (b) A rule forbidding solicitation on company premises during nonworking time, such as lunch breaks, is presumptively invalid.

CAVEAT—The Court considered a hospital's rule prohibiting solicitation by its employees at all times "in any area of the Hospital which is accessible to or utilized by the public," including lobbies, gift shop, cafeteria, entrances, corridors and sitting rooms. The hospital offered evidence of the necessity for the rule to prevent interference with patients' treatment and convalescence. The Court held that there was sufficient evidence to warrant the prohibition of solicitation in corridors and sitting rooms on floors used by patients. However, the rule was not justified with respect to the gift shop, cafeteria and lobbies on the first floor because those areas are not normally used by patients. See NLRB v. Baptist Hospital, — U.S. —, 99 S.Ct. 2598, 61 L.Ed.2d 2599 (1979).

LABOR LAW—EMPLOYMENT DISCRIMINATION

- (c) A rule forbidding the distribution of literature in working areas is presumptively valid, even though it is applicable to both working and nonworking time.
- (d) A rule forbidding the distribution of literature in nonworking areas on nonworking time is presumptively invalid. See CASE 8, below.

NOTE—No-solicitation and no-distribution rules must apply to all solicitation and distribution to be valid. A rule applicable only to union solicitation or distribution and not to charitable solicitations would be invalid.

4. The rights of employees to engage in solicitation or distribution may not be waived.

   e.g. The employer and the union agreed in their collective bargaining agreement that the company could enforce a rule prohibiting the distribution of literature in nonworking areas on nonworking time. In turn the employer permitted the union to use a bulletin board to communicate with employees. Was the employer's rule valid under these circumstances? Ans. No. The employer's rule violated the Act because employees who might be opposed to the union could not disseminate their views through literature. This interfered with their rights. The Court said that so long as the distribution is by employees to employees, and so long as the in-plant solicitation is on nonworking time, banning of that solicitation could interfere with their rights under the Act. Therefore, a union cannot waive the solicitation and distribution rights which employees have under the Act. See NLRB v. Magnavox Co., 415 U.S. 322, 94 S.Ct. 1099, 39 L.Ed.2d 358 (1974).

5. Employees may ordinarily wear union buttons or other emblems at any time. See Republic Aviation Corp. v. NLRB, 324 U.S. 793, 65 S.Ct. 982, 89 L.Ed. 1372 (1945).

6. The language used to frame no-solicitation and no-distribution rules is important. If the rule may be interpreted to be unlawfully broad, it will be found to be an 8(a)(1) violation. The reason is that the risk of ambiguity must be borne by the promulgator of the rule rather than by the employees who are supposed to abide by it.

CAVEAT—The use of the term "working time" in a rule is permissible because it is not ambiguous, but use of the term "working hours" renders the rule unlawfully broad. "The term 'working hours' connotes the period of time from the beginning to the end of a workshift. Thus, the use of that term in a no-solicitation or no-distribution rule is reasonably calculated to mean that employees are prohibited from engaging in any form of union solicitation or distribution of union literature from the time they 'clock in,' or begin their workshift, until the time they 'clock out,' or end their workshift. By contrast, the term 'working time' or 'work time' connotes the period of time that is spent in the performance of actual job duties, which would not include time alloted for lunch and break periods. Thus, the use of that term in a no-solicitation or no-distribution rule would clearly convey the meaning to employees that they were free to engage in solicitation or distribution during lunch and break periods which occur during their 'working hours.'" Essex Int'l, Inc., 211 NLRB 749 (1974).

7. An employer is not normally required to permit nonemployees to enter his premises to conduct organizing activities. See NLRB v. Babcock & Wilcox Co., 351 U.S. 105, 76 S.Ct. 679, 100 L.Ed. 975 (1956).

CAVEAT—Although the general rule is that an employer may bar nonemployee union organizers from its property, there are situations where that rule does not apply. "To gain access, the union has the burden of showing that no other reasonable means of communicating its organizational message to the employees exists or that the employer's access rules discriminate against union solicitation." Sears, Roebuck & Co. v. San Diego County Dist. Counsel of Carpenters, 436 U.S. 180, 98 S.Ct. 1745, 56 L.Ed.2d 209 (1978).

8. The Board has held that an off duty employee does not have the right to enter an employer's premises to engage in organizational activities if the rule prohibiting access is non-discriminatory and other means of communication are available.

e.g. An employer promulgated a rule in its employee handbook which stated: "An employee is not to enter the plant or remain on the premises unless he is on duty or scheduled for work." A majority of the Board concluded that where an employer's no-access rule denies all off-duty employees access to the premises for any purpose and is not discriminatorily applied only against employees engaged in union activities, the rule is presumptively valid absent a showing by the union that no adequate alternative means of communication is available to it. See GTE Lenkurt, Inc., 204 NLRB 921 (1973).

NOTE—Subsequent Board decisions have limited the rule in the Lenkurt case. The Board has held that such a rule is valid only if it:
  (a) limits access solely with respect to the interior of the plant and other working areas,
  (b) is clearly disseminated to all employees, and
  (c) applies to off-duty employees seeking access to the plant for any purpose and not just to those employees engaging in union activity.

The Board concluded that "except where justified by business reasons, a rule which denies off-duty employees entry to parking lots, gates, and other outside nonworking areas will be found invalid." Tri-County Medical Center, Inc., 222 NLRB 1089 (1976).

CASE 8—*prohibitions of union activities in the plant—the rules and exceptions*

The employer enforced a plant rule prohibiting "unauthorized distribution of literature of any description on company premises". Does this rule interfere with employee organizational rights?

Ans. Yes. The validity of rules restricting union solicitation or distribution of union literature on company property depends on the balancing of the right of employees to self-organization and the right of employers to maintain discipline in their plant. No solicitations are permitted when employees are supposed to be working. However, oral solicitation by employees is subject only to the restriction that it must be on non-working time in the absence of special circumstances which necessitate a broader rule. Distribution of literature must be on non-working time in non-working areas of the plant unless special circumstances are shown making the broad rule necessary. Since no such justification was shown in the present case, the broad company rule interfered with the exercise of Section 7 rights by employees and violated Section 8(a)(1) of the Act.

See Stoddard–Quirk Mfg. Co., 138 NLRB 615 (1962). See also Eastex, Inc. v. NLRB, 437 U.S. 556, 98 S.Ct. 2505, 57 L.Ed.2d 428 (1978).

NOTE—An ambiguous rule which may be interpreted by employees as restricting their rights is also invalid. Thus, a rule reading "no solicitation on company time" is invalid because employees may reason that since they are paid for breaks and lunch periods that is "company time", when actually those are periods when solicitations are permitted.

LEGAL GEMS—Discrimination Based on Race, Color, Religion, Sex or National Origin

1. The possibility that race discrimination might violate Section 8(a)(1) was first considered in a circuit court decision. It said that racial discrimination may violate Section 8(a)(1) if both of the following conditions are present:
   (a) it sets up a clash of interests between groups of employees which reduces their ability to work in concert to achieve their legitimate goals under the Act, and
   (b) it creates in the employees a docility which inhibits them from asserting their rights.
   This case was remanded to the NLRB for further factual findings. See United Packinghouse Workers Union v. NLRB, 416 F.2d 1126 (D.C.Cir.), cert. denied 396 U.S. 903, 90 S.Ct. 216, 24 L.Ed.2d 179 (1969).
2. On remand the Board concluded that the employer did not maintain a policy and practice of racial discrimination against its em-

ployees on account of their race or national origin as alleged. Thus, the Board did not reach the issue presented by the court. See Farmers' Cooperative Compress, 194 NLRB 85 (1971).

3. In a later case the Board considered that issue and stated: "[D]iscrimination based on race, color, religion, sex, or national origin, standing alone . . . is not 'inherently destructive' of employees' Section 7 rights and therefore is not violative of Section 8(a)(1) and (3) of the Act. There must be actual evidence, as opposed to speculation, of a nexus between the alleged discriminatory conduct and the interference with, or restraint of, employees in the exercise of those rights protected by the Act." Jubilee Mfg. Co., 202 NLRB 272 (1973), aff'd per curiam 504 F.2d 271 (D.C.Cir. 1974).

4. While discrimination based on race, color, religion, sex, or national origin does not violate Section 8(a)(1) per se, such discrimination may come within reach of the Act in certain situations:

   (a) Flagrant and irrelevant appeals to racial prejudice are grounds to set aside a representation election.

   (b) Concerted activity by employees to protest employer discrimination, whether actual or supposed, is protected by Section 7.

   (c) Refusal to bargain in good faith concerning the elimination of racial discrimination violates Section 8(a)(5).

   See Jubilee Mfg. Co., 202 NLRB 272 (1973), aff'd per curiam 504 F.2d 271 (D.C.Cir. 1974).

LEGAL GEMS—Domination or Assistance of Union

1. Section 8(a)(2) of the Taft-Hartley Act makes it an unfair labor practice for an employer "to dominate or interfere with the formation or administration of any labor organization or contribute financial or other support to it . . . ."

2. The purpose of this section is to make certain that the union representing employees is completely independent of the company and of company interference.

3. There is no distinction between AFL-CIO affiliated unions and unaffiliated, independent unions in the application of this Section.

4. Employer violations fall into two categories:

   (a) DOMINATION. A union is dominated by an employer if it was instigated or organized by supervisors and they control it or if supervisors subsequently are able to control or veto the actions of the union.

   (b) ASSISTANCE. Assistance is unlawful conduct which falls short of domination but still interferes with the employees' freedom in controlling the affairs of their union. An employer may not help in the formation or administration of the union, recognize it when it does not represent a majority of employees, or give financial assistance to it such as paying its attorney. See CASES 9 and 10, below.

CAVEAT—Cooperation with the union through collective bargaining must be distinguished from support which contains some degree of control or influence over the employees. An employer may give the union receipts from a vending machine, pay union stewards their usual wage if they investigate or process grievances during their usual workday, or permit the union to use a bulletin board in the plant, without violating the Act. See NLRB v. Post Pub. Co., 311 F.2d 565 (7th Cir. 1962). See also Cox, pp. 227–228.

LEGAL GEMS—Remedies for Domination or Assistance

1. If a union is proven to be "employer dominated" the Board orders the employer to disestablish it. This remedy prohibits the employer from recognizing or bargaining with the dominated union or its successor.

2. Unlawful assistance, which does not amount to domination, does not require that the union be disestablished, but the unlawful assistance must be discontinued by the employer.

3. If employer assistance helps the union to become the collective bargaining representative of the employees or to obtain a contract with the employer, the employer must withdraw recognition from the union until it is certified by a secret ballot election conducted by the NLRB. See CASE 10, below.

4. If the assistance does not affect the union's ability to bargain for the employees, the Board will not require withdrawal of recognition.

5. If the employer domination or assistance results in a contract requiring employees to join the union and they execute dues check-off authorization cards, the employer must reimburse employees for dues actually paid thereunder. See CASE 9, below.

6. All remedies are limited by the six months statute of limitations in Section 10(b) of the Act.

    e.g. If employer domination of a union occurred more than six months before the filing and service of the charge no finding of employer domination may be made. The reimbursement of union dues would only cover a period six months prior to the filing and service of the charge.

NOTE—For related union violations see Section 8(b)(1)(A), Chapter IX, Union Unfair Labor Practices, below. If picketing is involved, see Section 8(b)(4)(B), 8(b)(4)(C) and 8(b)(7), Chapter X, Picketing and Boycotts, below.

EMPLOYER UNFAIR LABOR PRACTICES

CASE 9—*competing unions—employer recognition prohibited*

Two rival unions were campaigning to organize the employees of Company Z. Union A notified the employer that it represented a majority of employees and filed a petition with the NLRB for an election. Two months later, while the petition was still pending, Union B showed the employer authorization cards signed by a majority of employees which authorized it to represent them. The employer then executed a contract with Union B which required employees to join the contracting union. Did the employer violate the Act by recognizing Union B and signing the contract with it?

Ans. Yes. The employer gave unlawful assistance to Union B by recognizing and bargaining with it when he knew that Union A was also engaged in an organizational drive and seeking to represent his employees. This unlawful assistance to Union B is remedied by withdrawing recognition. Since the contract required employees to join Union B, the employer's actions affected their terms and conditions of employment and also violated Section 8(a)(3) of the Act.

See Midwest Piping and Supply Co., Inc., 63 NLRB 1060 (1945). See also Shea Chem. Corp., 121 NLRB 1027 (1958).

NOTE—If there had not been rival claims for recognition, but had been only one union involved, recognition on the basis of authorization cards would have been permissible.

CASE 10—*recognition of minority union violates Section 8(a)(2)—good faith no defense*

During an organizing drive by Union X, it informed the employer, E, that it represented a majority of production and shipping employees. No other union was attempting to organize employees at that time. The union's claim was based on the number of authorization cards which employees had signed authorizing the union to represent them compared to the number of employees in the bargaining unit. No attempt was made to compare the names of the card signers with the names of employees in the unit. Thereafter, with both the union and E believing that the union represented a majority of employees, E signed an agreement granting exclusive recognition to the union. Two weeks later the union and E signed a collective bargaining agreement covering those employees. In fact the union did not represent a majority of employees when E recognized it, but the union acquired majority status by the time the collective bargaining agreement was executed. Unfair labor practice charges were brought against E and the union for recognition of the union at a time the union did not represent a majority of employees. Did the employer "contribute . . . support" to the union within the meaning of Section 8(a)(2)?

Ans. Yes. The grant of exclusive recognition to a minority union constitutes unlawful support of the union because the union so favored is given an advantage over others in securing the adherence of employees. The fact that E and the union acted in good faith is no defense because that would frustrate the right of employees to freely select a union to represent them. Although the union represented a majority of employees when the collective bargaining agreement was signed, the critical date is when the union was recognized. The later acquisition of majority status might indicate that the initial unlawful recognition afforded the union "a deceptive cloak of authority with which to persuasively elicit additional employee support." Thus, the act of recognizing the minority union as the exclusive representative of all employees was an unfair labor practice under Section 8(a)(2) of the Act. As a remedy the employer and union were ordered to cease giving effect to the collective bargaining agreement. The employer was ordered to cease recognizing the union unless and until it was certified by the Board, after a secret ballot election, as representing a majority of employees.

See International Ladies Garment Workers Union v. NLRB, 366 U.S. 731, 81 S.Ct. 1603, 6 L.Ed.2d 762 (1961).

NOTE—The Court also held that the union violated Section 8(b)(1)(A) by its acceptance of exclusive bargaining authority at a time when it did not in fact have the support of a majority of employees. Section 8(b)(1)(A) makes it an unfair labor practice for a union "to restrain or coerce employees in the exercise of the rights guaranteed in Section 7". See Chapter IX, Union Unfair Labor Practices, below.

LEGAL GEMS—Discrimination for Union Activities—Section 8(a)(3) and (4)

1. Section 8(a)(3) of the Taft-Hartley Act makes it an unfair labor practice for an employer "by discrimination in regard to hire or tenure of employment or any term or condition of employment to encourage or discourage membership in any labor organization . . . ," except by union security clauses.

2. Section 8(a)(4) of the Act makes it an unfair labor practice for an employer "to discharge or otherwise discriminate against an employee because he has filed charges or given testimony under this Act".

3. An employer may not hire, discharge or otherwise discriminate against an employee to encourage or discourage union activity.

4. If the effect of the employer's conduct is to discourage union activity, there is a violation of the Act regardless of motivation. Thus, anti-union motivation of the employer is not required for finding a violation.

5. In determining the lawfulness of the employer's actions some of the factors considered include:

    (a) independent violations of Section 8(a)(1),

    (b) whether the reason given for the employer's conduct was pretextual,

    (c) the timing of the employer's actions compared to when he learned of the protected activity of the employee, and

    (d) whether other employees were disciplined in the same way for the same offense.

    See CASE 11, below.

EMPLOYER UNFAIR LABOR PRACTICES

6. Discrimination regarding promotions, demotions, layoffs, transfers, and anything else affecting the employee's job is covered by this section because they affect terms and conditions of employment. See CASE 12, below.
7. An employer may contract with a union for a union shop. This requires employees to join the union after being employed thirty days.
8. If the union requests that an employee be discharged for failure to join a union in accordance with such a contract provision, the employer must discharge the employee unless he has reason to believe union membership was denied the employee or not offered on the same terms as given to other employees.

NOTE—A request by the union for an employer to discharge an employee for a reason other than his failure to tender dues and initiation fees uniformly required would violate Section 8(b)(2). If the employer took the requested action it would violate Section 8(a)(3).

CASE 11—*discharge for union activities unlawful*

X was an employee representative of the incumbent independent union. He repeatedly reported for work intoxicated, left work early without permission and engaged in other conduct which would warrant discharge. X joined a rival union which was seeking to raid the independent union. The day after the plant manager discovered that fact, X was discharged because of cumulative grievances against him. Is the discharge lawful?

Ans. No. An employer may discharge an employee for a good reason, a poor reason, or for no reason at all as long as the provisions of the Act are not violated. It is clear that the employer was willing to overlook all of X's shortcomings while he was a representative of the employer's favored, independent union. It was only when X joined the rival union that he was discharged. BUT FOR joining the rival union X would not have been discharged. Since joining the rival union precipitated X's discharge, it violated the Act.

See Edward G. Budd Mfg. Co. v. NLRB, 138 F.2d 86 (3rd Cir. 1943).

CASE 12—*discrimination regarding the hiring of employees unlawful*

Two employees who were active in supporting the union left their employment but continued to help the union and assist employees when they commenced a strike. When the strike ended, these two employees applied for employment as new employees, but the employer refused to hire them because of their activities in support of the union. Are prospective employees protected by the Act, and if so, what is the proper remedy?

Ans. Yes. The Act forbids "discrimination in regard to hire or tenure of employment . . . ." This clearly shows the intent of Congress to limit the power of an employer not only in terminating employment but also in denying

LABOR LAW—EMPLOYMENT DISCRIMINATION

employment. The proper remedy is to hire the discriminatees and pay them the money they lost by not having been hired originally. This is sanctioned by Section 10(c) which directs the Board to order such affirmative action that will effectuate the policies of the Act. There is no distinction between denying employment originally and discharging an employee because of his union activities.

> See Phelps Dodge Corp. v. NLRB, 313 U.S. 177, 61 S.Ct. 845, 85 L.Ed. 1271 (1941). See also Chapter IV, LEGAL GEMS—Computation of Back Pay, above, for an explanation of the method of computation of back pay.

LEGAL GEMS—Rights of Strikers

1. An employee may not be disciplined or discharged for participating in a strike or for honoring a picket line. See CASE 13, below.

2. There are two classifications of strikers:

    (a) ECONOMIC STRIKER. An economic striker seeks some economic benefit or recognition of his union. See GEMS 3-6, below.

    (b) UNFAIR LABOR PRACTICE STRIKER. An unfair labor practice striker seeks, as one of his purposes, to protest an unfair labor practice of his employer. See GEMS 7-9, below.

    NOTE 1—In comparatively rare situations where employees cease work to protest "abnormally dangerous" working conditions, they are not considered strikers and are given special protection under the act. See GEM 10, below.

    NOTE 2—Employees may waive their right to strike by agreeing to a no strike clause in their collective bargaining agreement. If employees strike in violation of a no strike clause in the contract, the employer could discharge all of them or pick and choose certain employees to be discharged. In such situations an employer may discharge the employees most active in causing the strike and/or the union officers or stewards for their failure to prevent the strike because such a strike is unprotected.

3. An employer has the right to continue to operate his business by REPLACING *economic* strikers. An employer does not have to re-employ a replaced *economic* striker, when the strike is terminated. See CASE 14, below.

4. A replaced economic striker does not lose forever his right to reinstatement with the company. It depends upon the availability of a job when he makes an unconditional offer to return to work.

    e.g. If production is *temporarily* cut back the employer must offer re-employment to the striker when full production is resumed *two months* later. See NLRB v. Fleetwood Trailer Co., 389 U.S. 375, 88 S.Ct. 543, 19 L.Ed.2d 614 (1967).

5. An economic striker remains an employee within the meaning of the Act even if he has been replaced. As an employee he is entitled to reinstatement if vacancies occur in the future, unless he has found substantially equivalent employment elsewhere or the employer has substantial and legitimate reasons to justify his failure to offer reinstatement to him. See Laidlaw Corp. v. NLRB, 414 F.2d 99 (7th Cir. 1969), cert. denied 397 U.S. 920 (1970).

6. If an economic striker is guilty of misconduct, such as preventing non-striking employees from entering or leaving the plant or throwing rocks at cars or employees entering or leaving the plant thereby endangering them, he may be disciplined or discharged.

7. An unfair labor practice striker is entitled to reinstatement upon his unconditional offer to return to work, even if the employer must terminate his replacement.

8. In addition to the right of reinstatement, unfair labor practice strikers are given more protection than economic strikers in other situations.

   (a) A no strike clause in a collective bargaining agreement does not apply to employees who strike to protest *serious* unfair labor practices of their employer. See Arlan's Dept. Store, 133 NLRB 802 (1961).

   (b) The provisions of Section 8(d) of the Act, which prohibit strikes during the 60 day insulated period prior to the termination of a contract, do not apply to unfair labor practice strikers. See Chapter VII, LEGAL GEMS—Duties During Contract Period of the Agreement, below.
   See CASE 15, below.

9. Misconduct which would be sufficient to discharge an *economic* striker may be insufficient cause for discharge of an *unfair labor practice* striker.

   e.g. The employer committed numerous unfair labor practices designed to destroy the union's majority status at its plant, and the employees began an unfair labor practice strike. The employer's misconduct included the refusal to bargain with the union, unlawful discharges, eviction of strikers from company owned dwellings, surveillance of union activities and unlawful solicitations of strikers to return to work. The employer discharged 77 strikers. The reasons were: (a) mass picketing preventing access to or from the plant, (b) demonstrations at private homes or the employment office, (c) activities of persons who directed the strike activity, and (d) individual acts of assault, threats or other misconduct. In determining whether strikers guilty of such misconduct should be ordered reinstated the employer's mass unfair labor practices which provoked the strike should be considered. In this case the employer's deliberate violations of the Act

LABOR LAW—EMPLOYMENT DISCRIMINATION

outweigh the mass picketing, demonstrations, and the responsibility of those employees who led such activities. Employees should not be denied reinstatement for that misconduct in the circumstances of this case for "reinstatement is the only sanction which prevents an employer from benefiting from unfair labor practices which may weaken or destroy a union." However, those strikers who assaulted nonstrikers or threatened members of their families, need not be offered reinstatement, whether this conduct was the reason for their discharge or occurred afterward. This conduct outweighs the employer's unfair labor practices and is "in part the product of personal vindictiveness or grievances." Such misconduct would be encouraged if the guilty strikers were ordered reinstated. Thus, some of the strikers who were discharged for cause were ordered reinstated because their misconduct was less serious than that of their employer, and it was the only remedy to prevent the employer from benefiting from its misconduct. See Kohler Co., 148 NLRB 1434 (1964), affirmed 345 F.2d 748 (D.C.Cir. 1965), cert. denied 382 U.S. 836, 86 S.Ct. 82, 15 L.Ed.2d 79 (1965).

NOTE—The Kohler case, above, was an exceptional case and attracted national publicity at the time of the strike. The reasons offered by the employer for denying reinstatement to the strikers would clearly be sufficient if there were only an economic strike. The misconduct would probably be sufficient to deny reinstatement if the employer's misconduct were less serious and not designed to provoke a strike.

10. Section 502 provides that employees may cease work and will not be considered on strike if working conditions are "abnormally dangerous." This is so even though there is a no strike clause in their collective bargaining agreement. However, to come within this provision the employees must show by "ascertainable objective evidence" that working conditions are "abnormally dangerous." Mere generalized belief is not sufficient to bring actions within this section of the act.

e.g. Three foremen at the Gateway Coal Co. mine failed to carry out prescribed safety procedures and made false entries in their log books with respect to the air flow into the mine. As a result, a reduction of the normal flow of air from 28,000 to 11,000 cubic feet per minute was not promptly discovered. However, even the reduced flow of air was in excess of the minimum requirements of state and federal laws. The miners met and decided not to work so long as the responsible supervisors had any duties regarding safety matters. Gateway continued to employ the supervisors, and brought an action in federal court to enjoin the strike. The Court first examined the collective bargaining agreement between the parties. Although the contract did not contain a no strike clause, it provided for arbitration of "all disputes and claims" and safety disputes were not specifically excluded. That language, together with national labor policy favoring arbitration, necessitated the conclusion that the safety disputes were arbitrable. Since the dispute was covered by final and binding arbitration the Court implied an agreement not to strike. The Court also considered whether a good faith belief by employees that working conditions were abnormally dangerous justified the strike. It held that since there was no ascertainable objective evidence that the mine was unsafe, the limited exception to a no strike obligation contained in Section 502 did not apply. The generalized belief of the miners that the mine was unsafe did not justify the strike and bring it within the provision of Section 502. Thus, Gateway was entitled to injunctive relief against the strike. See Gateway Coal Co. v. United Mine Workers, 414 U.S. 368, 94 S.Ct. 629, 38 L.Ed.2d 583 (1974).

CASE 13—*withholding of benefits to striking employees to which they were entitled held unlawful*

In the collective bargaining agreement the employer agreed to pay specified vacation benefits to employees who had worked a certain number of hours in the preceding year. It also provided that, in case of a layoff, termination or quitting, employees who had worked more than 60 days would be entitled to a pro rata share of their vacation benefits. The vacation benefits were to be paid on the Friday nearest July 1 of each year. The contract expired prior to July 1 and the employees commenced a strike. The employer continued to operate during the strike with non-strikers and replacements. When their vacation benefits were due the strikers asked for them, but the company refused claiming that all contract obligations had been terminated by the strike. However, shortly thereafter the company gave vacation pay as set out in the expired contract to those employees who were working, saying that this reflected a new "policy". May an employer refuse to pay benefits which accrued to striking employees under a terminated contract, while paying such benefits to striker replacements and non-strikers?

Ans. No. Paying accrued benefits to employees who are working and denying the same benefits to striking employees is clearly discriminatory and will discourage protected concerted activity. Since it is charged that this conduct violated Section 8(a)(3), the employer's motivation must be considered. Proof of an anti-union motivation may make conduct unlawful which would be lawful in other circumstances. Some conduct may be so inherently destructive of employee rights that even if the employer has some explanation for its actions an inference of improper motive may be drawn from the conduct itself. If the discriminatory conduct on employee rights is "comparatively slight" an anti-union motivation must be proven *if* the employer has legitimate business justification for the conduct. In this case the employer did not establish any legitimate reason for his actions, and since he engaged in discriminatory conduct which would discourage union membership, the employer violated Section 8(a)(3) of the Act.

LABOR LAW—EMPLOYMENT DISCRIMINATION

See NLRB v. Great Dane Trailers, Inc., 388 U.S. 26, 87 S.Ct. 1792, 18 L.Ed. 2d 1027 (1967).

CASE 14—*replacement of economic strikers—may not discriminate against union supporters*

Employees who were dissatisfied with the progress of contract negotiations commenced an economic strike in support of their bargaining demands and the employer began replacing them. When the strikers realized that their strike would not be successful they offered to return to work. Five of the striker replacements wanted to continue working so the employer reinstated all but five of the strikers. The five strikers who were replaced were the most active employees in support of the union and its strike. The five strikers who were not reinstated filed unfair labor practice charges with the NLRB. When employees who have struck for economic reasons offer to return to work after some replacements have been hired, may the employer pick and choose the employees he will re-employ up to the number of jobs available?

Ans. No. Discrimination in the re-employment of strikers based on their union activity violates the Act just as a discharge for that reason. When an employer has not caused the strike in some way by his unfair labor practices, he may continue his business during a strike by filling vacancies left by the strikers. He is not obliged to discharge striker replacements upon the conclusion of the strike in order to make jobs available for all strikers. However, in deciding what strikers to reinstate the employer may not discriminate on the basis of their union activities. Since the employer refused to re-employ them because of their union activities he violated the Act and must reinstate the five employees with back pay. The employer could have used criteria such as seniority or ability in determining who should not be re-employed.

See NLRB v. Mackay Radio & Telegraph Co., 304 U.S. 333, 58 S.Ct. 904, 82 L.Ed. 1381 (1938).

NOTE 1—If the employer committed unfair labor practices which caused or prolonged the strike he could not hire permanent replacements for the strikers. The unfair labor practice strikers would be entitled to reinstatement upon their unconditional offer to return to work.

NOTE 2—An employer may not offer a 20-year seniority credit to striker replacements and employees who abandoned a strike, even if that is necessary to continue operations during an economic strike. Such an action is so disruptive of employee rights protected by the Act that it may not be excused by showing that it was motivated by business exigencies. The super-seniority offered employees affects all strikers, whereas permanent replacement, proper under, *Mackay Radio,* case 14 above, affects only those strikers actually replaced. Further, super-seniority will forever divide the employees and be re-emphasized in future layoffs. It will hamper bargaining and tend to deter future protected activity, whereas striker replacement ceases to be an issue once a strike is over. Therefore, giving non-strikers super-seniority would be disruptive of labor relations and contrary to the policies of the Act as it unlawfully discriminates against employees engaging in

EMPLOYER UNFAIR LABOR PRACTICES

protected activity. See NLRB v. Erie Resistor Co., 373 U.S. 221, 83 S.Ct. 1139, 10 L.Ed.2d 308 (1963).

NOTE 3—If the job of an economic striker is abolished or absorbed into another job for economic reasons, the employer is not obligated to reinstate the striker. See Teamsters Local 200 v. NLRB (P & V Atlas Industrial Center), 233 F.2d 233 (7th Cir. 1956).

CASE 15—*limitation on strikes in contract and Act not applicable to unfair labor practice strikes*

The employer executed a collective bargaining agreement with the Carpenters' Union which contained a no strike clause. Toward the end of that contract Union X began to organize the employees. The employer did not want to deal with Union X as the representative of its employees, and unlawfully assisted a third union, the Pulp Workers, in organizing its employees. Neither Union X nor the Pulp Workers filed a petition for an NLRB election during the 90 to 60 day period before the end of the Carpenters contract. The Carpenters gave the 60 day notice required by Section 8(d) of their desire to negotiate a new contract. During that 60 day period before the collective bargaining agreement expired by its terms, the employer discharged an employee because of his support of the Carpenters' Union. That action precipitated a strike. Four months after the strike began the employees who were on strike made an unconditional offer to return to work. The employer refused to reinstate the strikers and they were discharged. The strikers contended that the refusal to reinstate them after their unconditional offer to return to work constituted an unfair labor practice under Section 8(a)(3). The employer contended that the strikers were not protected because: (a) the strike began when the no strike clause in the contract was in effect, and (b) Section 8(d) made a strike unlawful during the 60 day period after the statutory notice. Are either of the employer's contentions valid?

Ans. No. (a) Although the Carpenters' Union agreed to refrain from "any strike" during the term of the collective bargaining agreement, that term must be interpreted as applying only to economic strikes. This is so because the contract itself deals with the economic relationship of the parties. Furthermore, the Act was designed to protect the rights of employees and the waiver of such rights will not be inferred without strong reason. Employees should be permitted to protect their rights by engaging in a strike where the employer attempts to deny those rights by commission of unfair labor practices. Thus, the no strike clause applies only to economic strikes and not to unfair labor practice strikes. (b) The purpose of Section 8(d) was to prevent strikes for "termination or modification" of an existing contract during a 60 day period of renegotiation. The purpose of the present strike was to protest the unfair labor practices of the employer. Therefore, Section 8(d) is not applicable. The unfair labor practice strikers are entitled to reinstatement with back pay from the date that they made an unconditional offer to return to work.

See Mastro Plastics Corp. v. NLRB, 350 U.S. 270, 76 S.Ct. 349, 100 L.Ed. 309 (1956).

LABOR LAW—EMPLOYMENT DISCRIMINATION

LEGAL GEMS—Temporary or Permanent Plant Closing

1. A "lockout" is a temporary shutdown of a plant by an employer to gain some bargaining concession or discourage union activity. It is an employer's weapon, just as the strike is the union's weapon.

2. A lockout may be legal or be an unfair labor practice depending upon the surrounding circumstances.

3. An employer may lock out employees after bargaining to an impasse in order to bring economic pressure on the union to modify its bargaining position, so long as the bargaining impasse was not caused by the employer's unfair labor practices. See CASE 16, below.

4. A lockout solely to discourage union activity, or as a reprisal for union activity, is an unfair labor practice.

5. An employer has the absolute right to terminate permanently its entire business operation for any reason, including reprisal for union activity of its employees.

6. A partial closing of a business may be an unfair labor practice under Section 8(a)(3) if it is motivated by a "purpose to chill unionism in any of the remaining plants of the single employer and if the employer may reasonably have foreseen that such closing will likely have that effect." See CASE 17, below.

★CAVEAT—The closing of one of several plants in a business is distinguished from going out of business entirely because the partial closing may discourage employees at the other plants from exercising their right to join a union.

7. An employer may not remove its business to another location for anti-union considerations. This is known as a "run away shop".

CASE 16—*employer may lockout employees after impasse*

The employer was engaged in the business of repairing ships and operated shipyards in four cities for that purpose. The business was highly seasonal with most of the work being done in the winter months. The employer and unions representing the employees began contract negotiations in May and continued bargaining into August without reaching an agreement. Employees continued to report for work after the contract expired, but the parties had bargained to an impasse and no further meetings had been scheduled. Because of previous strikes at the company the employer was concerned with the possibility of a strike when business increased in the fall or when emergency repairs on a ship were required. The employer closed two shipping yards completely and laid off a substantial number of employees at a third yard because of the unresolved labor dispute, although the union said that they did not intend to strike. The lockout continued until a contract was agreed upon two and one-half months later. May an employer lock out employees during a labor dispute to bring economic pressure to bear in support of his legitimate bargaining position after an impasse is reached in bargaining?

56

Ans. Yes. To violate Section 8(a)(1) the action must interfere with rights guaranteed in Section 7. The Board found that the lockout interfered with the employees' rights to bargain and their right to strike. The Supreme Court reversed. It found that the above facts do not show an attempt to frustrate bargaining, but only to resist the union demands and obtain a modification of them. This is not inconsistent with the employees' right to bargain collectively. That an employer can pre-empt the possibility of a strike and leave the union with nothing to strike against is not an unlawful intrusion upon the union's right to strike. That right to strike is not unlimited. There is nothing in the Act which states that the right to strike carries with it the right to determine when a work stoppage will occur or its length. Thus, a lockout does not unlawfully interfere with the union's right to strike. Section 8(a)(3) requires an intention to discourage union membership or otherwise discriminate against the union. There is no evidence to show that was the employer's motive. The purpose and effect of the lockout was to bring pressure on the union to modify its bargaining demands. Thus, a lockout after bargaining to an impasse does not violate Section 8(a)(1) or (3) of the Act when its sole purpose is to bring economic pressure on the union in support of its bargaining demands.

See American Shipbuilding Co. v. NLRB, 380 U.S. 300, 85 S.Ct. 955, 13 L.Ed.2d 855 (1965).

NOTE 1—Several employers were members of a multiemployer bargaining group which negotiated together with the union representing their employees. After the parties bargained to an impasse the union struck only one member of the employer bargaining group, and the employees continued to work for the other employers. In response to that whipsaw strike the employers which were not struck locked out their employees who were represented by the union. All employers continued business with temporary replacements. The Court held that there was no violation of the Act in operating with temporary replacements while regular employees were locked out. Such action was no more destructive of employee rights than the lockout itself, which was lawful. The action of the employers was defensive; it was designed to counter the effect of the whipsaw strike. The employers did not act with an anti-union motivation, but to serve a legitimate business purpose, the preservation of the multiemployer bargaining group. Thus, no unfair labor practice was committed. See NLRB v. Brown, 380 U.S. 278, 85 S.Ct. 980, 13 L.Ed.2d 839 (1965).

NOTE 2—A lockout before a bargaining impasse is reached may also be lawful. e. g., An employer is bargaining in good faith with a union which has represented its employees for a number of years. They reach agreement on many issues but cannot agree on a work assignment and several minor issues. The union, which has struck over the work assignment in the past, threatens to strike. Although the parties have not bargained to an impasse, the employer, which is engaged in a highly seasonal business and fears "unusual harm" from a strike during the busy season, may lock out the employees. However, each case in this area must be determined on its own facts. See Lane v. NLRB, 418 F.2d 1208 (D.C.Cir. 1969).

LABOR LAW—EMPLOYMENT DISCRIMINATION

CASE 17—*discriminatory closing of entire business lawful*

After a majority of employees voted in an NLRB election, to be represented by a union, the employer's president called a meeting of its board of directors to consider closing the plant. It was decided that there was little hope of achieving competitive costs for the operation with the advent of the union, so they voted to liquidate the corporation. Two months after the election all operation ceased and the machinery and other equipment were sold at auction. The union filed charges alleging that the employer's actions constituted unlawful discrimination against its employees because they selected a union to represent them. May an employer terminate its entire business for discriminatory reasons?

Ans. Yes. An employer has the absolute right to terminate its *entire* business for any reason, including anti-union motivation. However, a discriminatory *partial* closing may have repercussions on what remains of the business, affording the employer leverage for discouraging employees in the exercise of their protected rights in much the same way as found in a "run away shop". The court held that if the persons exercising control over a plant which is being closed for anti-union reasons: (a) have an interest in another business, whether or not it is engaged in the same line of commercial activity as the closed plant, by which the employer may benefit from the discouragement of unionization in that business; (b) close the plant with the purpose of achieving that result; (c) occupy a relationship to the other business which might lead employees to believe that plant would be closed if they engage in union activities, then an unfair labor practice under Section 8(a)(3) has been established. The case was remanded for a determination of the purpose and of the effect of the closing on other aspects of the employer's business based upon the above criteria.

See Textile Workers Union v. Darlington Mfg. Co., 380 U.S. 263, 85 S.Ct. 994, 13 L.Ed.2d 827 (1965).

VI. GOOD FAITH BARGAINING

LEGAL GEMS—Good Faith Bargaining—Introduction

1. Section 8(a)(5) of the National Labor Relations Act, as amended makes it an unfair labor practice for an employer "to refuse to bargain collectively with the representatives of his employees. . . ."

2. The employer's duty to bargain may arise after:

    (a) voluntary recognition of the union,

    (b) certification that the union represents a majority of employees by the NLRB after a secret ballot election of employees in an appropriate unit, or

    (c) unfair labor practice proceedings whereby the employer is ordered to bargain with the union because substantial violations of the Act have caused the union to lose its majority status and prevent a fair election.

3. The bargaining obligation normally continues for one year following certification, after which there is a rebuttable presumption that the union continues to represent a majority of employees.

4. Mandatory subjects of bargaining include all matters reasonably related to "wages, hours, and other terms and conditions of employment."

5. The employer's bargaining obligation extends only to the union which is the exclusive representative of the employees. Although an employer may adjust grievances presented by an individual employee, it is not required to do so.

LEGAL GEMS—The Concept of Good Faith Bargaining

1. The Act provides in Section 8(a)(5) that it is an unfair labor practice for an employer "to refuse to bargain collectively with the representatives of his employees, subject to the provisions of Section 9(a)."

2. Section 9(a) of the Act provides that the bargaining representative of the employees shall be:

    (a) selected by a majority of the employees,

    (b) in an appropriate unit,

    (c) as the *exclusive* representative of *all* the employees in the bargaining unit, and

    (d) "for the purposes of collective bargaining in respect to rates of pay, wages, hours of employment, or other conditions of employment".

LABOR LAW—EMPLOYMENT DISCRIMINATION

NOTE—Union A may include representatives from other unions on its bargaining team as long as they bargain solely on behalf of the employees represented by Union A in the absence of a showing of bad faith. Neither an employer nor a union may select or veto the persons employed to negotiate for the other side. See General Electric Co. v. NLRB, 412 F.2d 512 (2d Cir. 1969).

3. Section 8(d) of the Act defines "good faith bargaining" as the *mutual* obligation of the employer and the union to:

   (a) meet at reasonable times,

   (b) confer in good faith with respect to wages, hours, and other terms and conditions of employment, and

   (c) execute a written contract incorporating any agreement reached, if requested by the other party.

4. Section 8(d) also states that the obligation to bargain "does not compel either party to agree to a proposal or require the making of a concession." See Chapter VII, LEGAL GEMS—Duties During Contract Period of the Agreement, below, for Section 8(d) requirements regarding the modification or termination of a collective bargaining agreement.

5. Good faith bargaining requires an open mind and a sincere purpose of reaching an agreement.

NOTE—The manner and extent of negotiations necessary to satisfy the requirement of bargaining in good faith vary according to each situation. Factors are considered such as: reasonableness of a party's position, holding to a pre-determined position during negotiations, and repeated failure to be available for bargaining meetings or to meet for a reasonable length of time. See CASE 19, below.

6. In one case the Board said that the essential ingredient of good faith bargaining is "the serious intent to adjust differences and to reach an acceptable common ground." NLRB v. Insurance Agents' Int'l Union, 361 U.S. 477, 80 S.Ct. 419, 4 L.Ed.2d 454 (1960).

7. In determining whether a party has bargained in good faith the Board may not pass on the desirability of the substantive terms of the collective bargaining agreement. The Board should analyze the *quality* of bargaining as a whole; merely insisting on the inclusion of a particular clause by one party is not normally a per se violation. See CASE 18, below.

See generally Cox, "The Duty to Bargain in Good Faith," 71 Harv. L.Rev. 1401 (1958).

GOOD FAITH BARGAINING

CASE 18—*insisting on clause giving employer great control over employment terms not unlawful per se*

The union submitted a proposed collective bargaining agreement to the employer which contained a provision for arbitration of all grievances. The employer objected to unlimited arbitration, and proposed a management functions clause. That clause listed matters such as promotions, discipline and work scheduling as the responsibility of management and excluded them from arbitration. After a number of bargaining sessions the parties agreed to many contract terms, but no agreement was reached on the proposed management functions clause. The union filed an unfair labor practice charge with the NLRB contending that the employer had failed to bargain in good faith. While the union's charge was being litigated the parties agreed on a contract with a modified management functions clause. However, some terms and conditions of employment were still excluded from arbitration. The Board concluded that the employer's action in bargaining for such a clause constituted a per se violation of Section 8(a)(5) and (1) of the Act. Specifically, the Board held that bargaining for a clause under which management retained responsibility for certain conditions of employment was an unfair labor practice because it was "in derogation of" the statutory rights of employees to bargain collectively as to conditions of employment. Did the Board analyze the requirement of good faith bargaining correctly?

Ans. No. Although the Act requires the parties to bargain in good faith, Section 8(d) expressly provides that the obligation to bargain collectively does not compel either party to agree to a proposal or to make a concession. In this case the employer could have rejected the union's proposal for unlimited arbitration without committing an unfair labor practice. However, a management functions clause was offered as a counterproposal. The mere fact that the management functions clause covered certain conditions of employment did not violate the Act per se as had been held by the Board. The duty to bargain collectively must be enforced by application of the good faith bargaining standards of Section 8(d) to the facts of each case. If the per se violation as found by the Board were enforced, employers in every industry would be prohibited from bargaining for a management functions clause when the union declined to accept it. Such clauses are common in collective bargaining agreements. The Board has no power to pass on the desirability of the substantive terms of labor agreements. The evidence, viewed as a whole, did not show that the employer refused to bargain in good faith by reason of its bargaining for a management functions clause. Therefore, the Board's order relating to a per se violation in seeking that clause was not enforced.

See NLRB v. American Nat. Ins. Co., 343 U.S. 395, 72 S.Ct. 824, 96 L.Ed. 1027 (1952).

NOTE—The Court referred to the employer's proposal as a management functions clause. This is more commonly known as a management rights clause. Sometimes it is termed a management prerogatives clause.

LABOR LAW—EMPLOYMENT DISCRIMINATION

CASE 19—*bad faith bargaining shown by course of conduct*

General Electric operated plants in all fifty states with 250,000 employees, of whom 120,000 were represented by various unions. In preparing for contract negotiations for its represented employees the company solicited comments from local management concerning the type and level of benefits that employees desired. These were then formed into specific proposals and their cost and effectiveness analyzed. The company said that it would take all facts into consideration and hold nothing back when it made a "fair, firm offer" to the union. The company determined to take this "product" and "sell" it to its employees and the general public through publicity prior to and during negotiations. The company was willing to accept union suggestions based on facts which it may have overlooked, but the mere fact that the union disagreed would not be grounds for the company to change its position. The company denounced the traditional give-and-take of bargaining as dishonest and injurious to the company's credibility. Before formal bargaining sessions began, the employer informed the union that it would institute a contributory insurance plan for all employees, but if the union objected, only unrepresented employees would receive the benefit. The union demanded bargaining on the plan, but the employer claimed that the present agreement waived bargaining. The union continued its objections, and the plan was placed into effect for unrepresented employees only. When the union made its proposals the employer publicly denounced them saying that they might cost many employees their jobs through increased foreign competition. The theme of the message, which was publicized on radio, TV, newspapers, plant publications, and other media, was that the company, not the union, was the best protector of employee interests. The company complained that the union proposals were excessive, but when the union asked for cost estimates the company refused saying that it was referring to the "level of benefits". After the company presented its "fair, firm offer" to the union it released its prepared publicity the following day, although the union asked the company to delay publicity until it had the opportunity to examine the proposals and offer changes. The union renewed its request for cost information so that it could re-allocate its demands and still come within the company's cost framework, but the company refused. The company placed most of its proposals into effect for unrepresented employees before the expiration of the contract with the union, which was contrary to past practice. The union was unwilling to accept the company offer and no progress was made in negotiations. The union commenced a strike when the contract expired, but employees returned to work after three weeks when the strike proved ineffective. The union charged the employer with bargaining in bad faith. Did the employer's conduct constitute bargaining in bad faith, as charged by the union?

Ans. Yes. In reaching this result the following issues were raised: (a) Did the institution of the insurance plan, even though limited to unrepresented employees, violate the Act? Yes. The facts warrant the conclusion that the company intended to show the employees that the union could not gain more for them than the company was prepared to offer. This impaired the union's ability to represent the employees. The company's defense that the union had waived its right to bargain about the plan was rejected, and the court pointed out that the granting of benefits to unrepresented employees discriminated against represented employees just as giving a cash bonus to non-union employees would unlawfully discourage union activity. (b) Did the company unlawfully refuse to furnish relevant and necessary information to the union in bargaining? Yes. Based on Truitt Manufacturing, case 20, below, the court found that the employer's failure to furnish the information regarding the cost of various proposals within a reasonable time, although rejecting the union demands as "astronomical" or "costly", violated the Act. In other areas of negotiation the union had to weigh the cost of wage increases against improved fringe benefits. Unless the employer answered the union's genuine, non-burdensome requests for cost information, it could not bargain intelligently on those issues and arrive at a reasoned decision, particularly those involving a re-allocation of benefits within the company's cost framework. That the exact information requested was not available does not excuse the employer's obligation to advise the union what information could be furnished and providing the union with relevant information that is available. (c) May an employer bargain directly with locals representing employees when it was currently bargaining with the International concerning those employees? No. The employer had recognized the international union as the representative of all the locals in prior negotiations and had bargained on a national level. When a strike was imminent, the company broke that pattern and dealt separately with several union locals at various plants making a more favorable offer to them than was offered at the national negotiations. In breaking the established pattern of single negotiations covering all plants, the employer breached its bargaining duty. An employer has a continuing obligation to recognize the international as the exclusive bargaining representative and may not make any offer to local unions at a particular plant when negotiations for that plant are being conducted on a national level. (d) Was there an overall failure to bargain in good faith by the employer? Yes. A determination of overall good faith—or lack of it—in bargaining involves a consideration of the totality of the conduct of the party charged. Acts which are not in themselves unfair labor practices may support an inference that a party is bargaining in bad faith. The employer's bad faith bargaining is demonstrated by the above violations (specifically, presenting the insurance proposal on a take-it-or-leave-it basis, failing to provide relevant and necessary cost-information to the union, and bypassing the international in an attempt to deal directly with some locals) and the following conduct: (i) The company made vague and evasive responses to detailed union proposals. (ii) When the union finished presenting its proposals, the company, instead of offering counter-proposals or commenting specifically on the union proposals, offered prepared lectures on the causes of economic instability. (iii) The company took some unreasonable positions and then defended them with no apparent purpose except to avoid yielding to the union. For example, the company selected a date to start pension and insurance benefits, arbitrarily changed the dates several times with inconsistent explanations, and finally selected the "appropriate" date. While the company could insist on any date it chose, its manner of responding to the union on this matter reflected on its philosophy of bargaining. (iv) When it was apparent that the strike would fail, the company insisted that the union consent to the contract unconditionally. When the union protested that the memorandum prepared by the company for its signature was too vague, the company refused to submit more detailed language and the union signed without ever seeing the final contract language. (v) The company argued that it granted the union many concessions during negotiations, but an analysis of them showed that these were only on minor points and did not have much substance. These factors, considered as a whole, were designed to degrade the union in the eyes of its members and the general public. The "firm, fair offer" was designed to show the uselessness of the union. The extensive publicity picturing the company as the true defender of the employees interest emphasized this and inhibited true bargaining. The court concluded: "The aim, in a word, was to deal with the union through the employees, rather than with the employees through the union." Thus, the overall conduct of the employer constituted bad faith bargaining and was violative of the Act.

    See NLRB v. General Electric Co., 418 F.2d 736 (2d Cir. 1969), cert. denied 397 U.S. 965 (1970).

NOTE 1—The court summarized its own decision as follows: "We do not today hold that an employer may not communicate with his employees during negotiations. Nor are we deciding that the 'best offer first' bargaining technique is forbidden. Moreover, we do not require an employer to engage in 'auction bargaining,' or, as the dissent seems to suggest, compel him to make concessions, 'minor' or otherwise. . . . We hold that an employer may not so combine 'take-it-or-leave-it' bargaining methods with a widely publicized stance of unbending firmness that he is himself unable to alter a position once taken. It is this specific conduct that GE must avoid in order to comply with the Board's order."

NOTE 2—The bargaining technique employed by General Electric in CASE 19 above, is known as "Boulwarism". It was named after the company's chief negotiator. There have been no later cases where the "best offer first" strategy was used.

LEGAL GEMS—Obligations Arising During Collective Bargaining

1. A party must, upon request, make available evidence to support his bargaining position.
2. The test is whether the information sought is "relevant and necessary" in bargaining.

    CAVEAT—In cases where the union seeks information as to specific aspects of the employer's financial condition or profits, a specific need for that information must be shown. See **CASES** 20 and 21, below.

3. An employer may not change any term or condition of employment while bargaining with the union unless the parties have bargained to an impasse. In such a situation the employer may put its last offer into effect. See CASE 22, below.

CASE 20—*employer required to show financial records if ability to pay at issue*

The employer and union were bargaining over a new contract. The union demanded a 10¢ hourly wage increase, but the employer offered 2½¢. The employer argued that its average wage was already more than the average wage of its competitors and it had to remain competitive. Any increase more than 2½¢ would "break the company." The union demanded to see financial records of the company to substantiate its position. The company refused, contending that its financial records were confidential and not a matter of bargaining. Does good faith bargaining require an employer to disclose financial records to support its position that it cannot grant a wage increase for economic reasons?

Ans. Yes. Good faith bargaining requires that claims made by either party be honest claims. If an employer asserts that it cannot grant a wage increase for economic reasons, it is incumbent on the employer to substantiate that claim. Otherwise an employer could make such a claim mechanically and negotiation would be fruitless. If the union sees some evidence of the employer's claim, it might reduce or withdraw its demand. The court pointed out, however, that the particular circumstances of each case must be considered before a determination can be made whether the obligation to bargain in good faith has been met.

See Truitt Mfg. Co. v. NLRB, 351 U.S. 149, 76 S.Ct. 753, 100 L.Ed. 1027 (1956).

CASE 21—*employer not required to show financial records if ability to pay is not at issue*

The employer operated several service stations on the West Virginia Turnpike. During negotiations with the union the employer took the position that no wage increase was warranted because it intended to "remain competitive" with service stations in the surrounding area, and would pay only the prevailing wage rate for the area. The employer conducted various wage surveys and concluded that no service station in the area paid higher wages to its employees. The results of these surveys were made available to the union and the employer refused to grant a wage increase based upon his conclusions from those surveys. The union asked for financial data to show the employer's inability to pay. The employer answered that it was not pleading inability to pay, but only that it was unwilling to give more economic benefits than other service stations in the surrounding area. These other stations were not located on the turnpike and, therefore, did not compete directly with the employer. Did the employer violate the Act by refusing to furnish the requested information?

Ans. No. In considering whether a party has bargained in good faith all of the surrounding circumstances must be considered. If the employer meant by the phrase "to remain competitive" that a wage increase would force it to increase prices over those of its competitors and hence lose business the employer would, in effect, be pleading inability to pay and would be required to disclose financial records. However, the employer only said that he would not pay more than the operators of other service stations in the area. Regardless of the effect that a wage increase would have on the employer's competitive position, it is legally entitled to take the position that it will pay no more than the area wage scale. This is "hard bargaining", but it is not unlawful in this case, as it was in CASE 20, above.

See Charles E. Honaker, 147 NLRB 1184 (1964).

LABOR LAW—EMPLOYMENT DISCRIMINATION

CASE 22—*unilateral change in employment terms of employer during negotiations held unlawful*

During contract negotiations the employer changed his sick leave policy, granted salary increases to employees greater than previously offered to the union, and granted merit increases to 40 percent of the bargaining unit employees. All of these matters had been discussed during negotiations, but no agreement had been reached on them. Did the employer's actions violate his duty to bargain in good faith as the union charged?

Ans. Yes. A refusal to negotiate *in fact* as to a term or condition of employment violates Section 8(a)(5) of the Act even though the employer bargains in good faith concerning all other subjects. The unilateral change of conditions of employment being negotiated is similarly a violation for it circumvents the duty to bargain and frustrates the objectives of good faith bargaining as much as a flat refusal to bargain. Granting benefits as was done in the present case can only undercut the union's bargaining position and suggest to employees that they do not need a union to obtain increased benefits. Overall subjective bad faith bargaining is not required for a finding that a party has bargained in bad faith concerning a particular matter. A change in working conditions while bargaining continues is a violation of the employer's duty to bargain in good faith.

See NLRB v. Katz, 369 U.S. 736, 82 S.Ct. 1107, 8 L.Ed.2d 230 (1962).

NOTE—If the parties have bargained to an impasse (i. e., each party has reached a position in bargaining where neither will make any more concessions) then the employer may place his last offer to the union into effect. However, the impasse must not have been caused by the employer's bad faith bargaining and he may not give the employees more than he has previously offered through the union.

LEGAL GEMS—Obtaining Bargaining Rights

1. The employer's duty to bargain can arise when:
   (a) the employer voluntarily recognizes the union,
   (b) the union wins an NLRB election and is certified by the Board, see Chapter XII, Representation Proceedings, below, or
   (c) the union demands bargaining for a group of employees constituting an appropriate unit, the union represents a majority of those employees, and the employer commits substantial unfair labor practices making it unlikely that a fair election can be held. See CASE 23, below.

2. If the employer shows by his actions that a bargaining request would be futile, no demand is required by the union to create a bargaining obligation for the employer.

3. An employer can insist on an NLRB election before recognizing the union if he does not engage in substantial unfair labor practices which would make a fair election impossible. See CASE 24, below.

GOOD FAITH BARGAINING

4. A union is not required to choose between proceeding to an election and filing a refusal to bargain charge. A union can participate in an election and if it loses, it can then file objections to the election and a refusal to bargain charge. See Bernel Foam Products Co., Inc., 146 NLRB 1277 (1964).

5. No bargaining duty can arise after a valid election in which the union has lost. For this reason, the union must file objections to the election based upon the employer's unfair labor practices. See Chapter XII, Representation Proceedings, below.

6. There is no required form for the bargaining demand. It may be a letter or telephone call, but it must be unambiguous and indicate what employees the union seeks to represent. Those aspects of good faith bargaining peculiar to unions are considered under Section 8(b)(3). See Chapter IX, Union Unfair Labor Practices, below.

7. A union may demonstrate its majority status in the bargaining unit by:

    (a) winning an election, the usual method,

    (b) obtaining signed authorization cards from a majority of employees and being voluntarily recognized by the employer, or

    (c) calling a strike which is engaged in by a majority of employees.

CASE 23—*obtaining bargaining rights without an election after substantial employer violations*

Four cases were consolidated for hearing, three of which are pertinent here. In each of three cases the union conducted an organizational campaign, obtained authorization cards from a majority of employees in an appropriate unit, and then, demanded recognition. Each employer refused to recognize the union on the ground that authorization cards were inherently unreliable indicators of employee desires and conducted its own anti-union campaign in which the employers committed various unfair labor practices. In Company A the union did not petition for an election, but filed unfair labor practice charges. At Company B the union petitioned for an election, but it was not conducted because the union filed unfair labor practice charges. An election was conducted at Company C and the employees rejected the union, but the Board set the election aside because of the employer's unfair labor practices. To remedy the unfair labor practices, each employer was ordered by the Board to bargain with the union. The employers appealed. Was the Board justified in its ruling?

Ans. Yes. Three issues were presented in this case: (a) Can a union obtain bargaining rights for employees by means other than an NLRB election? Yes. Section 9(a) of the Act refers to the union as one "designated or selected" by a majority of employees without specifying how the representative is to be chosen. That language is the same as used in the original Wagner Act where it was recognized that a union could establish its majority status by a strike or possession of cards signed by a majority of employees authorizing the union to represent them. There is nothing in the legislative history of the present Act contrary to these decisions which would limit the employer's duty to bargain to those situations where the union has been certified by the NLRB. Thus, a union may establish its majority status without an election and require an employer to bargain with it. (b) Are cards signed by employees authorizing the union to represent them sufficiently reliable to establish the majority status of the union? Yes. An employee who signs a card which clearly authorizes a union to represent him should be bound by it unless he is deliberately misled by the solicitor into disregarding the language used on the card. The subjective motivation of the employee in signing the card is not relevant. Further, when the employer has committed unfair labor practices designed to thwart the union activity of the employees, authorization cards may be the only reliable method of ascertaining the true desires of employees. Thus, a union may establish its majority status by authorization cards signed by employees. (c) Is the remedy of ordering an employer to bargain with the union appropriate where the employer's unfair labor practices interfere with the holding of a fair election? Yes. The lesser remedy of posting a notice signed by the employer informing employees of their rights and assuring them that the employer will not violate the Act in the future may not be adequate after the employer has succeeded in destroying the union's majority status or the conditions necessary for a fair election. The most suitable remedy for extensive unfair labor practices in those circumstances would be a bargaining order. On the other hand minor or less extensive unfair labor practices, because of their minimal impact on the election machinery, would not warrant the issuance of a bargaining order. Based on the answers to these questions the court then remanded the cases to the Board for a determination of the effect of the unfair labor practices and whether a fair election could be conducted.

See NLRB v. Gissel Packing Co., 395 U.S. 575, 89 S.Ct. 1918, 23 L.Ed.2d 547 (1969).

NOTE 1—The Board's original reasoning in the Gissel case, above, was that the employers' unfair labor practices after the recognition demands showed that each employer did not refuse to recognize the union because of a good faith doubt of its majority status, but to gain time to destroy the union's majority. The Supreme Court said that the employer's good faith was largely irrelevant. In remanding the case to the Board for additional findings based on Gissel the Fifth Circuit summarized the court's holding: "Under the Gissel holding a bargaining order may issue where: (a) the union had valid authorization cards from a majority of the employees in an appropriate bargaining unit; (b) the employer's unfair labor practices, although not 'outrageous' and 'pervasive' enough to justify a bargaining order in the absence of a card majority, were still serious and extensive; (c) 'the possibility of erasing the effects of past practices and of ensuring a fair election (or a fair rerun) by the use of traditional remedies, though present, is slight'; and (d) employee sentiment can best be protected in the particular case by a bargaining order." NLRB v. American Cable Systems, Inc., 414 F.2d 661 (5th Cir. 1969).

NOTE 2—The *Gissel* decision affirmed the Board's rule in Cumberland Shoe Corp., 144 NLRB 1268 (1963), enforced 351 F.2d 917 (6th Cir.

1965) that an authorization card which is unambiguous on its face may be used to establish the union's majority status unless the employee was led to disregard the wording on the card by being told that its "only" or "sole" purpose was to obtain an election. In *Cumberland* employees were told "the purpose of the card was to secure an election." Since the solicitor did not say the "only" purpose of the card was an election, and the card authorized the union to represent the employee, the card was valid to obtain bargaining rights.

NOTE 3—A dual purpose card authorizes the union to obtain an election or to represent the employee in collective bargaining. It is usually counted toward the union's majority. See Aero Corp. v. NLRB, 363 F.2d 702 (D.C.Cir. 1966), cert. denied 385 U.S. 973, 87 S.Ct. 510, 17 L.Ed. 2d 436 (1966).

CASE 24—*employer's right to insist on NLRB election under the Act*

The union demanded recognition based upon authorization cards signed by a majority of employees in an appropriate bargaining unit. When the employer refused to recognize the union, the union petitioned for an election. However, the employer stated that it would not abide by the results of an NLRB election, if one were conducted, on the ground that the union's organizational campaign had been improperly assisted by company supervisors in violation of Section 8(a)(2), making it a company assisted union. The union withdrew its election petition and renewed its demand for recognition, but the company again declined to recognize the union. Thereupon the union struck for recognition and filed an unfair labor practice charge based upon the company's refusal to bargain. There was no allegation that the employer engaged in any unfair labor practice besides refusing to bargain in violation of Section 8(a)(5). The Board held that the employer was not guilty of an unfair labor practice solely because it refused to accept evidence of the union's majority status other than the result of a Board election. The question of whether the employer acted in good faith was not deemed relevant by the Board. The court of appeals reversed the Board. It held that if the employer had doubts as to the union's majority status, it could and should test its doubts by petitioning for an election. The court concluded that inasmuch as Congress in 1947 authorized employers to file their own representation petitions, the burden was on them to file such a petition if they refused to recognize the union after it demanded recognition. That decision was appealed to the Supreme Court. Should the employer be required to recognize the union?

Ans. No. The Court reviewed the legislative history and concluded that Congress authorized employer petitions to eliminate the discrimination against employers which had previously existed. There was no suggestion in the legislative history that Congress wanted to place the burden of obtaining a representation election on the employer. The Court concluded: "In light of the statutory scheme and the practical administrative procedural questions involved, we cannot say that the Board's decision that the union should go forward and ask for an election on the employer's refusal to recognize the authorization cards was arbitrary and capricious or an abuse of discretion." Absent an agreement to permit the majority status to be determined by means other than a Board election, or employer unfair labor practices which impair the election process, a union with authorization cards purporting to represent a majority of the employees has the burden of taking the next step in invoking the Board's election procedure if recognition is refused. The refusal to bargain charge was dismissed.

See Linden Lumber Div., Summer & Co. v. NLRB, 419 U.S. 301, 95 S.Ct. 429, 42 L.Ed.2d 465 (1974).

LEGAL GEMS—The Employer's Bargaining Obligation

1. A collective bargaining agreement supersedes any existing individual employment contract. See **CASE 25**, below.

2. An employer may not negotiate with individual employees if they are represented by a union.

3. After a union has been certified by the Board as the representative of a majority of employees in an appropriate unit, the employer must bargain in good faith with that union for one year. This is known as the certification year.

4. If the union loses its majority status during the certification year, the employer is normally required to continue to recognize and bargain with the union.

   e.g. The union won an NLRB election by a vote of eight to five. Before the union was formally certified by the Board, which is five days after the election if no objections are filed, a majority of employees signed a statement that they did not want to be represented by the union and gave the statement to their employer. The union was certified, but the employer refused to bargain with it. The union filed a refusal to bargain charge with the NLRB. Did the employer violate Section 8(a)(5)? Ans. Yes. An employer is obligated to bargain with the union during the year following its certification as representing a majority of employees. The purpose of this rule is to promote industrial peace, and there are reasons for all parties to abide by it. (a) A union so should be given time to negotiate for the employees. (b) The employer should not be encouraged to delay bargaining in the hope that the union will lose the support of a majority of employees. (c) The employees must be impressed with the "solemn and costly" election procedure and abide by their decision for a period of one year. Thus, the employer violated Section 8(a)(5) by refusing to bargain with the union. See Brooks v. NLRB, 348 U.S. 96, 75 S.Ct. 176, 99 L.Ed. 125 (1954).

5. For a period of one year following the certification there is a rebuttable presumption that the union continues to represent a majority of bargaining unit employees.

6. A bargaining order to remedy an unfair labor practice requires an employer to bargain for a reasonable period, which is usually considered to be one year from the date of the order. See CASE 26, below.

7. The Board decides whether an employer or union has bargained in good faith.

8. The Board may not decide what bargainable subjects should or should not be included in the contract. Neither may it compel agreement on a specific subject. See CASE 27, below.

CASE 25—*individual employee privileges subservient to collective interests under Act's scheme of collective bargaining*

The employer offered an employment contract to any individual employee who desired to sign it. Each contract provided in pertinent part that the company would furnish work to the employee at a certain rate and the employee agreed to work for a period of one year. About 75 percent of the employees signed such employment contracts, but this was not required. A union filed a petition with the Board and was certified after an election. However, the employer refused to bargain with the union concerning the terms of employment for employees with whom it had individual employment contracts. The union filed unfair labor practice charges alleging that the employer bargained in bad faith. May an individual employment contract voluntarily signed by an employee be used to prevent or postpone bargaining with the certified bargaining representative of all the employees?

Ans. No. Individual contracts, regardless of the circumstances that justify their existence or their terms, cannot be used to defeat or delay the procedures prescribed by the Act. The purpose of the Act is to promote collective bargaining rather than individual agreements, so the latter cannot be used to frustrate the purposes of the Act. Even if an employee is able to obtain better terms of employment because of his own skills than a union might obtain for all employees, the majority rules. If the union which represents the employees negotiates a contract the special advantage of an individual may become a contribution to the collective result. Thus, the privileges of an individual employee become subservient to the collective interests of all employees.

See J. I. Case Co. v. NLRB, 321 U.S. 332, 64 S.Ct. 576, 88 L.Ed. 762 (1944).

CASE 26—*duration of a bargaining order*

The employer was ordered to bargain with the union in order to remedy its unfair labor practices. However, while the union's unfair labor practice charge was being investigated, the union lost its majority status through a turnover of employees unrelated to the employer's unfair labor practices. Based on this fact the employer refused to bargain with the union. Will an employer be ordered to bargain with the union to remedy the employer's unfair labor practices even when the union has lost its majority status through no fault of the employer?

Ans. Yes. The bargaining order is designed to remedy the employer's unlawful refusal to bargain. Some procedural delay is necessary to investigate and litigate alleged unfair labor practices. If an employer were permitted to escape the remedy when the union lost its majority, then the employer would be given the opportunity to benefit from a refusal to abide by the law. This would only encourage delay. A bargaining relationship once rightfully established must be permitted to exist and function for a reasonable period in which it can be given a fair chance to succeed.

See Franks Bros. Co. v. NLRB, 321 U.S. 702, 64 S.Ct. 817, 88 L.Ed. 1020 (1944).

NOTE—In CASE 26, above, the court required bargaining for a "reasonable time". In Mar–Jac Poultry Co., 136 NLRB 785 (1962) the Board held that an employer was required to bargain with a union for one year from the execution of a settlement agreement just as he is required to bargain for one year after a union certification. For a further discussion of this problem see Pepe, "Certification Year Rule and the Mar–Jac Poultry Extension", 19 Labor L.J. 335; Freilicher, "More on Mar–Jac", 19 Labor L.J. 743.

CASE 27—*board cannot require parties to agree to a specific contract clause*

In contract negotiations the union asked for a dues check-off clause whereby the employer would deduct dues owed to the union by its members upon submission of a proper authorization by the employee. The employer did not object to the union's demand because of any general principle or policy against making deductions from employees' wages. In fact it deducted charges for items like insurance and contributions to charities. Furthermore, at another plant it already had a dues check-off arrangement with the bargaining representative of those employees. The company refused on the ground that it was "not going to aid and comfort the union". Efforts by the union to obtain some sort of compromise on its dues check-off request met with the response that it was the "union's business" and the company was not going to provide any assistance. The Board concluded that the company failed to bargain in good faith concerning the check-off clause because it maintained its position only to frustrate bargaining. In order to remedy the unfair labor practice, the Board ordered the employer to agree to a dues check-off clause. Does the Board have authority to order a party to agree to a specific contract clause in order to remedy a refusal to bargain on that clause?

Ans. No. While the Board has the power to require employers and unions to negotiate, it is without power to compel a company or a union to agree to any substantive contractual provision of a collective bargaining agreement. "It is implicit in the entire structure of the Act that the Board acts to oversee and referee the process of collective bargaining, leaving the results of the contest to the bargaining strength of the parties. It would be anomalous indeed to hold that while Section 8(d) prohibits the Board from relying on a refusal to agree as the sole evidence of bad faith bargaining, the Act permits the Board to compel agreement in that same dispute." One of the fundamental policies of the Act is freedom of contract and "allowing the Board to compel agreement when the parties themselves are unable to do so would violate the fundamental premise on which the Act is based—private bargaining under governmental supervision of the procedure alone, without any official compulsion over the actual terms of the contract." Thus, the employer was not ordered to agree to a dues check-off clause, but only to bargain in good faith on that subject.

See H. K. Porter Co., Inc. v. NLRB, 397 U.S. 99, 90 S.Ct. 821, 25 L.Ed.2d 146 (1970).

LEGAL GEMS—Subjects for Bargaining

1. A bargaining subject is one which the parties are permitted to bargain on and which can be included in the collective bargaining agreement. There are two classifications of bargainable subjects:

   (a) A *mandatory* or *compulsory* subject is anything covered by the phrase "wages, hours, and other terms and conditions of employment."

       e.g. A no-strike clause, the length of the contract, retroactivity, the interpretation, administration, and modification of the contract, merit increases, rates for new jobs, bonuses, rental of company houses, and the price of meals furnished by the employer.

   (b) A *permissive* subject of bargaining is a subject that may be included in the collective bargaining agreement, but as to which the parties are not forced to bargain.

       e.g. A strike vote of employees before engaging in a strike, performance bonds, or an industry promotion fund are permissive bargaining subjects.

2. A non-bargainable subject is one on which no bargaining is permitted. This may occur because the subject *must* be included in the contract on request or because it *may not* be included in the contract.

       e.g. The exclusive recognition of a union must be agreed to by the employer and therefore must be included in the contract on request. A closed shop is illegal and therefore may not be agreed to by the parties or included in a collective bargaining agreement.

3. The parties must bargain in good faith on *mandatory* bargaining subjects and can maintain their position until an impasse is reached.

4. The parties may negotiate on *permissive* bargaining subjects, but they may not insist that their position be agreed to by the other party in order to reach agreement on a contract. In other words

a party may not bring negotiation to an impasse on a permissive subject. See CASE 28, below.

5. To be a mandatory subject of bargaining the subject must fall within the meaning of "wages, hours, and other terms and conditions of employment." The following tests may aid in determining whether a subject of bargaining is mandatory:

   (a) Has the subject matter settled some term or condition of employment?

   e.g. A hiring hall is concerned with initial employment and, therefore, is covered by this test.

   (b) Does the subject regulate the relations between the employer and employees?

   e.g. A hiring hall governs the standards to be applied to prospective employees and, therefore, regulates relations between employer and employees. See CASE 28, below.

6. A refusal to bargain on a *mandatory* bargaining subject is an unfair labor practice. By contrast, a refusal to bargain on a *permissive* subject of bargaining is not an unfair labor practice.

   e.g. The benefits received by employees from a health insurance plan are mandatory bargaining subjects. However, the identity of the carrier of the employee insurance, if it does not affect employee benefits, is only a permissive subject. Thus, the employer may insist that a particular company handle the insurance program.

7. The employer may not take action which unilaterally changes a "term" or "condition" of employment.

   e.g. If an employer desires to subcontract out some work performed by bargaining unit employees, he must first notify the union and, upon demand, bargain with the union on the *decision* to subcontract and its *effect* on the represented employees. See CASE 29, below.

8. The employer has a duty to give a union notice before subcontracting work performed by bargaining unit employees and an opportunity to bargain upon request by the union. The duty to bargain normally arises in the following situations:

   (a) the employer proposes to take some action which will effect some changes in existing employment conditions,

   (b) the contracting out was a departure from established practice, or

   (c) it has or may have a significant impairment of job tenure, employment security, or reasonably anticipated work opportunities for those in the bargaining unit.

   See Westinghouse Electric Corp., 150 NLRB 1574 (1965).

GOOD FAITH BARGAINING

NOTE—Subcontracting (or any other action short of going out of business completely) with an anti-union motivation would be unlawful.

9. Where there is a *partial* closing of facilities by an employer the Board has held that since there is an impact on employees, it constitutes a "condition of employment" and bargaining is required on the *decision*.

   e.g. An employer closed one of two plants solely for economic reasons without bargaining with the union. Employees represented by the union were terminated. The Board treated the employer's action as a partial closing of the business and found that the employer was obligated to bargain on the actual decision to close the plant. The Board distinguished the Darlington decision, CASE 17, above, because this was a partial closing and not a complete shutdown of the business. The Board concluded that the reasoning of the Supreme Court in its Fibreboard decision, see CASE 29, below, controlled. See Ozark Trailers, Inc., 161 NLRB 561 (1966).

   NOTE—The reasoning of the Board in Ozark Trailers has not been followed by courts of appeal, which have based their decisions on whether the change is one "primarily about the conditions of employment" or is instead "fundamental to the basic direction of a corporate enterprise." NLRB v. Royal Plating & Polishing Co., 350 F.2d 191 (3rd Cir. 1965); Morrison Cafeterias Consolidated, Inc., 177 NLRB 591 (1969), modified 431 F.2d 254 (8th Cir. 1970); International Union, UAW v. NLRB, 470 F.2d 422 (D.C.Cir. 1972).

10. The Board has recognized that where the partial sale of a business was part of the employer's plan to divest itself of all similar operations, the decision was at the "core of entrepreneurial control" and bargaining on the decision was not required.

    e.g. General Motors operated a truck center where new and used trucks and coaches were sold at retail. Subsequently General Motors sold certain personal property and equipment at that center and sublet the premises to a buyer who became a General Motors franchised dealer. The conversion of the self-owned outlet into an independently owned and operated franchized dealership was part of the employer's national policy. Management of the business passed to the franchized dealer, and the employees were terminated when the new operator hired its own employees. The union representing General Motors' employees filed unfair labor practice charges against the company alleging, inter alia, that the company violated Section 8(a)(5) by refusing to bargain concerning its decision to sell. The Board stated: "A decision to withdraw capital from a company-operated facility and relinquish operating control to an independent dealership is very much 'at the core of entrepreneurial control.'" Thus, the Board concluded that the decision to sell was not a mandatory subject of bargaining under Section 8(a)(5). See General Motors Corp., 191 NLRB 951, enforced 470 F.2d 422 (D.C.Cir. 1972).

11. Courts of appeal have developed the following rules with respect to the partial closing of a business:

(a) If the decision appears to be primarily designed to avoid the bargaining agreement with the union, or if it produces no substantial change in the operations of the employer, the courts have required bargaining.

e.g. The unilateral transfer of work from a union plant to a nonunion plant three miles away was held to violate the Act. See Weltronic Co. v. NLRB, 419 F.2d 1120 (6th Cir. 1969), cert. denied 398 U.S. 938, 90 S.Ct. 1841, 26 L.Ed.2d 270.

(b) If the decision resulted in the termination of a substantial portion of the employer's business, or involved a major change in the nature of its operations, no bargaining has been required.

(i) The court held that an employer which sold its dairy products through employee driver-salesmen and independent contractors, and unilaterally changed its distribution system to use only independent contractors was not required to bargain with the union about that decision. The NLRB had ordered reinstatement of the terminated driver-salesmen with backpay, but the court refused to enforce the Board Order because the decision was based on the economics of operation, and to require bargaining "would significantly abridge its freedom to manage its own affairs." NLRB v. Adams Dairy, Inc., 350 F.2d 108 (8th Cir. 1965), cert. denied 382 U.S. 1011, 86 S.Ct. 619, 15 L.Ed.2d 526.

(ii) A company was faced with the economic necessity of either moving its business or consolidating the operations of its failing business. The employer decided to close a plant without bargaining with the union on its decision instead of moving the plant to another location. The court refused to enforce a Board decision which found that the employer's conduct violated the Act. The court reasoned that since the decision was made for economic reasons, and it involved a management decision to recommit and reinvest funds in its business, bargaining on the decision itself was not mandatory. See NLRB v. Royal Plating and Polishing Co., 350 F.2d 191 (3rd Cir. 1965).

See generally Gorman, pp. 517–523.

GOOD FAITH BARGAINING

CAVEAT—The examples in GEMS 9-11, above, involve the duty to bargain under Section 8(a)(5) concerning the *decision* to close part of a business for valid economic reasons. It is well settled that an employer must bargain about the *effects* of such a decision on employees. This includes severance pay, accrued vacation and other benefits, and any other appropriate topics. Where the closing or work transfer is discriminatory, it violates Section 8(a)(3). See CASE 17, above.

CASE 28—*party may not insist permissive bargaining subjects be included in contract*

The employer insisted that its collective bargaining agreement include a "ballot" clause requiring a secret ballot vote of employees before engaging in a strike, and a "recognition" clause which recognized only the local union. The international union with which the local was affiliated, and which had been certified as bargaining agent by the NLRB, was excluded as a party to the contract. The international union filed charges with the NLRB contending that the employer's position violated Section 8(a)(5) of the Act. Was the employer's bargaining position an unfair labor practice?

Ans. Yes. Section 8(a)(5) and Section 8(d) establish the obligation to bargain in good faith with respect to "wages, hours, and other terms and conditions of employment." The duty to bargain is limited to subjects which are covered by that phrase. An employer or union may insist that a contract include its proposal relating to a mandatory subject, but may not insist that a contract include other subjects. The "ballot" clause relates to the procedure to be followed by employees before a strike. It does not settle any term or condition of employment. The "recognition" clause excludes the certified representative of the employees as a party to the contract. That is an evasion of the statutory duty of the employer. Although it was lawful for the employer to *propose* the "ballot" and "recognition" clauses, they were not mandatory bargaining subjects. They were only permissive bargaining subjects, and since the union refused to agree to them, the employer violated Section 8(a)(5) by *insisting* that they be included in the contract.

See NLRB v. Wooster Div. of Borg-Warner Corp., 356 U.S. 342, 78 S.Ct. 718, 2 L.Ed.2d 823 (1958).

CASE 29—*subcontracting as a mandatory subject of bargaining*

The union which had represented the employer's maintenance employees for a number of years requested negotiations on a new contract. In previous negotiations the employer had explained its desire to effectuate certain economics in the work done by the maintenance employees, but the union would not agree. Just before the expiration of the current contract, the employer announced that it had contracted out all maintenance work for economic reasons. May a com-

LABOR LAW—EMPLOYMENT DISCRIMINATION

pany subcontract all work performed by bargaining unit employees for economic reasons without giving the union the opportunity to bargain over the decision?

Ans. No. The failure to notify and give the union the opportunity for meaningful bargaining over the decision to subcontract work which would eliminate all bargaining unit jobs violates the Act. It is not necessary to show anti-union motivation. Such contracting out is encompassed by the phrase "terms and conditions of employment" in Section 8(d) of the Act. The words clearly cover the termination of employment which contracting out of work in this case involves. To insure meaningful bargaining on this matter the Board has the power to order the *status quo ante,* i. e., the resumption of maintenance operations by the company and the reinstatement with back pay of all employees affected by the employer's unilateral action. The unilateral subcontracting by the employer violated Section 8(a)(5) of the Act.

See Fibreboard Paper Products Corp. v. NLRB, 379 U.S. 203, 85 S.Ct. 398, 13 L.Ed.2d 233 (1964). See also CASE 32 in Chapter VII, below, for another remedy.

LEGAL GEMS—Collective Bargaining—Rights of Individual Employees

1. Section 9(a) contains a proviso which gives individual employees "the right at any time to present grievances to their employer and to have such grievances adjusted, without the intervention of the bargaining representative, as long as the adjustment is not inconsistent with the terms of a collective bargaining contract or agreement then in effect: *Provided further,* That the bargaining representative has been given opportunity to be present at such adjustment."

2. Despite the provision of Section 9(a), the Act does not protect the "right" to present grievances directly to an employer by making it an unfair labor practice for an employer to refuse to consider such grievances presented outside the contractual grievance procedure.

3. Employees may not circumvent their collective bargaining representative and insist on bargaining directly with their employer over matters being handled by their union under the contractual bargaining procedure. See CASE 30, below.

4. An employee may not compel an employer to arbitrate his individually presented grievance unless the collective bargaining agreement specifically confers such a right on him. That is so because the union is the sole agency empowered to do so as the employees' exclusive bargaining representative under the Act. See Black-Clawson Co. v. International Ass'n of Machinists, 313 F.2d 179 (2nd Cir. 1962).

CASE 30—*no duty to bargain with subgroup of employees who are represented by union*

Several employees complained to their union that their employer, a department store, was discriminating on the basis of race in making assignments and promotions. The union investigated and filed a grievance. There was a collective bargaining agreement in effect which prohibited discrimination, provided grievance machinery with final and binding arbitration, and contained a no strike clause. The employees were dissatisfied with the grievance procedure and refused to participate. At a meeting of the employer and union representatives to negotiate the grievance, the employees demanded that the company president meet with them to work out a program dealing with the discrimination. When the president referred them to the personnel director, the employees instead of meeting called a news conference to make their views public. Then the employees picketed the store urging a public boycott "until black people have full employment and are promoted justly." The employer after first warning the employees, discharged two of the picketing employees for attempting to bargain directly with the company over terms and conditions of employment as they affected racial minorities. Does the Act protect such employee activity in view of the national policy against racial discrimination in employment?

Ans. No. The Act did not protect the concerted activities of employees where they bypassed the union and picketed the store. The union was the exclusive bargaining agent of the employees regarding terms and conditions of employment. "In establishing a regime of majority rule, Congress sought to secure to all members of the unit the benefits of their collective strength and bargaining power, in full awareness that the superior strength of some individuals or groups might be subordinated to the interest of the majority." To prevent a "tyranny of majority over minority interests," a union must represent the interests of all employees fairly. In this case the complaint of the employees was covered by the contract and their grievance was being processed. The union has an interest "in not seeing its strength dissipated and its stature denigrated by subgroups within the unit separately pursuing what they see as separate interests." The fact that the grievance alleged racial discrimination does not warrant an exception to the rule of exclusive representation contained in Section 9(a). The attempt by some employees to circumvent contractual procedures was unprotected concerted activity. Thus, the employer was not obligated to bargain with the separate group of employees, but only with their union representative. Since the action of the employees was not protected, the discharges were upheld.

See Emporium Capwell Co. v. Western Addition Community Organization, 420 U.S. 50, 95 S.Ct. 977, 43 L.Ed.2d 12 (1975).

VII. THE COLLECTIVE BARGAINING AGREEMENT

LEGAL GEMS—The Collective Bargaining Agreement—Introduction

1. Good faith bargaining, discussed in the preceding chapter usually leads to a collective bargaining agreement between the company and the union.

2. The collective bargaining agreement reflects those issues where there has been both negotiation and agreement. See LEGAL GEMS—The Collective Bargaining Agreement, Typical Clauses, below.

3. Even after the agreement has been entered into, the duty to bargain in good faith continues.

4. The collective bargaining agreement is a special type of contract because it is affected not only by basic contract law, but also by national labor policy as reflected in labor laws passed by Congress and by court decisions.

5. Collective bargaining agreements typically provide for the machinery of arbitration. This is because the contract cannot cover all aspects of the employer-employee relationship. As a result there is an extensive body of law with respect to arbitrations under collective bargaining agreements.

6. Final and binding arbitration is a device particularly suited to the resolution of labor disputes because it is quicker than court litigation and because labor arbitrators have developed expertise in such matters.

7. There is no such thing as a standard collective bargaining agreement. Each contract must be tailored to the needs and desires of the employees, union and company involved.

8. The common names for typical clauses found in collective bargaining agreements are given below along with the summarized contents of such clauses or brief explanations of them.

See generally Cox, pp. 567–581.

LEGAL GEMS—The Collective Bargaining Agreement—Typical Clauses

INTRODUCTORY NOTE—The scope and coverage of any collective bargaining agreement varies from plant to plant and union to union. The following GEMS identify typical clauses found in many agreements.

COLLECTIVE BARGAINING AGREEMENT

1. *Recognition.* The employer recognizes the union as the exclusive collective bargaining representative of a specific group of employees. This is called the bargaining unit.

2. *Successorship.* The contract is binding on purchasers of the employer, and successors and assigns of both parties.

3. *Management rights.* The company retains all rights not limited in the contract, including the right to manage its business, direct the work force, and maintain safety and efficiency of its operations.

4. *Union Shop.* All newly hired employees are required as a condition of continued employment after thirty days to join the union. Present employees are required to join after thirty days from the execution of the contract.

5. *Dues Check-Off.* Employees who submit written authorizations to the employer will have their dues deducted from their pay and the company will remit their dues to the union.

6. *Probationary employees.* Newly hired employees will be on probation for the first thirty days of their employment, and a discharge during that period will not be subject to the grievance procedure.

7. *Discipline and discharge.* Employees shall observe reasonable rules and regulations established by the employer. All disciplinary actions are subject to the grievance procedure.

8. *Discrimination.* Management agrees not to discriminate against employees because of their union activities, race, sex, age or national origin.

9. *Seniority.* The parties agree to use the length of service of employees, which may be plant wide or by department, for purposes such as layoff and recall. It may also be a factor in the transfer or promotion of employees.

10. *Working conditions.* Management agrees to permit the union to use a company bulletin board; union representatives are permitted to confer with employees on company time concerning grievances; employees who are union stewards will be paid for time spent on union business during the normal work day. (This is not unlawful assistance. See Chapter V, LEGAL GEMS—Domination or Assistance of Union, above.); the company will post a seniority list; the company will post all vacant jobs and employees may bid on those jobs; and, job vacancies will be filled on the basis of the employee's ability and seniority.

11. *Work schedule.* The normal work week is defined as are circumstances under which employees receive over-time pay. Shift times including night shift premiums are also set forth.

12. *Rates and classifications.* Wage rates and job classifications of bargaining unit employees, including rate progression are listed.

13. *Holidays.* Paid holidays are listed.

14. *Vacations.* A schedule of vacations is set forth which will be based on the length of service of the employee.

15. *Other pay provisions*:

    (a) Bereavement pay for an absence due to a death in the employee's immediate family.

    (b) Jury duty allowance for an employee if he is called to serve on a jury.

    (c) Call-in pay when an employee reports for work and there is no work available, but the company failed to notify the employee not to report for work.

16. *Pension and insurance programs.* The employer agrees to establish or continue its pension, hospitalization, life and accident insurance plans. Employees may be required to contribute in order to participate in some of these plans.

17. *Grievance procedure.* This usually consists of at least three steps:

    (a) An employee and his union steward present their complaint orally to the foreman who has authority to settle it.

    (b) If the matter is not settled, it is reduced to writing and the union steward and officers confer with management.

    (c) If no agreement is reached, the aggrieved party may submit the matter to arbitration which is binding on all parties.

18. *Arbitration.* The mechanics of taking the case to arbitration are set forth in the contract.

19. *No strike or lock-out.* The union agrees not to engage in any type of work stoppage, and the employer agrees not to lock-out employees during the term of the agreement.

20. *Separability.* The parties intend each contract clause to be separable from other clauses and if one clause is declared invalid that will not affect the validity of other clauses in the contract.

21. *Re-opening.* This is a clause used only occasionally in contracts permitting the negotiation of a specific item before the expiration of the whole contract.

    e.g. A three-year contract may have a wage reopener clause after two years to permit negotiation of wages for the third year of the contract.

22. *Wrap-up clause.* The contract is the full settlement of all issues which were the subject of collective bargaining between the parties and no such issues shall be subject to negotiation during the term of the agreement.

23. *Duration of contract.* The expiration date of the contract is set, which is usually one, two or three years from its inception. Some contracts provide that they will automatically be renewed for one

COLLECTIVE BARGAINING AGREEMENT

year unless a notice to terminate is given to the other party 60 days before the expiration of the contract.

LEGAL GEMS—Duties During Contract Period of the Agreement

1. Collective bargaining does not end with the execution of a collective bargaining contract, rather it is a continuing process. As new problems arise either party may require the other to meet and bargain.

2. Section 8(d) provides that during the term of a collective bargaining agreement neither party may modify or terminate the agreement unless it:

    (a) gives the other party 60 days' written notice;

    (b) offers to meet with the other party to negotiate;

    (c) notifies the Federal Mediation and Conciliation Service and any appropriate state agency within 30 days of "(a)" above, if no agreement has been reached; and

    (d) continues in full force and effect the terms of the existing contract for 60 days after "(c)" above or the contract expires, whichever is later.

3. Section 8(d) does not apply to matters which are not included in the collective bargaining agreement because as to such matters then there is no "modification or termination" of the agreement. See CASES 31 and 32, below.

4. Longer time periods have been established under Section 8(d) for health care institutions before a union may strike or an employer may lockout employees.

    (a) Where a collective bargaining agreement is in effect, 90 days' notice must be given to the other party of intent to terminate the contract, and 60 days' notice must be given to the Federal Mediation and Conciliation Service (FMCS) and any appropriate state agency.

    (b) Where there is no collective bargaining agreement 30 days' notice of a dispute must be given to the FMCS and any appropriate state agency.

NOTE—Upon receiving notice, the FMCS is required to mediate the dispute.

5. If an employee engages in a strike without complying with Section 8(d), he loses his employee status and with it the protection of the Act, and thus can be discharged.

LABOR LAW—EMPLOYMENT DISCRIMINATION

CASE 31—*wage re-opening clause limits employer's duty to bargain*

The employer and union were parties to a two-year contract which provided for re-opening after one year on the subject of wages. When the union re-opened negotiations it requested bargaining on wages, changes in the existing group insurance program and the establishment of a pension plan. The employer refused to bargain on any subject except wages. May a party compel bargaining during the term of a contract on any bargainable subject?

Ans. No. If a subject is contained in a collective bargaining agreement, neither party can compel bargaining on it during the term of the contract unless it is so provided in the contract. However, if the subject was not previously negotiated by the parties, one party can compel bargaining on it during the contract term. Since pensions had never been discussed by the parties, the employer violated the Act by not negotiating with the union on that subject. Group insurance was covered by the collective bargaining agreement and the employer was not obligated to bargain on that subject.

See NLRB v. Jacobs Mfg. Co., 196 F.2d 680 (2d Cir. 1951).

NOTE—Mere discussions of a subject during contract negotiations do not constitute a waiver of subsequent bargaining on that subject. Section 8(d) is not applicable to mid-term negotiation of a subject not covered by the contract if it does not "modify or terminate" the contract itself. See NLRB v. C & C Plywood Corp., 384 U.S. 903, 86 S.Ct. 1337, 16 L.Ed. 2d 357 (1967).

CASE 32—*bargaining required when jobs are eliminated*

In reorganizing its trucking operations for economic reasons, the employer unilaterally instituted changes in its method of handling in-bound and out-bound freight. This reduced high operating costs by eliminating inefficiency and resulted in the permanent layoff of about one-third of the employees in the bargaining unit. Must an employer bargain with the union concerning a reorganization which will eliminate a substantial number of bargaining unit jobs?

Ans. Yes. Although the employer has the right to determine the need for a reorganization of its operation to make it more efficient, "the Act imposed upon it the obligation to notify the Union of its reorganization plan and to afford the Union an opportunity to negotiate concerning changes in the plan itself, the manner and timing of the implementation of the plan, and the effects of the changes on employees whose jobs were to be eliminated." The Board emphasized that the *consent* of the union was not necessary before the employer could effect a reorganization, but the employer must at least bargain to an impasse before taking any action. The Board did not order a resumption of the *status quo ante* as in the *Fibreboard* case, CASE 29, above, to remedy the refusal to bargain because the work had not been transferred to any other group of employees, nor had any new employees been hired to perform the work of the terminated employees. Requiring the employer to resume its inefficient practices would be inequitable especially since the employer's action was motivated solely by economic considerations. Since the employer subsequently bargained with the union concerning the effect of the changes upon its employees, the employer was ordered to give all terminated employees back pay from the date of their termination to the date of bargaining with the union.

See Dixie Ohio Express Co., 167 NLRB 573 (1963). Compare CASE 17, above.

LEGAL GEMS—Enforcement of a Collective Bargaining Agreement

1. Section 301 of the Act provides that a collective bargaining agreement is enforceable in any federal district court having jurisdiction of the parties, without regard to the amount in controversy or citizenship of the parties.

2. In addition to conferring jurisdiction, the Act authorizes federal courts to fashion a body of federal law for the enforcement of collective bargaining agreements. This includes the power to order specific performance of an agreement to arbitrate grievances. See Textile Workers Union v. Lincoln Mills of Alabama, 353 U.S. 448, 77 S.Ct. 923, 1 L.Ed.2d 972 (1957).

3. Since national labor policy favors the arbitrability of labor disputes, a court will order arbitration of a grievance unless there is an express provision in the contract excluding the matter from arbitration. See CASES 33 and 34, below.

    e.g. Union A represented production and maintenance employees, and Union B represented salaried, technical employees. The employer had separate contracts with each union. Union A filed a grievance which asserted that certain employees in the engineering laboratory, represented by Union B, were performing production and maintenance work. Union A desired to arbitrate the grievance, but the employer refused. The employer contended: (a) the NLRB had exclusive jurisdiction, and (b) since only one union was willing to arbitrate the dispute, an award might not end the controversy. Should a court compel arbitration? Ans. Yes. (a) The fact that the NLRB could resolve the dispute through its machinery does not prevent a party from submitting a grievance to arbitration under the contract. (b) Although Union B will not be a party to the arbitration proceedings, "the arbitration may as a practical matter end the controversy or put into movement forces that will resolve it." If the dispute is taken to the Board after the arbitration award, the Board may give weight to the arbitration award. However, if the Board disagreed with the arbiter, the Board's ruling would take precedence. The dispute should go to arbitration as this may resolve the matter. See Carey v. Westinghouse, 375 U.S. 261, 84 S.Ct. 401, 11 L.Ed.2d 320 (1964).

LABOR LAW—EMPLOYMENT DISCRIMINATION

4. In determining whether a grievance is arbitrable under the contract, a court may not consider the merits of a grievance, but only whether the grievance is arguably within the scope of the grievance provision of the contract. See CASE 34, below.

5. A court will not review an arbitrator's decision on the merits because it is final and binding on the parties. See CASE 35, below.

6. State courts also have jurisdiction to enforce collective bargaining agreements, but they must apply federal law. See CASE 36, below.

CASE 33—*court may compel arbitration of grievance*

The collective bargaining agreement between the parties provided for arbitration of grievances and contained a no-strike clause. It also provided that employees would be employed and promoted on the basis of seniority "where ability and efficiency are equal". An employee who was injured on the job filed a claim for workmen's compensation. That claim was settled on the basis of the employee having a 25 percent permanent disability. The employee then sought re-employment based on his seniority. The company refused, and the employee filed a grievance which the company refused to arbitrate on the grounds that: (a) the employee was estopped from making the claim because of his settlement of the workmen's compensation claim on the basis of a permanent disability; (b) the employee was unable to perform the work required; and (c) this type of issue was not arbitrable. The union brought suit to compel arbitration of the grievance. May a party be compelled to process a grievance to arbitration when it appears from the wording of the contract that it is without merit?

Ans. Yes. The union claimed that the company had violated a specific provision of the contract. The company took the position that it had not violated that clause. There was, therefore, a dispute involving the interpretation of the contract. National labor policy favors arbitration and courts may not determine the merits of a grievance which the parties have agreed to submit to arbitration. A contract which provides for the submission of all questions of contract interpretation to arbitration limits the functions of the court to ascertaining whether the matter, on its face, is governed by the contract. Whether the grieving party is right or wrong is a matter for the arbitrator to determine. Therefore, the company was directed to arbitrate the grievance.

See United Steelworkers of America v. American Mfg. Co., 363 U.S. 564, 80 S.Ct. 1343, 4 L.Ed.2d 1403 (1960).

CASE 34—*court favors arbitration of disputes*

Company A laid off a number of employees and contracted the maintenance work formerly done by them to Company B. The employees of Company B, which included some laid off employees of Company A, were paid lower wages and worked on Company A's property. Some employees of Company A filed a grievance alleging that this constituted a partial lock-out and was discriminating in violation of the contract. The contract contained no-strike and no-lock-out clauses. It also provided that disputes over the meaning of the contract were subject to arbitration, but not "matters which are strictly a function of management". Company A refused to arbitrate the grievance and the union brought suit to compel arbitration. Is the grievance concerning contracting out work subject to arbitration?

Ans. Yes. The grievance procedure is part of the continuous collective bargaining process. Although the question of arbitrability is for the court to decide, in the absence of any express provision excluding a particular grievance from arbitration, the matter must be left to arbitration. This is particularly true in the present case where the clause excluding matters from arbitration is vague and the arbitration clause is broad. A labor contract is unlike other contracts in that the parties are not free to break off negotiations if they cannot agree. The choice of entering or not entering a relationship has already been determined when bargaining begins. The entire employment relationship is involved in collective bargaining and "the grievance machinery of collective bargaining is at the very heart of the system of industrial self-government." Thus, matters are left to an arbitrator who has special knowledge of the factors involved in this field, rather than to the courts. Arbitration of the grievance was directed.

See United Steelworkers of America v. Warrior & Gulf Navigation Co., 363 U.S. 574, 80 S.Ct. 1347, 4 L.Ed.2d 1409 (1960).

CASE 35—*court will not review arbitrator's decision on merits*

The employer and the union had a collective bargaining agreement which provided for final and binding arbitration to settle all disputes. When one employee was discharged, a group of employees struck in protest. The employer refused to permit those employees to return to work, and the matter was arbitrated. The arbitrator found that the conduct of the employees warranted only a ten-day suspension and ordered them reinstated with back-pay, but was not clear on how the back pay should be computed. Will an arbitrator's decision be enforced by the court when it is unclear or ambiguous?

Ans. Yes. The interpretation of the contract rests solely with the arbitrator because it was his construction of the contract which the parties bargained for. Insofar as the arbitration decision concerns the construction of a contract, courts may not overrule the arbitrator merely because they believe that the contract should be interpreted differently; for then the arbitration award would not be final. The case was remanded so the parties could complete the arbitration and determine the exact amount of back pay due.

See United Steelworkers of America v. Enterprise Wheel & Car Corp., 363 U.S. 593, 80 S.Ct. 1358, 4 L.Ed.2d 1424 (1960).

CASE 36—*federal law prevails over state law in resolving dispute under collective bargaining agreement*

The collective bargaining agreement between the company and the union provided for the settlement of disputes by a board of arbitration, the decision of which was binding on the parties. The contract did not contain a no-strike clause, and the employees struck to protest the discharge of an employee. The employer obtained an injunction against the strike and sued the union in a state court for damages. When a suit is brought in a state court under Section 301, must the state court apply federal law as opposed to the applicable state law?

Ans. Yes. Where there is a conflict, the state law must give way to the federal law. Otherwise, individual contract terms might have different meanings under state and federal law, and that would have a disruptive influence on the negotiation and administration of collective bargaining agreements. In the present case the union struck to settle a dispute which the contract provided would be settled exclusively by arbitration and, therefore, the union violated the terms of the contract under federal law. The fact that the contract did not contain a no-strike clause did not make the strike permissible. The contract imposed the duty to submit the dispute in question to arbitration. A "strike to settle a dispute which a collective bargaining agreement provides shall be settled exclusively and finally by compulsory arbitration constitutes a violation of the agreement." This rule is consistent with federal labor legislation to promote the arbitral process as a substitute for economic warfare between employers and unions. Since the union was obligated to settle the grievance by arbitration, a no-strike clause was implied and the union's strike rendered it liable to the employer for damages.

> See Local 174, Teamsters, Chauffeurs, Warehousemen, & Helpers of America v. Lucas Flour Co., 369 U.S. 95, 82 S.Ct. 571, 7 L.Ed.2d 593 (1962).

LEGAL GEMS—Obligations of Successor Employers

1. Successorship occurs when one business succeeds to the business of another. This may occur after a merger, reorganization, purchase of assets or purchase of stock. After a successorship there may be a question as to the obligations of the new employer under the collective bargaining agreement of the former employer.

2. A successor may expressly agree to assume the obligations of the existing collective bargaining agreement as part of the acquisition of the business, in which event the successor is bound by the terms of the existing agreement.

3. Where state law requires the successor to assume the obligations of the predecessor employer, the successor must arbitrate grievances arising under the predecessor's collective bargaining agreement. See CASE 37, below.

4. Unless the successor agrees to assume the existing collective bargaining agreement, it normally does not bind the successor. However, if the work force remains substantially unchanged, the successor must recognize and bargain with the union which represented employees of the predecessor. See CASE 38, below.

5. Where the work force changes so that the union which represented employees of the precedessor no longer represents a majority of

employees, there is no duty to recognize or bargain with the union. See CASE 39, below.

CAVEAT—The refusal of the successor to retain employees of the predecessor because of their union membership would violate Section 8(a)(3) of the Act.

6. The purchaser of a business, with knowledge that the seller has committed unfair labor practices, may be held jointly and severally liable with the seller to remedy those unfair labor practices.

e.g. X was ordered by the NLRB to reinstate with back pay an employee who had been unlawfully discharged. X sold his business to Y without complying with the Board order. Y continued X's business without interruption or substantial change in the method of operation and was a successor to X's business. Y was a bona fide purchaser of the business with knowledge of the Board order. May the Board order Y to reinstate the employee with back pay? Ans. Yes. The Board's power to remedy unfair labor practices includes authority to issue an order against a successor where necessary to effectuate the policies of the Act. A successor can protect itself against unfair labor practice liability when negotiating the purchase by securing an indemnity clause. However, the employee who was unlawfully discharged would be without a meaningful remedy if the successor were not liable. Thus, the Board may order a successor to remedy the unfair labor practices of its predecessor. See Golden State Bottling Co., Inc. v. NLRB, 414 U.S. 168, 94 S.Ct. 414, 38 L.Ed.2d 388 (1973).

CASE 37—*duty to arbitrate may survive merger and bind successor*

Company A, which had a contract covering its eighty employees, was purchased by Company B, which had 300 employees, none of whom was represented by a union. The employees of Company A went to work with the employees of Company B. There was no successorship clause in the contract. The union and Company B were unable to agree on the effect of the merger on the collective bargaining agreement so the union sued Company B one week before the end of the contract to compel arbitration. The suit was based on Section 301 of the Act which gives federal courts jurisdiction to hear suits for breach of collective bargaining agreements. May arbitration be compelled?

Ans. Yes. Two issues were presented to the court: (a) When the contracting company is merged into another company, may the court decide whether the arbitration provisions of the contract survive? Yes. It is for the court to determine whether the contract does in fact create the duty to arbitrate in any given set of circumstances. This is done by applying federal law which controls. However, state law may be utilized to assist the development of correct principles. Here the state law contains the rule that in merger situations the surviving corporation is liable for the obligations of the disappearing corporation. Thus, a collective bargaining agreement, just as any other contract, may impose duties on the buyer under state law. The Court held that the successor employer was required to arbitrate with the union under the terms of the contract, in circumstances as here, where the business entity remains the same and only the owner of the business changes. A company will consummate a merger for business considerations. National labor policy requires that this be balanced by some protection for the employees involved. Unless arbitration can be compelled the employees would have no remedy. Therefore, some of their rights will survive a merger. (b) Are terms and conditions of employment after the merger subject to the grievance machinery of the contract when those rights will bind the employer after the expiration of the contract? Yes. If a matter is subject to the grievance procedure during the term of the contract, it will not lose its arbitrability just because the resolution of the problem will have effects after the expiration of the contract (e. g., the seniority rights of employees in Company A and Company B). No distinction is made between procedural or substantive matters in determining arbitrability of any issue.

See John Wiley & Sons, Inc. v. Livingston, 376 U.S. 543, 84 S.Ct. 909, 11 L.Ed.2d 898 (1964).

CASE 38—*successor has duty to recognize union if majority of work force unchanged*

A large employer contracted with Wackenhut Corp. for plant protection services. Four months before that contract was to expire Wackenhut signed a three year collective bargaining agreement with a union covering the guards employed. However, Burns Security Services was awarded the contract to provide plant protection services when the contract with Wackenhut expired. Burns hired 27 Wackenhut guards and brought in 15 of its own guards from other locations. The union demanded that Burns recognize it and honor its contract with Wackenhut. Burns refused and the union filed a charge with the NLRB alleging that Burns' refusal violated Section 8(a)(5). The Board held that Burns must recognize the union and honor the contract, and it ordered Burns to reimburse employees for any loss of pay because of any changes made in contract terms. The court of appeals upheld the Board's order to bargain, but refused to enforce the order requiring Burns to honor the existing union contract. That decision was appealed to the Supreme Court. Should the decision of the court of appeals be affirmed?

Ans. Yes. After noting that the union had been certified less than four months earlier and that a majority of Burns' employees had been employed by the former contractor, the Court applied what it described as consistent holdings that "a mere change of employers or of ownership in the employing industry is not such an 'unusual circumstance' as to affect the force of the Board's certification within the normal operative period if a majority of employees after the change of ownership or management were employed by the preceding employer." That result would be different if Burns had not hired a majority of its employees from the group represented by the recently certified union. However, a successor em-

COLLECTIVE BARGAINING AGREEMENT

ployer could not lawfully refuse to hire former employees solely because they were members of a union. In discussing the question whether the successor contractor must honor the predecessor's contract, the Court reaffirmed its statement in the H. K. Porter decision, CASE 27, above, in which it said: "While the Board does have power . . . to require employers and employees to negotiate, it is without power to compel a company or union to agree to any substantive contractual provision of a collective bargaining agreement. . . . [A]llowing the Board to compel agreement when the parties themselves are unable to agree would violate the fundamental premise on which the Act is based— private bargaining under governmental supervision of the procedure alone, without any official compulsion over the actual terms of the contract." On the contract question the Court also discussed other types of successorships, such as merger, stock acquisition, reorganization, or assets purchase, and it noted that to hold either the union or the new employer bound by a previous contract may result in serious inequities. "A potential employer may be willing to take over a moribund business only if he can make changes in corporate structure, composition of the labor force, work location, task assignment, and nature of supervision. Saddling such an employer with the terms and conditions of employment contained in the old collective-bargaining contract may make these changes impossible and may discourage and inhibit the transfer of capital. On the other hand, a union may have made concessions to a small or failing employer that it would be unwilling to make to a large or economically successful firm." While a successor employer may sometimes agree to be bound by an existing union contract, or under certain circumstances the Board might properly find as a matter of fact that the successor had assumed the obligations under the old contract, such duty does not follow as a matter of law from the mere fact that a new employer is doing the same work in the same place with the same employees as his predecessor. Thus, Burns was required to recognize and bargain with the union, and the failure to do so violated Section 8(a)(5). However, Burns was not obligated to honor the contract between Wackenhut and the union.

    See NLRB v. Burns Int'l Security Services, Inc., 406 U.S. 272, 92 S.Ct. 1571, 32 L.Ed.2d 61 (1972).

NOTE 1—The minority opinion in the five to four Burns decision concurred in the ruling that Burns was not bound by the contract, but dissented from the ruling that Burns must bargain with the certified union. They noted that there was no showing how many of the 27 Wackenhut employees had voted for the union and, therefore, there was no evidence that a majority of Burns' 42 employees wanted the union. Moreover, they pointed out that Burns had been treated as a "successor" in the sense that it had taken over the assets of Wackenhut, whereas in fact Burns acquired nothing from Wackenhut, but merely displaced it by bidding lower for the contract to furnish plant protection services. The minority opinion would require the Board to disregard the successorship question and determine the representation of Burns employees by the usual procedures applicable to employers generally.

NOTE 2—The Court distinguished its decision in Wiley v. Livingston, CASE 37, above, in which it held that where one company is merged into another, and state law makes the successor liable for the obligations of the disappearing corporation, the successor remains liable under an arbitration clause in the contract. The arbitrator may determine to what extent, if any, the surviving company is bound by other provisions of the existing union contract. The Court noted that suit in that case was based on Section 301 of the Act to enforce the collective bargaining agreement, whereas suit in the Burns case was based on a violation of Section 8(a)(5). National labor policy favoring arbitration was important in the Wiley case, but the provision of Section 8(d) that neither party can be required to agree to any particular contract term was the important factor in Burns. A subsequent decision by the Supreme Court, CASE 39, below, casts doubt on the validity of that distinction and thus limits the application of the Wiley rationale.

NOTE 3—The Court made another distinction between the Wiley and Burns cases. Wiley involved the merger of two companies and the extent of the successor's duty to arbitrate under the predecessor's contract. In Burns there was no merger or sale of assets. Burns and a competitor bid on work and Burns was successful. Burns hired enough of the predecessor's employees to require it to bargain with the union, but that fact was not sufficient to compel Burns to honor its competitor's collective bargaining agreement.

NOTE 4—Under the Burns decision a successor may change pre-existing contract terms upon commencing business until the duty to bargain arises. That duty occurs when the full employee compliment is hired, and it is known that the union represents a majority of employees. Burns changed the terms and conditions of employment as the guards were hired before its bargaining obligation arose. In those circumstances Burns did not violate the Act when it changed terms and conditions of employment and refused to be bound by the contract of its predecessor. However, after Burns completed its hiring and knew that a majority of its employees had been represented by the union, the obligation to recognize the union and negotiate arose.

CASE 39—*successor has no duty to recognize union if work force substantially changed*

Company B purchased the personal property used by a restaurant and motor lodge from A, which also agreed to lease the land and buildings to B. A had a collective bargaining agreement covering its restaurant employees and another contract with the same union covering its motel employees. Both contracts contained arbitration clauses and provided that they would be binding on "successors, assigns, purchasers, lessees or transferees." The purchase agreement specifically provided that B would not assume A's labor agreements or recognize the union. After reaching agreement on the sale A terminated all of its employees and B hired its own work force. When B commenced operations it employed 33 persons in the restaurant and twelve in the motor lodge. Of these employees only nine of the restaurant employees and none of the motor lodge employees had been among the 53 employees of A. None of A's supervisory personnel was hired by B. The union filed the present action against A and B. The suit sought an injunction to compel arbitration under the collective bargaining agreements to determine B's obligation to A's employees. It was brought under Section 301 of the Act and was based on the Wiley decision, CASE 37, above. A admitted that it was bound to arbitrate under its contract. However, B, the successor, contended that it was not obligated to arbitrate or bargain with the union under the Burns decision, CASE 38, above. Must B, the successor, recognize and bargain with the union?

Ans. No. The Court reviewed its past decisions in Wiley, which was a Section 301 suit, and Burns, which arose from NLRB unfair labor practice proceedings. The Court noted that both cases were governed by the Labor Management Relations Act, and the fact that a different forum was chosen to initiate each of the two cases was not a sufficient basis to distinguish them. The Court found that the Wiley case was not applicable to the present proceedings because: (a) Wiley involved a merger, as a result of which the initial employing entity completely disappeared. In contrast, the present case involved only a sale of some assets, and the initial employer remained in existence as a viable corporate entity with substantial revenues from the lease of the restaurant and motor lodge. (b) The merger in Wiley was conducted against a background of state law which embodied the general rule that in merger situations the surviving corporation is liable for the obligations of the disappearing corporation. The disappearance of the original employing entity in the Wiley merger meant that unless the union were afforded some remedy against Wiley, it would have no means to enforce the collective bargaining obligations of the merged corporation which might be applicable. (c) Most important, in Wiley the surviving corporation hired all of the employees of the disappearing corporation. Those employees continued to perform the same work on the same products under the same management at the same work place as before the change in the corporate employer. In the present case B hired its own independent work force which included only nine of the 53 former employees and none of the former supervisors. For those reasons the Wiley decision was not applicable. Nothing in federal labor laws requires an employer which purchases the assets of a business to hire all of the employees of the predecessor. If the rule were otherwise employees of the predecessor would be deemed employees of the successor, dischargeable only in accordance with the provisions of the contract and subject to the grievance and arbitration provisions thereof. However, B was not required to retain any of A's employees, and, in the circumstances of this case, was not required to honor any provision of A's contract with the union. Thus, B cannot be compelled to arbitrate with the union. The Court concluded that since there was no substantial continuity of identity in the work force hired by B with that of A, and no express or implied assumption of the agreement to arbitrate, B was not required to arbitrate any alleged obligation to former employees.

See Howard Johnson Co. v. Hotel & Restaurant Employees Detroit Local Joint Bd., 417 U.S. 249, 94 S.Ct. 2236, 41 L.Ed.2d 46 (1974).

NOTE—There was no evidence in the Howard Johnson case, above, that the successor discriminated in its hiring practices in any way against the employees of the predecessor. Thus, the failure to hire all the employees of the predecessor was not an unfair labor practice under Section 8(a)(3).

LEGAL GEMS—The NLRB and Arbitration Proceedings

1. If a breach of contract is also an unfair labor practice, the aggrieved party may:

    (a) file charges with the NLRB,

    (b) pursue his contractual remedy, or,

    (c) both.

2. The Board is not precluded from adjudicating unfair labor practices even though they may also have been the subject of an arbitration proceeding. However, the Board will defer to an arbitration award under certain circumstances.

3. The justification for deferral to arbitration is based upon national labor policy.

    (a) Section 203(d) of the Act, referring to the Federal Mediation and Conciliation Service, states: "Final adjustment by a method agreed upon by the parties is hereby declared to be the desirable method for settlement of grievance disputes arising over the application or interpretation of an existing collective bargaining agreement."

    (b) Decisions of the Supreme Court, such as the Steelworkers Trilogy, have encouraged arbitration. See CASES 33, 34, and 35, above.

4. The NLRB will honor an arbitration award and dismiss a subsequent unfair labor practice charge based on the same facts as a matter of policy where:

    (a) the proceedings appear to have been fair and regular,

    (b) all parties agreed to be bound by them, and

    (c) the decision of the arbitration panel was not clearly repugnant to the purposes and policies of the Act.

NOTE—This rule was applied to discharges as well as "technical" contract violations. See Spielberg Mfg. Co., 112 NLRB 1080, (1955) and CASE 40, below.

5. The policy of honoring arbitration awards which had already been rendered was expanded to include pending arbitration awards. See Dubo Mfg. Co., 142 NLRB 431 (1963).

6. A later decision announced a deferral policy with respect to matters which the parties *could* arbitrate under their collective bargaining agreement. If the alleged unfair labor practice involved an interpretation of the collective bargaining agreement, and it was subject

COLLECTIVE BARGAINING AGREEMENT

to the grievance/arbitration provisions of that contract, then the NLRB will defer to the contractual procedure. The Board noted the following factors in reaching its decision:

(a) the parties had a long history of collective bargaining,

(b) there was no union animus, that is, anti-union motivation,

(c) the employer desired to submit the dispute to arbitration,

(d) the contract provided for arbitration of the disputed matter,

(e) the resolution of the unfair labor practice issue depended on the interpretation of the contract, and

(f) the decision of the arbitrator would most probably resolve the issue presented to the Board.

See Collyer Insulated Wire, 192 NLRB 837 (1971).

7. The Board's policy announced in the Collyer decision **GEM 6**, above, was gradually expanded to include unfair labor practices other than refusal to bargain situations.

e.g. In one case the Board said that if the employer's discriminatory motivation in a discipline or discharge case could have been submitted to the arbitrator but was not in order to later proceed with unfair labor practice charges before the Board, the Board will nevertheless accept the arbitrator's award. The purpose of that rule was to avoid trial of the same facts before two forums. See Electronic Reproduction Service Corp., 213 NLRB 758 (1974).

8. Subsequently, with a change of Board membership, its deferral policy was reexamined and modified.

(a) The Board held that it would not apply the Collyer deferral policy to cases alleging a violation of Section 8(a)(1), 8(a)(3), 8(b)(1)(A), or 8(b)(2) of the Act. See General American Transportation Corp., 228 NLRB 808 (1977).

(b) The Board affirmed its policy of deferring 8(a)(5) and 8(b)(3) charges if they meet the Collyer criteria, as listed in **GEM 6**, above. See Roy Robinson Chevrolet, 228 NLRB 828 (1977).

NOTE—Presumably, only refusal to bargain charges will be deferred under the present Board policy. However, Board decisions only cover the Sections of the Act referred to above.

CAVEAT—A breach of contract is not necessarily an unfair labor practice. To be an unfair labor practice the breach *must* materially affect a "term or condition of employment" and *must not* depend primarily on the interpretation of an ambiguous contractual provision or be "essentially one involving a contract dispute, making it reasonably probable that arbitration will put the statutory infringement finally at rest in a manner sufficient to effectuate the policies of the Act." C & S Industries, 158 NLRB 454 (1966).

LABOR LAW—EMPLOYMENT DISCRIMINATION

CASE 40—*arbitration award binding on parties*

The company and union were parties to a collective bargaining agreement which contained union shop and dues check-off clauses. An employee withdrew his authorization for the company to deduct his dues and he failed to pay his dues to the union. After he was delinquent for 60 days, the union requested his discharge. The company continued to employ him and the union filed a grievance under the contract to obtain the employee's discharge. Upon the expiration of the collective bargaining agreement, a state right to work law became operative. The company denied the grievance on the ground that the state right to work law prohibited it from enforcing the union shop clause in the old contract. The union took the grievance to arbitration. The arbitrator found that the company failed to perform its contractual obligation by not discharging the employee, but ruled that because of the state right to work law, the employee should be treated as having been re-employed as of the expiration of the contract with his seniority unbroken except for job tenure. The employee was later laid off with other employees because of his reduced seniority. He filed a charge with the NLRB alleging that the union violated the Act by pursuing the grievance to arbitration and compelling the company to put into effect the arbitrator's award which resulted in his layoff. He also alleged that the employer violated the Act by complying with the arbitrator's decision. Should the arbitrator's award have been honored by the parties?

Ans. Yes. Arbitration is an instrument of national policy for compromising contractual differences and the award is honored in the present case because: (a) the union processed the grievance to final and binding arbitration as provided in the contract; (b) the company's contractual obligation to discharge the employee was fully litigated before the arbitrator; and (c) an impartial arbitrator decided the question in a well reasoned decision after a full and fair hearing. Although the employee involved was not present at the hearing, the company defended his position, and, therefore, his presence was not required. The Board will not substitute its judgment for that of the arbitrator because his decision was not "palpably wrong" and not "clearly repugnant to the purposes of the Act". That the remedy of the Board may have been different from that of the arbitrator is not controlling. Therefore, neither the company nor the union violated the Act by their actions in reducing the seniority or laying off the employee involved.

See International Harvester Co., 138 NLRB 923 (1962), enf'd 327 F.2d 784 (7th Cir. 1964), cert. denied 377 U.S. 1003, 84 S.Ct. 1938, 12 L.Ed.2d 1052 (1964).

VIII. PUBLIC SECTOR BARGAINING

LEGAL GEMS—Public Sector Bargaining—Introduction

1. The public sector comprises those institutions which are supported by taxes. It includes federal, state and local governments and agencies.

2. A public employee is a person who is employed by a federal, state or local government or agency.

NOTE—For purposes of collective bargaining the term public employee usually excludes elected officials and political appointees. It may also exclude supervisors and other employees depending on the wording of the applicable statute.

3. Public sector bargaining may be divided according to:

    (a) laws governing employees of the federal government, and

    (b) state laws regulating labor relations of state employees.

4. The federal government lacks constitutional authority to regulate labor regulations of state employees.

    e.g. The federal government attempted to apply federal minimum wage and overtime laws of the Fair Labor Standards Act to employees of hospitals, nursing homes, schools, local transit operations, policemen and fire fighters employed by the states and their political subdivisions. That was held unconstitutional because such authority was not granted to Congress by the Commerce Clause, Article I, Section 8(3) of the Constitution. The Court said that in attempting to regulate wages paid by states in their sovereign capacities, Congress impaired the ability of the states to function effectively. Congress may not exercise its power to regulate commerce so as to force directly upon the state its choices as to how essential decisions regarding the conduct of integral government functions are to be made. See National League of Cities v. Usery, 426 U.S. 833, 96 S.Ct. 2465, 49 L.Ed.2d 245 (1976).

5. Most states have labor laws which affect employees of state and local governments. These laws vary widely from state to state depending on political pressures and needs within each state.

6. Those states with labor laws have based them largely on federal laws.

7. The major difference between public and private sector bargaining is this: if negotiations reach an impasse in the private sector, the union may strike. In the public sector, since most states prohibit strikes by their employees, the union is unable to exert lawfully the usual pressure by a strike.

LABOR LAW—EMPLOYMENT DISCRIMINATION

NOTE—The union may be able to attain its goals by exerting political pressure against the state agency involved and by influencing public opinion.

8. Two reasons are often given for prohibiting strikes by public employees:

   (a) State employees should not be allowed to disrupt the functions of government by a strike of its employees.

   (b) Public employees should be treated differently from employees of private businesses because governmental employers have no profit motive as private employers.

LEGAL GEMS—Collective Bargaining in the Federal Government

1. The right of federal employees to organize and bargain with the government developed slowly.

   (a) Employees of the postal service were permitted to join unions under the Lloyd-LaFollette Act of 1912.

   (b) Executive Order No. 10988 of 1962 specifically recognized the right of employees of the administrative branch of government to organize and negotiate with their agency on certain terms and conditions of employment.

   (c) Bargaining rights of federal employees were strengthened by subsequent Executive Orders.

   (d) In 1969 the Federal Labor Relations Council was established to administer the program of employee-management relations in the federal government.

   (e) The Federal Service Labor Management and Employee Relations Law was enacted in 1978 and sets forth a comprehensive codification of the rights of federal employees. See GEM 5, below.

2. Most nonsupervisory government employees are covered by Executive Orders which give them the right to form, join and assist unions. Employees also have the right to refrain from joining any union.

3. Agencies must give exclusive recognition to unions representing a majority of employees in an appropriate unit after a secret ballot election. This procedure is based on similar provisions of the Taft-Hartley Act.

4. Unfair labor practices were established similar to those in the Taft-Hartley Act. Both the government agencies and unions are subject to those unfair labor practices.

5. The Federal Service Labor Management and Employee Relations Law was enacted as part of Title VII of the Civil Service Reform Act of 1978. See Title 5, Part III, Subpart F, Chapter 71 of the

U. S. Code. This gives the force of law to the government-employee labor relations program which was previously based on Executive Orders. Important provisions of the new law include:

(a) establishment of an independent agency, the Federal Labor Relations Authority, which is modeled after the NLRB and will investigate and enforce unfair labor practice charges against the government and unions, and

(b) expansion of matters subject to collective bargaining and arbitration.

6. With respect to collective bargaining, the new law:

(a) reserves to management the right to make decisions on matters not subject to bargaining, such as:

   (i) wages and salaries,

   (ii) compulsory payment of union dues,

   (iii) agency mission,

   (iv) budget,

   (v) organization,

   (vi) number of employees, and

   (vii) internal security.

(b) permits, but does not require, bargaining on methods, means and technology of conducting agency operations,

(c) retains the right of employees to form, join or assist labor organizations or to refrain from such activities.

7. The Act continues the prohibition of strikes by federal employees, as well as picketing which interferes with government operations. This prohibition of strikes by employees of the federal government has been held constitutional.

   e.g. The Postal Clerks, a union which represented employees of the Post Office Department, sought a declaratory judgment that a statute and Executive Order prohibiting strikes by government employees was unconstitutional. It also challenged the requirement that employees sign an affidavit agreeing not to strike while employed by the government. The Postal Clerks based their contention on employees' First Amendment rights of association and free speech. The request for a declaratory judgment was denied. "At common law no employee, whether public or private, had a constitutional right to strike in concert with his fellow workers. Indeed, such collective action on the part of employees was often held to be a conspiracy. When the right of private employees to strike finally received full protection, it was by statute, Section 7 of the National Labor Relations Act, . . . It seems clear that public employees stand on no stronger footing in this regard than private employees and that in the absence of a statute, they too do not possess the right to strike." Since there is no constitutional right to strike, the government may condition employment on a promise not to strike. Thus, the federal statute and Executive Order prohibiting strikes by government employees is constitutional. Since the government may prohibit strikes by its employees it may also require employees to sign an affidavit agreeing not to strike. See United Federation of Postal Clerks v. Blount, 325 F.Supp. 879 (D.C.D.C.1971), affirmed without opinion, 404 U.S. 802, 92 S.Ct. 80, 30 L.Ed.2d 38 (1971).

LEGAL GEMS—Labor Relations Under State Laws

1. The right to organize and bargain collectively is specifically recognized in about 35 states.

2. An agency is usually established in states to administer its public sector bargaining laws. That agency will:

    (a) define the appropriate bargaining unit and conduct an election among those employees to determine whether they wish union representation, and

    (b) investigate unfair labor practice charges and prosecute where a violation has been found.

NOTE—State agencies are often modeled after the NLRB.

3. Employees who are usually covered by state labor laws include:

    (a) policemen,

    (b) fire fighters,

    (c) teachers, and

    (d) civil service employees of state governments and their political subdivisions.

4. Some state labor laws also include:

    (a) health care employees,
    (b) transit system employees,
    (c) nonprofessional school employees, and
    (d) college professors.

5. The following state employees are generally excluded from coverage of state labor laws:

    (a) elected or appointed officials, and

    (b) supervisors and managerial employees.

6. Some states also exclude from coverage of their labor laws:

    (a) part time employees, and

    (b) employees dealing with confidential labor relations matters.

PUBLIC SECTOR BARGAINING

LEGAL GEMS—Representation Elections in the States

1. Most states provide for an election to determine the collective bargaining representative of employees.
2. The state agency which conducts the election usually determines the appropriate bargaining unit.
3. Bargaining units generally exclude supervisors and managerial employees.
4. After a majority of employees in an appropriate unit has selected a union to represent them, the agency must recognize and bargain with that union.

NOTE—States which provide for elections usually permit objections to the results of the elections to be filed. Some states have specifically adopted the NLRB rule in **CASE 77**, below, in determining whether an election should be set aside.

LEGAL GEMS—Collective Bargaining Agreements for State Employees

1. Collective bargaining agreements covering public sector employees usually set forth the rights and duties of management and the signatory labor organization. They also contain certain terms of employment and a grievance procedure.
2. Terms and conditions of employment which may be the subject of collective bargaining are generally defined by statute.
3. Sometimes a grievance procedure is established by state law.
4. Since most states prohibit strikes by public employees, state law often provides for mediation and arbitration when there is an impasse in negotiations. A typical state law might provide as follows:
   (a) Initially there is mediation of the dispute. The mediator attempts to narrow the issues in dispute and offer compromises. This is advisory in nature.
   (b) Fact finding may be utilized if mediation fails. In this step the parties present their cases to the fact finder who investigates the claims of the parties. He then makes findings of fact and recommendations to the parties. This step is also advisory in nature.
   (c) If fact finding fails, some states permit employees to strike. Other states provide for arbitration which may be binding on the parties or merely advisory.
5. Union shop clauses, which require the employee to join a union are prohibited in most states. However, there is a growing minority of states which require employees who are not union members to pay a sum less than the normal union dues to defray union costs of negotiating and administering the collective bargaining agreement.

LABOR LAW—EMPLOYMENT DISCRIMINATION

LEGAL GEMS—State Labor Relations—Unfair Labor Practices

1. The rights of public sector employees generally are modeled after the National Labor Relations Act, as amended.

    (a) Employer unfair labor practices often parallel Section 8(a) of the NLRA. See Chapter V, above.

    (b) Union unfair labor practices are usually similar to Section 8(b) of the NLRA, but most state laws do not deal with secondary boycotts. See Chapter IX, above.

2. Many states impose the duty to represent all bargaining unit employees fairly, just as unions are obligated to do in the private sector.

3. A breach of contract is an unfair labor practice in some states and subject to the jurisdiction of some state agencies. In other states contract enforcement is handled by the courts unless the same set of facts constituting the breach of contract also establishes the unfair labor practice. This latter course is the procedure followed under the Taft-Hartley Act.

4. Governmental agencies and unions in some states commit an unfair labor practice by refusing to comply with the decision of an arbiter.

5. In addition, many states make a strike or work slowdown an unfair labor practice.

6. The prohibition of strikes by public employees of states has been upheld as constitutional in numerous state courts.

    e.g. In the state of New York the Taylor Law prohibited strikes by public employees. D, the president of a union, and D's union were found guilty of violating that law and appealed, contending that it was unconstitutional under the Fourteenth Amendment because it deprived employees of due process of law. The court said that the state law was valid so long as the prohibition of strikes by public employees was reasonably calculated to achieve a valid state policy in an area open to state regulation. The government-employee relationship must take into account the ability of the government to perform its essential functions, and through budgeting of government resources, establish priorities among services. The ability of the government to establish priorities among its services would be destroyed if its employees could engage in strikes which deprive the public of essential services. Furthermore, strikes by some government employees could result in gains to them wholly disproportionate to services rendered by them at the expense of the public and other public employees. "The consequence would be the destruction of democratic legislative processes because budgeting and the establishment of priorities would no longer result from the free choice of the electorate's representatives but from the coercive effect of paralyzing strikes of public employees." Thus, the Taylor Law's prohibition of strikes by public employees reasonably effectuates a valid state policy and is constitutional. See City of New York v. De Lury, 23 N.Y.2d 175, 295 N.Y.S.2d 901, 243 N.E.2d 128 (1968).

7. If there is an unlawful strike by public employees most courts will enjoin peaceful picketing. This is so even where state law prohibits the issuance of an injunction in similar circumstances involving private employers. See Anderson Federation of Teachers v. School City of Anderson, 252 Ind. 558, 251 N.E.2d 329 (1969), cert. denied 399 U.S. 928, 90 S.Ct. 2243, 26 L.Ed.2d 794 (1970).

8. A public employee commission is usually established to administer the unfair labor practice provision of state laws.

IX. UNION UNFAIR LABOR PRACTICES

LEGAL GEMS—Union Unfair Labor Practices—Introduction

1. In 1947 the Taft-Hartley Act amended the National Labor Relations Act to add union unfair labor practices. The purpose of the amendments was to balance some of the advantages given to unions under the Wagner Act by imposing corresponding duties on them. Subsequent amendments added additional union unfair labor practices to the Act.

2. Section 8(b)(1)(A) makes it an unfair labor practice for a union to restrain or coerce employees in the exercise of rights guaranteed in Section 7 of the Act. It is the union's duty under 8(b)(1)(A) to represent all employees in the bargaining unit fairly.

3. A union may regulate its own internal affairs by imposing discipline on its members, provided that such discipline is not contrary to the policies of the Act or to public policy.

4. Section 8(b)(1)(B) makes it an unfair labor practice for a union to restrain or coerce an employer in the selection of its representatives for the purposes of collective bargaining or the adjustment of grievances.

5. Section 8(b)(2) makes it an unfair labor practice for a union to cause or attempt to cause an employer to discharge or otherwise discriminate against an employee except for the failure to tender periodic dues and initiation fees uniformly required when the collective bargaining agreement contains a union security clause.

6. Section 8(b)(3) requires a union to bargain in good faith with the employer.

7. Section 8(b)(5) prohibits a union from requiring payment of excessive or discriminatory fees to join the union when membership is required under a union security clause.

8. Section 8(b)(6) prohibits "featherbedding," which is payment for work not performed.

9. Section 8(g) places certain restrictions on the right to strike against health care institutions.

NOTE 1—The above unfair labor practices are discussed in this Chapter.

NOTE 2—Section 8(b)(4) and (7) place limitations on union picketing and boycotts. Those subjects are analyzed in Chapter X, Picketing and Boycotts, below.

UNION UNFAIR LABOR PRACTICES

LEGAL GEMS—Section 8(b)(1)(A)—Restraint or Coercion of Employees

1. Section 8(b)(1) makes it an unfair labor practice for a *union* "to restrain or coerce (A) employees in the exercise of the rights guaranteed in Section 7: *Provided*, That this paragraph shall not impair the right of a labor organization to prescribe its own rules with respect to the acquisition or retention of membership therein".

2. This section is the counterpart of Section 8(a)(1) which prohibits *employer* interference, restraint or coercion.

3. Under this section a union may not threaten or assault employees or a supervisor in the presence of employees, or engage in similar misconduct designed to intimidate employees. See **CASE 41**, below.

4. It is not a valid defense to an 8(b)(1)(A) charge for the union to show that its threats were unsuccessful.

5. During a strike a union may not prevent employees from entering or leaving the plant.

6. Section 8(c) provides that the "expressing of any views, argument, or opinion . . . shall not constitute or be evidence of an unfair labor practice. . . ." This section which is known as the "free speech" provision of the Act, applies to employers and unions, alike.

7. Section 8(c) means that mere name calling during a strike is not an unfair labor practice.

8. Union responsibility for the acts of strikers is determined by the ordinary rules of agency. One decision stated that "a union is liable for the acts of an agent within the scope of his general authority as agent even though the union has not specifically authorized or subsequently ratified, or indeed may have forbidden, the act in question. The Board also holds that authorization or ratification may be manifested by conduct, sometimes even passive acquiescence as well as by words." Lithographers and Photoengravers Int'l Union (Holiday Press), 193 NLRB 11 (1971).

    e.g. In a strike which has been authorized by a union, that union is normally responsible for the acts of authorized pickets. "Threats and the employment of force on a picket line, even though forbidden, are reasonably to be expected, and so 'within the scope of employment of pickets for which the labor organization is responsible.'" Teamsters Local 327 (Coca-Cola Bottling Works of Nashville), 184 NLRB 84, 94 (1970); United Furniture Workers (Colonial Hardwood Flooring Co.), 84 NLRB 563, 587 (1949). See also **CASE 41**, below.

LABOR LAW—EMPLOYMENT DISCRIMINATION

CASE 41—*union responsible for picket line misconduct*

The employer and union could not agree on a new contract and the union called a strike. However, not all employees participated in the strike. As some non-striking employees left the plant, a larger group of strikers followed the employees home and shouted "dirty scabs" and other epithets at them. On other occasions during the strike, striking employees shouted threats of physical violence at employees who reported for work, and blocked the driveway to the plant parking lot, and massed in front of all plant entrances. (a) Do these acts violate the Act? (b) Is the union responsible for the acts of the strikers?

Ans. (a) Yes. (b) Yes. There are three essential elements of a violation. There must be: (1) restraint or coercion, (2) by a labor organization or its agent, and (3) against employees in the exercise of their rights guaranteed in Section 7 of the Act. The conduct of the strikers in following the employees for some distance was designed to intimidate them in the exercise of their right to refrain from striking and, therefore, was an unfair labor practice. It is immaterial that the unlawful conduct failed to deter the employees from crossing the picket line afterward. Likewise, threats to employees and preventing employees from reporting for work by blocking the driveway and mass picketing are also unfair labor practices. Section 8(c) of the Act guarantees free speech to unions and employers and permits the expressing of opinions if they do not contain a threat. Shouting at the non-strikers and calling them names was not an unfair labor practice because of the free speech provision. Threats of physical violence, blocking the driveway to the plant parking lot, even for just a short time, and mass picketing restrained and coerced employees in the exercise of their right to refrain from striking and report for work and all violated Section 8(b)(1)(A) of the Act. In determining union responsibility for the acts of the strikers the Board applied the following rules of agency: (1) The burden of proof was on the party asserting the existence of the agency relationship. (2) The union must have consented to the acts of the employees. This is called authorization or ratification and may be shown by affirmative conduct, or passive acquiescence, as well as by words. (3) If the agent was acting in the general scope of his authority, the principal will be bound. In the present case those tests were applied to the local union which was directly involved in the strike and its international union which assisted it. A local union officer was in charge of the strike. He was frequently present at the plant with the strikers and actually participated in some of the unlawful incidents. He did not attempt to prevent any of the unlawful incidents, and therefore, the local union is responsible for them. The international union was also held responsible. An international representative was assigned to assist its local in the strike. The international representative was present during some of the unlawful acts and made no attempt to stop or to disavow the acts. The conduct of the local and international representatives constituted a ratification of the unlawful acts of the strikers and both unions are responsible.

See International Longshoremen's & Warehousemen's Union, CIO, Local 6 (Sunset Line & Twine Co.), 79 NLRB 1487 (1948).

NOTE—Unfair labor practice charges were brought against the United Mine Workers (UMW) and its District 2 for mass picketing, threats and acts of violence during a strike in violation of Section 8(b)(1)(A). The two unions contended that they were not responsible for the acts of the striking employees and non-employees who joined the strikers and participated in the strike. That defense was rejected. District 2 called a meeting of employees who voted to strike and District 2 organizers were present at the picketing locations directing the strike. Thus, District 2 was responsible for the actions of the strikers. The UMW, the certified bargaining representative of the striking employees, was also responsible for the strike misconduct because its representatives participated in negotiations with the employer during the strike, it appointed the District 2 organizer who was in charge of the strike, its representative visited the picket locations during the strike, and a UMW representative vetoed a settlement of the charges by District 2. The fact that District 2 representatives instructed pickets not to engage in unlawful activity or violence was no defense because the unions made no attempt to enforce the instructions. Thus, both the UMW and its District 2 conducted the strike as a joint venture, and both were responsible for the misconduct of the pickets. See United Mine Workers of America and United Mine Workers of America, District 2 (Solar Fuel Co.), 170 NLRB 1581 (1968).

LEGAL GEMS—Union's Duty to Represent Employees in the Bargaining Unit

1. A union has the duty to represent all employees in the bargaining unit. For example, a union may not discriminate against an employee because of his race. See CASE 42, below.

2. A union must consider all employee grievances in good faith, but it is not obligated to process those grievances which it believes have no merit.

3. The union is not obligated to process a grievance to arbitration to fulfill its duty of fair representation. It only must give it fair consideration.

CAVEAT—A union may not refuse to process a grievance because an employee is not a member of the union, because he criticized the policies of the union at a meeting, or because he engaged in any other activities which are protected in Section 7 of the Act. See Port Drum Co., 170 NLRB 555 (1968); International Union of Electrical, Radio and Machine Workers, AFL–CIO, Local 485 (Automotive Plating Corp.), 170 NLRB 1234 (1968). In both cases the Board ordered the union to process the grievances to arbitration and it retained jurisdiction in the event that the ordered remedy did not prove adequate.

4. The Board has held that a breach of the duty to fairly represent employees in the bargaining unit violates Section 8(b)(1)(A) and Section 8(b)(2) of the Act. The duty to represent employees fairly

is implied from the privilege of exclusive representation. See CASES 43 and 44, below.

CASE 42—*duty to represent all employees in bargaining unit fairly*

An independent union consisted of two locals: Local 1 was comprised of white employees, and Local 2 was comprised of Negro employees. The two locals were jointly certified and each local signed a contract with the employer covering its members and other employees of like color in the bargaining unit. When the contracts expired Local 1 signed a new contract, but Local 2 was not able to reach agreement. Pursuant to the contract with Local 1 the employer followed job-bidding procedures. In doing so it accepted and considered requests for the job opening which had been designated as available only to white workers. The employer refused to accept the bid of a Negro employee, and he filed a grievance with Local 1. Local 1 refused to process the grievance. May a union refuse to process a grievance for a bargaining unit employee?

Ans. No. The bargaining agent for employees must represent all employees in the bargaining unit without discrimination. Since Local 1 refused to process the grievance of an employee because of his race, it breached its duty to represent him fairly. This restrained and coerced the employee in the exercise of his right to have a grievance processed by his bargaining representative and violated Section 8(b)(1)(A). The union's actions also violated Section 8(b)(2) because the contract caused racial discrimination in terms and conditions of employment. The refusal to bargain with the employer about the grievance also constituted a violation of Section 8(b)(3). A union which practices racial discrimination cannot be given aid under Section 9 of the Act. Because the certified Locals signed contracts based on race and administered the contracts so as to perpetuate racial discrimination in employment, their certifications were rescinded.

See Independent Metal Workers Union, Local 1 and Local 2, Hughes Tool Co., 147 NLRB 1573 (1964). See also CASES 43 and 44, below.

CASE 43—*union's duty to bargaining unit employees—differing views of court and Board*

The contract between the employer and the union provided that any employee could have a leave of absence without losing his seniority during the slack season, which was defined in the contract as April 15 to October 15. Employee A, after receiving permission from his employer, commenced his leave on April 12, which was three days early. He did not secure a waiver of this contract provision from the union. Due to an illness the employee did not return to work in the fall until October 30. The union at the request of several other employees demanded that the company move employee A to the bottom of the seniority list because he failed to return to work on October 15 as required by the contract. The union started to process this grievance, but when it learned that the employee's late return was excused because of illness it changed its claim and demanded a reduction in seniority because the employee left work before April 15. The employer agreed to the

UNION UNFAIR LABOR PRACTICES

union's demand. Employee A was a member of the union, and there was no reason for the union to discriminate against him. The employee filed charges against the union and the company. Does discrimination by a union against an employee for reasons unrelated to union or protected concerted activity violate the Act?

Ans. No. The Board found that the union acted for "irrelevant, unfair or invidious" reasons, and that established the unfair labor practice. The court refused to enforce the Board order and held that the union's actions must be designed to encourage union membership and be related to the union or protected concerted activity of the employee and must encourage or discourage union membership before a violation of the Act can be found. In other words, the test is: If the employer acted for the same motive as the union did, would the employer violate Section 8(a)(3)? In the present case the union may have treated the employee unfairly, but not unlawfully. Since the union's request to the employer was lawful, the employer did not violate the Act by reducing the seniority of the employee.

See NLRB v. Miranda Fuel Co., Inc., 326 F.2d 172 (2d Cir. 1963).

NOTE 1—Although the court did not enforce the Board order in CASE 43, above, the Board in subsequent cases has maintained that a union owes a duty of fair representation to all employees in the bargaining unit and has not applied the test of whether the particular action of the union encourages union membership. See CASE 42, above.

NOTE 2—Company A purchased Company B and consolidated operations at A's plant. Union X, which represented employees of A and B before the consolidation, signed an agreement with A to dovetail (integrate) the seniority of B's employees who were transferred to work with A's employees. Two years later when A laid off a substantial number of employees for economic reasons, Union X renegotiated the seniority agreement so that for purposes of layoff and recall the employees who transferred from B had their seniority endtailed (placed at bottom of list) to that of A's employees. This resulted in the layoff of employees formerly employed by B before A's employees. The Board found that the union's actions were not motivated by a good faith effort to represent all employees, but to assure the election of a union officer by the numerically superior employees of A at the expense of B's employees. This breached the union's duty of fair representation. The employer and union were directed to dovetail the seniority of employees in accordance with the original agreement and make B's employees whole for any loss of earnings. See Barton Brands, Ltd., 213 NLRB 640 (1974).

NOTE 3—An employee may have the right to bring suit individually against a union for breach of its duty of fair representation. See Chapter XI, Other Rights of Employees, and CASES 65, 66 and 67, below.

CASE 44—*failure to process grievance in good faith violates Section 8(b)(1)(A)*

The collective bargaining agreement between Local 12 and the company provided for plant wide seniority. However, by custom, separate seniority lists were maintained for white and Negro employees. That system limited job opportunities available for Negroes. The company maintained segregated lunch room and rest room facilities. Eight Negro employees were laid off at a time when white employees with less plant wide seniority were permitted to work because they held jobs restricted to white employees. The laid off Negroes filed a grievance with Local 12 asking for back pay for the period of their unlawful layoffs, and to end the company's segregated plant facilities. Local 12 refused to process the grievance and the Negroes appealed to the union's international president. The president ordered Local 12 to process the grievance. Instead of processing the grievance, Local 12 negotiated an agreement with the company to end some racial discrimination at the plant and to recall the laid off Negro employees. Unfair labor practice charges were filed against Local 12 for failure to process the grievance, for back pay, and to terminate the remaining segregation at the plant. The Board determined that the union's conduct constituted an unfair labor practice and ordered Local 12 to process the grievance and submit contract proposals to end racial discrimination. Local 12 sought court review of the Board's order. Should the Board's order be enforced?

Ans. Yes. A union does not breach its fiduciary duty of fair representation by the mere failure to process a grievance if it is done in good faith. If the union concludes after a good faith investigation of the merits of the grievance that the claim is insubstantial, it may refuse to take further action. However, in the present case the evidence showed that Local 12 failed to act in good faith. It disregarded the instructions of its international president to process the grievance, and the negotiations with the company failed to settle the claims involving back pay and segregated plant facilities. The evidence shows that the union failed to process the grievance for arbitrary and discriminatory reasons. In refusing to represent the Negro employees in a fair and impartial manner Local 12 violated Section 8(b)(1)(A) by restraining those employees in the exercise of their Section 7 right to bargain collectively through their chosen representatives. That the actions of Local 12 may not have directly encouraged or discouraged union membership does not change that determination because such a showing is not necessary to establish a violation of Section 8(b)(1)(A). Local 12 was ordered to process the grievance through arbitration and submit contract proposals to the company to prohibit racial discrimination.

See Local 12, Rubber Workers v. NLRB, 368 F.2d 12 (5th Cir. 1966). See also Truck Drivers Local 568 v. NLRB, 379 F.2d 137 (D.C.Cir. 1967).

LEGAL GEMS—Section 8(b)(1)(A)—Union's Right to Govern Its Internal Affairs

1. The right of a union to regulate its internal affairs means that it may fine or impose other discipline on *members* who violate lawful union rules. However, union discipline may not violate public policy. See CASES 45 and 46, below.

    e.g. Union A represents clerical employees at a plant and calls a lawful strike to support its bargaining demands. Union B represents the production employees at the same plant and has a contract in effect with the employer which contains a

UNION UNFAIR LABOR PRACTICES

no-strike clause. May Union B fine its members who cross the picket line? Ans. No. A union may not fine, suspend or expel a member for refusing to violate a no-strike clause. A union is not free to discipline its members when the reason for its action contravenes a public policy, which, in this case, requires parties to abide by the terms of their collective bargaining agreement. See Local 12419, International Union of District 50 (National Grinding Wheel Co.), 176 NLRB 628 (1969).

2. Although a union may fine or otherwise discipline *members* who violate union rules, the union has no power to discipline a person who has lawfully resigned from the union.

    e.g. A collective bargaining agreement contained a maintenance of membership clause requiring employees who were union members to remain members in good standing "as to payment of dues" as a condition of employment for the duration of the contract. After the contract expired the employees commenced a strike to support the union's bargaining demands. The union members, in addition to voting to strike, also voted to fine any member aiding or abetting the employer during the strike. Thereafter, some employees sent letters of resignation to the union and returned to work. The union fined those employees one day's pay for each day they worked. The employees filed charges with the NLRB alleging that the fines violated their Section 7 right "to refrain from any or all" union activities. The Supreme Court held that where there were no restrictions or by-laws governing resignation from the union, the law required "that the member be free to refrain in November from the actions he endorsed in May and that his Section 7 rights are not lost by a union's plea for solidarity or by its pressures for conformity and submission to its regime." The Court held that once an employee lawfully resigns from the union, it can take no action against the employee for violating a union rule. The Court did not decide what restraints, if any, a union could impose on its members to limit their right to resign. Thus, the fine of employees who resigned from the union violated Section 8(b)(1)(A). See NLRB v. Granite State Joint Board, Textile Workers Local 1029, 409 U.S. 213, 93 S.Ct. 385, 34 L.Ed.2d 422 (1972). See also Booster Lodge 405, I. A. M. v. NLRB, 412 U.S. 84, 93 S.Ct. 1961, 36 L.Ed.2d 764 (1973).

3. The statutory purpose of the Act requires that employees must be free at all times to utilize the processes of the Board and a union commits an unfair labor practice if it restrains employees in exercising that right.

LABOR LAW—EMPLOYMENT DISCRIMINATION

4. A union may not compel employees to exhaust internal union remedies before filing unfair labor practice charges. See CASE 47, below.

5. A union *may expel or suspend* a member who files a petition to decertify the union because such conduct by the union is a defensive action to protect the existence of the union. See CASE 48, below.

6. A union *may not fine* a member for filing a decertification petition because this does not help a union to defend itself, and it discourages employees from utilizing the Board's processes. See NOTE 2 after CASE 48, below.

NOTE—In some industries it is common for employees to retain their union membership after they have been promoted to supervisory positions. For an analysis of union discipline of supervisor-members see LEGAL GEMS—Section 8(b)(1)(B)—Restraint or Coercion of Employer, below.

CASE 45—*union may fine members for crossing picket line*

A local union called a lawful economic strike to support its bargaining demands after a vote of employees and authorization from its international. During the strike some union members crossed the union's picket line and worked. When the strike ended and all employees returned to work, the local brought charges against employees who crossed their picket line for violating the union's constitution and by-laws. A hearing was conducted and all the charged members were found guilty of "conduct unbecoming a union member." They were fined various amounts between $20 and $100. Some union members refused to pay and the local union brought suit to collect the fines. The employer filed a charge alleging that the action of the union restrained and coerced the employees in their right to cross a picket line and work. The contract between the employer and the union required all employees to become and remain "a member of the union to the extent of paying his monthly dues . . . ." May a union fine members who cross a lawful picket line?

Ans. Yes. An economic strike is a weapon used by unions to achieve their bargaining demands. Provisions in the union constitution and by-laws designed to protect this right were commonplace when the Taft-Hartley Act was passed and still are found and applied. The legislative history of the Taft-Hartley Act shows that Congress did not intend to interfere with the internal affairs of unions. There is no evidence in the legislative history of the Act that shows a Congressional intent to render enforcement of such provisions unlawful. A union may proceed in accordance with its constitution and by-laws and impose a reasonable fine on members and sue in an appropriate court to collect those fines. The Act only prohibits a union from attempting to enforce internal regulations to affect the member's employment status for non-payment of the fine. That is, a union may not request that an employee be discharged because he fails to pay a fine, even though it may sue to collect it.

UNION UNFAIR LABOR PRACTICES

See NLRB v. Allis-Chalmers Mfg. Co., 388 U.S. 175, 87 S.Ct. 2001, 18 L.Ed.2d 1123 (1967).

NOTE—A union may suspend from membership and fine a member for exceeding a union established production quota. In sustaining the union's action the court noted: (a) the production ceiling did not violate the collective bargaining contract, (b) the union enforced a validly adopted rule, (c) the rule concerns itself with a legitimate union interest, (d) the union's actions are not contrary to the purposes of the Act, and (e) the rule is reasonably enforced against union members who are free to leave the union and escape the rule. See Scofield v. NLRB, 394 U.S. 423, 89 S.Ct. 1154, 22 L.Ed.2d 385 (1969).

CASE 46—*NLRB lacks authority to determine reasonableness of otherwise valid union discipline*

The employer and the union were parties to a collective bargaining agreement. When the old contract expired there was an 18 day strike before a new contract was signed. Both contracts provided that employees had to retain their union membership during the term of the contract, but employees were not required to join the union if they were not already members. Some employees who were union members crossed the union picket lines to work during the strike without resigning from the union. The union fined those members, and when the members did not pay the fine, the union sued them in a state court. A charge was filed against the union with the NLRB. It alleged that the union violated Section 8(b)(1)(A) because the fines of members were unreasonable. The NLRB said that it would not attempt to regulate the internal affairs of unions by ruling on the reasonableness of disciplinary fines levied against members. The Board reasoned that the validity of fines under the Act did not depend on their being reasonable in amount. Was that decision correct?

Ans. Yes. The Supreme Court said that "the Board was warranted in determining that when the union discipline does not interfere with the employee-employer relationship or otherwise violate a policy of the National Labor Relations Act Congress did not authorize it 'to evaluate the fairness of union discipline meted out to protect a legitimate union interest.'" That means that the NLRB should not rule upon the reasonableness of an otherwise valid union fine. However, if the union sues to collect the fine in a state court, that court has authority to determine whether the fine is reasonable, and reduce excessive fines. State courts may draw on their experience in areas of the law apart from labor relations to determine the reasonableness of fines. Thus, the reasonableness or unreasonableness of a fine does not determine whether the union has violated Section 8(b)(1)(A). In this case, the fines levied against employees for activities while they were union members did not violate the Act.

See NLRB v. Boeing Co., 412 U.S. 67, 93 S.Ct. 1952, 36 L.Ed.2d 752 (1973).

NOTE 1—In CASE 46, above, the union also levied fines against employees who had resigned from the union. The Court held that such fines violated the Act because they interfered with the employees' right to refrain from union activities. It also held that employees who crossed the picket line prior to their resignation from the union could be fined only for work performed prior to their resignation.

NOTE 2—Remedies for union disciplinary action under state law are discussed below. See Chapter XI, LEGAL GEMS—Rights of Union Members Under State Law, below.

CASE 47—*union may not limit employees' right to utilize Board's processes*

An employee filed a charge with his local union and alleged that its president had violated the constitution of the international. The local found in favor of its president after a hearing. The employee did not pursue the intra-union appeals procedure, but filed a charge with the NLRB. The local then processed a charge against the employee because he did not exhaust his internal union remedies, as required by its constitution, before filing his charge with the Board. The employee was found guilty by the union and expelled. The charge filed with the NLRB was dismissed because of lack of merit. The employee filed a second charge with the Board and claimed that his expulsion from the union for filing the original charge was unlawful. May a union expel a member for his failure to comply with the union's constitution and exhaust internal union remedies before filing a charge against the union with the Board?

Ans. No. A union has the freedom of self-regulation where its legitimate internal affairs are concerned. In the present case, however, the union attempted to regulate access of a member to the machinery established by Congress to protect his rights. Public policy requires that there be as much freedom to ask the Board for relief as there is to petition any other department of government for redress of grievances. Any coercion used to discourage, retard or defeat access to Board procedures is beyond the legitimate interest of a union and violates the Act.

See NLRB v. Industrial Union of Marine and Shipbuilding Workers of America, AFL–CIO, 391 U.S. 418, 88 S.Ct. 1717, 20 L.Ed.2d 706 (1968).

CASE 48—*union may expel member to protect itself*

Price, an employee represented by Union A for a number of years and a union member filed a petition with the NLRB to decertify his union. Union B intervened in those proceedings. An election was conducted which was won by Union A. Some members of Union A filed charges with their union against Price charging that by filing the decertification petition he violated the union's constitution. The union suspended Price from membership and prevented him from attending meetings for five years. Price filed a charge with the Board claiming that the union discipline violated Section 8(b)(1)(A). May a union suspend a member who files a decertification petition with the Board?

Ans. Yes. Although the suspension of union membership is restraint or coercion within the meaning of the Act, a union has the right to regulate its own internal affairs. Price sought to remove his union as bargaining agent which was a very real attack on the union's existence. The union has the right to protect itself in such a situation. "Otherwise, during the preelection campaign the member could campaign against the union while remaining a member and therefore privy to the union's strategy and tactics." Therefore, the union was permitted to suspend the member to protect itself when he tried to decertify it.

    See Price v. NLRB, 373 F.2d 443 (9th Cir. 1967), cert. denied 392 U.S. 904, 88 S.Ct. 2051, 20 L.Ed.2d 1363 (1968).

NOTE 1—A union may not suspend a member for filing a decertification petition and then attempt to collect dues from him during the period of suspension. This would be a continuing form of coercion and have a discouraging effect upon a member's decision to invoke the Board's representation processes. Further, collection of dues was not necessary to preserve the union's existence. See Local 4186, United Steelworkers of America, AFL–CIO (McGraw Edison Co.), 181 **NLRB** 992 (1970).

NOTE 2—Public policy forbids a union to penalize a member because he seeks the aid of the Board. An exception to that rule permits a union, as a matter of self-defense, to expel a member who tries to decertify it. Fining a member who files a decertification petition is not a defensive action. It does not help the union defend itself. A fine can only be punitive and discourage members from seeking access to the Board's processes. The member could still campaign against the union while remaining a member and therefore privy to its strategy and tactics. Therefore, fining a member for filing a decertification petition is coercive and violates Section 8(b)(1)(A). See International Molders' and Allied Workers Union, Local No. 125, AFL–CIO (Blackhawk Tanning Co.), 178 NLRB 208 (1969), enforced 442 F.2d 92 (7th Cir. 1971).

LEGAL GEMS—Section 8(b)(1)(B)—Restraint or Coercion of Employer by Union

1. Section 8(b)(1) makes it an unfair labor practice for a *union* "to restrain or coerce . . . (B) an *employer* in the selection of his representatives for the purposes of collective bargaining or the adjustment of grievances".

2. A union may not refuse to bargain with the representatives selected by the employer to bargain for it, or strike or picket to obtain that object.

    e.g. A union may not strike to support a bargaining demand that foremen, whose duties include the adjustment of employee grievances, be union members. That would limit the employer's choice of foremen to union members and give the union power to force the discharge or demotion of foremen by expelling them from the union. An equally divided Supreme Court sustained the holding of the lower court that the union's action restrained and coerced the employer in the selection of his bargaining representative for the adjustment of grievances. See International Typographical Union, AFL-CIO v. NLRB, 365 U.S. 705, 81 S.Ct. 855, 6 L.Ed.2d 36, rehearing denied 366 U.S. 941, 81 S.Ct. 1658, 6 L.Ed.2d 853 (1961). The court also found that the union's attempt to gain preferential treatment for union members violated Section 8(b)(2) and by this conduct it breached its duty to bargain in good faith.

3. A union may not discipline a supervisor in his capacity as a union member for engaging in activities related to collective bargaining or the adjustment of grievances. A union may discipline supervisor-members who engage in other activities, such as performing struck work. See **CASE 49**, below.

CASE 49—*supervisor-members subject to discipline by union for crossing picket line*

Employees began an economic strike and set up a picket line at the entrances to the company. Supervisors, some of whom were members of bargaining units represented by the striking unions, and some of whom were represented by other unions, crossed the picket line and performed work normally done by nonsupervisory employees then on strike. The unions involved later fined and took other disciplinary action against the supervisors. The supervisors filed charges with the NLRB contending that the discipline violated Section 8(b)(1)(B) because it interfered with the performance of their duties as supervisors. May a union discipline supervisor-members who cross a picket line and work during a strike?

Ans. Yes. The Court analyzed the legislative history of Section 8(b)(1)(B) as follows: "Nowhere in the Legislative history is there to be found any implication that Congress sought to extend protection to the employer from union restraint or coercion when engaged in any activity other than the selection of its representatives for the purposes of collective bargaining and grievance adjustment. The conclusion is thus inescapable that a union's discipline of one of its members who is a supervisory employee can constitute a violation of Section 8(b)(1)(B) only when that discipline may adversely affect the supervisor's conduct in performing the duties of, and acting in his capacity as, grievance adjuster or collective bargainer on behalf of the employer." The Court held that since the supervisors in the present case were not engaged in collective bargaining, the adjustment of grievances, or any activities related thereto when they crossed the picket line and performed struck work, the union could discipline them. Although the application of this rule in the present case would prevent the employer from having the full loyalty of its supervisors, the Court noted that an employer "is at liberty to demand absolute loyalty from his supervisory personnel by insisting, on pain of discharge, that they neither participate in, nor retain membership in, a labor union. . . . Alternatively, an employer who wishes to do so can permit his supervisors to join or retain their membership in labor unions, resolving such conflicts as arise through the traditional procedures of collective bargaining." Since the

UNION UNFAIR LABOR PRACTICES

employer chose the latter course, he cannot now complain that the Act should be interpreted to protect the supervisors. Therefore, a union may discipline any supervisor-member who crosses a picket line to work. The charge against the union was dismissed.

See Florida Power & Light Co. v. International Bhd. of Electrical Workers Local 641, 417 U.S. 790, 94 S.Ct. 2737, 41 L.Ed.2d 477 (1974).

NOTE—Where supervisor-members crossed a picket line, but performed only supervisory duties during a strike, the union violated Section 8(b)(1)(B) when it fined them. See American Broadcasting Companies v. Writers Guild, 437 U.S. 411, 98 S.Ct. 2423, 57 L.Ed.2d 313 (1978).

LEGAL GEMS—Section 8(b)(2)—Discharges Caused by Unions

1. Section 8(b)(2) protects employees from the union causing their discharge by making it an unfair labor practice for a union "to cause or attempt to cause an employer to discriminate against an employee in violation of subsection (a)(3) or to discriminate against an employee with respect to whom membership in such organization has been denied or terminated on some ground other than his failure to tender the periodic dues and the initiation fees uniformly required as a condition of acquiring or retaining membership".

2. This does not, however, limit the union's right to ask for a discharge of an employee pursuant to a valid union security clause.

3. An employer and union may contract for an exclusive hiring hall whereby the employer agrees to hire only employees referred to it by the union.

4. The union may not discriminate in the operation of its exclusive hiring hall. This means a union must refer employees based upon some objective criteria and must treat members and non-members alike. For example, the first employee to sign up is the first dispatched.

5. A union may request the discharge of an employee who does not comply with the hiring hall requirements. See **CASE 50**, below.

6. If an employee is not required to clear through a union hall to obtain work, the union is not held to the standard in **GEM 4**, above, because the employee can obtain employment by applying directly with the company.

CASE 50—*exclusive hiring hall requires employer to hire all employees through hall*

The Teamsters Union had a contract with a number of trucking companies which required employers to hire casual employees through the union. The union agreed to refer employees on the basis of their seniority in the industry without regard to union membership. An employee who was a union member obtained

LABOR LAW—EMPLOYMENT DISCRIMINATION

casual employment by applying for work directly with the employer. When the union discovered this it requested his discharge because the employee had not been hired through the union as required by the contract. The employer complied with the union's request and discharged the employee. Does a collective bargaining agreement providing that all employees be hired through the union unlawfully encourage union membership?

Ans. No. There is no express ban of hiring halls in the Act. The Act only prohibits discrimination which encourages or discourages union membership. While the very existence of a union hiring hall encouraged union membership, this was not unlawful. The situation was similar to a union which obtains increased wages and improved working conditions through collective bargaining. Obtaining those benefits would tend to increase union membership. However, that would not be unlawful because it was not accomplished by discrimination. The agreement establishing the present exclusive hiring hall provided that it was to be operated without discrimination based on union membership, and it was not unlawful as long as it conformed to that contract provision. An exclusive hiring hall must be operated without discrimination. Thus, the union did not violate the law by contracting for the exclusive hiring hall and by obtaining the discharge of an employee who failed to comply with the hiring hall provisions. The request for and subsequent discharge of that employee by the employer did not violate the Act.

Local 357, International Bhd. of Teamsters, Chauffeurs, Warehousemen & Helpers of America v. NLRB, 365 U.S. 667, 81 S.Ct. 835, 6 L.Ed.2d 11 (1961).

NOTE—In CASE 50, above, there was an exclusive hiring hall and the employee had to comply with its rules and regulations. By contrast if there is no valid exclusive hiring agreement between the employer and the union, an employee may not be required to abide by union rules in order to work for an employer. A union may not request the discharge of such an employee because he failed to comply with a union rule which required employees to register at the union hall before obtaining employment. The purpose of asking for the discharge of the employee was to coerce union members into compliance with its rules and practices. This would strengthen the union's control of its members. If the union could obtain the discharge of an employee, it would be regarded as a strong union. Non-members would be encouraged to join the union because it was "a strong organization whose favor and help was to be sought and whose opposition was to be avoided." The effect of the union's action on non-members would be to encourage membership. However, union members have the right to refrain from observance of the union rules without penalty of discharge, unless there is an exclusive hiring arrangement with the employer. The union violated the Act by requiring and obtaining the discharge of the employee for failure to comply with a union rule, when there was *no* valid exclusive hiring hall agreement in effect. See Radio Officers' Union v. NLRB, 347 U.S. 17, 74 S.Ct. 323, 98 L.Ed.2d 455 (1954).

UNION UNFAIR LABOR PRACTICES

LEGAL GEMS—Remedies for Union Unfair Labor Practices

1. If the Board finds that a union has committed an unfair labor practice, it will order the union to take specific action to remedy the violation. No punitive damages are awarded.

2. If the union coerces or discriminates, it must post a notice for 60 days stating that it will not commit the unfair labor practices found.

3. A union must give back pay to an employee whom it unlawfully caused to be discharged. See Chapter IV, LEGAL GEMS—Computation of Back Pay, above.

4. A union which prevents an employee from working because of an unlawful strike or because it has physically injured him is not required to give him back pay. See Progressive Mine Workers v. NLRB, 187 F.2d 298 (7th Cir. 1951); International Union of Operating Engineers, Local 513 (Long Constr. Co.), 145 NLRB 554 (1963).

   e.g. During a strike three union officials threatened physical harm to employees who crossed the picket line and truck drivers who handled the products of the struck employer. Strikers attempted to wreck one truck while it was being driven. The Board found that the union conduct violated Section 8(b)(1)(A). Although the union's conduct prevented some employees from working the Board refused to order the union to make them whole by ordering back pay as a remedy. The Board reasoned that remedies other than back pay were available to prevent the occurrence of violence and the remedy of back pay might interfere with the right of employees to strike. See Union de Tronquistas de Puerto Rico, Local 901, International Brotherhood of Teamsters (Lock Joint Pipe & Co.), 202 NLRB 399 (1973).

NOTE—For a further discussion of remedies see Chapter IV, Procedure and Remedies, below.

LEGAL GEMS—Section 8(b)(3)—Union's Duty to Bargain

1. Section 8(b)(3) makes it an unfair labor practice for a *union* "to refuse to bargain collectively with an employer. . . ."

2. This is the counterpart of the *employer's* duty to bargain in good faith, as contained in Section 8(a)(5) of the Act.

3. Section 8(d) defines collective bargaining and Section 9(a) sets forth the requirements to be a bargaining agent. See Chapter VI, Good Faith Bargaining, above. These sections apply to unions the same as to employers.

4. The notice requirements of Section 8(d), discussed in Chapter VII, The Collective Bargaining Agreement, above, are equally applicable to unions and employers.

LABOR LAW—EMPLOYMENT DISCRIMINATION

NOTE 1—A union must give 60 days' notice to terminate a contract under Section 8(d)(4). A union may not strike in support of its demands until that 60 day period has expired even though the contract has, by its terms, expired. A union violates Section 8(b)(3) if it strikes before complying with the sixty-day notice requirement. See Carpenters District Council of Denver & Vicinity, AFL–CIO (Rocky Mountain Prestress, Inc.), 172 NLRB 793 (1968).

NOTE 2—Where the employer is a health care institution a 90 day notice is required instead of the usual 60 day notice. See Chapter VII, LEGAL GEMS—Duties During Contract Period of the Agreement, above, and LEGAL GEMS—Section 8(g)—Strikes Against Health Care Institutions, below.

5. The union must represent all employees in the bargaining unit without regard to their union membership. See CASE 47, above.

6. The use of economic pressure, even if it is illegal or unprotected by the Act, is not, by itself, inconsistent with the duty of the union to bargain in good faith. See CASE 51, below.

e.g. A union strike during negotiations while a contract was in effect, in violation of a no-strike clause, does not necessarily mean that the union has bargained in bad faith. See Cheney California Lumber Co. v. NLRB (Lumber & Sawmill Workers Local 2647), 319 F.2d 375 (9th Cir. 1963).

CASE 51—*unlawful conduct during negotiations does not mean that union bargained in bad faith*

Prudential Insurance Company was negotiating a collective bargaining agreement to cover its agents in 35 states and the District of Columbia. While the union was bargaining in good faith, and after the existing contract expired, it announced that its members would engage in the following on-the-job activities designed to harrass the company: (a) the agents refused to solicit new business, and, when writing new business was resumed, they refused to comply with the company's reporting procedures, (b) the agents refused to participate in a company promotional campaign, (c) they reported late to district offices and refused to perform their customary duties, (d) they engaged in "sit-in-mornings" and left as a group at noon, (e) they refused to attend business conferences arranged by the company, (f) they demonstrated and picketed at various offices, and (g) they distributed literature and solicited policy holders to sign a petition directed at the company. May lack of good faith by a union be inferred from the type of economic pressure that it attempts to put on the employer?

Ans. No. The use of economic pressure by the parties to a labor dispute is not an exception to some policy; it is part and parcel of the process of collective bargaining. The use of economic pressure is not in itself inconsistent with the duty to bargain in good faith. The employees engaged in a "sit-in" and a "slowdown" which are unprotected activities for which the employees could have been disciplined. However, this does *not* mean that these activities constituted a refusal to bargain on the part of the union. The Board may not act as an arbitrator and say what economic weapons the parties may use in seeking to gain acceptance of their bargaining demands. To permit that would put the Board in a position to influence the substantive terms of the collective bargaining agreement. As the devices of the parties were limited the Board's influence would be increased. However, this is contrary to our national labor policy which is to permit the parties to work out their own agreement. Since the Board may not enter the area of the substantive aspects of collective bargaining, it may not conclude that a party has bargained in bad faith based on the type of economic pressure which is exerted by one party. The Board may find, for example, that a sit-in is unlawful and issue an appropriate order to remedy that conduct, but the Board may not find a refusal to bargain based upon such conduct. The Company could have disciplined the employees, for their unprotected conduct, but the conduct could not impute bad faith to the union.

See NLRB v. Insurance Agents' Int'l Union, 361 U.S. 477, 80 S.Ct. 419, 4 L.Ed.2d 454 (1960).

LEGAL GEMS—Section 8(b)(5)—Discriminatory or Excessive Union Initiation Fees

1. If an employee must join a union because of a union security clause in the contract between his employer and the union, his initiation fee must not be excessive or discriminatory under Section 8(b)(5) of the Act.

2. In determining the lawfulness of an initiation fee, Section 8(b)(5) requires the Board to consider, "among other relevant factors, the practices and customs of labor organizations in the particular industry, and the wages currently paid to the employees affected".

    e.g. The union which represented broadcast technicians at ABC and NBC in New York had an initiation fee of $150. When regular employees were on vacation during the summer and also during the football season, both networks hired seasonal employees who were required to join the union. In order to encourage the employment of laid off union members on these seasonal jobs, the union raised its initiation fee to various amounts up to $1,000 depending on the weekly earnings of employees. Ninety percent of the employees involved earned $130 to $140 per week and were required to pay an initiation fee of $500. The Board found that the new initiation fee schedule was discriminatory and excessive. It discriminated against nonmembers of the union and discouraged them from seeking the seasonal jobs. It also unfairly favored laid off union members since they would not have to pay the new, higher fee. The initiation fee was also excessive based upon that charged by another union in the area which represented other broadcast technicians. See New York Local 11, National Association of Broadcast Employees and Technicians, AFL-CIO (NBC), 164 NLRB 242 (1967).

LEGAL GEMS—Section 8(b)(6)—Featherbedding—Payment for Work Not Performed

1. "Featherbedding" is receiving payment for work which has not been performed and which will not be performed.

2. Section 8(b)(6) attempts to limit featherbedding practices by making it an unfair labor practice for a union "to cause or attempt to cause an employer to pay or deliver or agree to pay or deliver any money or other thing of value, in the nature of an exaction, for services which are not performed or not to be performed".

3. This section has been strictly construed. It only prohibits payments when no work is performed. See CASE 52, below.

4. A demand for payment for unwanted or unnecessary work, if related to the usual job of employees, is permitted.

   (a) Some advertisers give newspapers their ads already impressed on a matrix which permits the by-passing of a step in the printing process. A union does not violate the Act by insisting that publishers pay for the work thus avoided by having employees perform the work at a later date. Even though there is no use for the reproduced compositions and they are promptly melted down, the work is done by the employee with the employer's consent and the union can ask for the work. Since the union may lawfully ask for the work, it does not commit an unfair labor practice by demanding that the employees be paid for performing the work. See American Newspaper Publishers Ass'n v. NLRB, 345 U.S. 100, 73 S.Ct. 552, 97 L.Ed. 852 (1953).

   (b) A company was engaged as the general contractor for a $21 million project. It negotiated a contract with the Teamsters which required the company to employ a union steward who had no duties except checking the union cards of incoming truck drivers. When that contract expired the company refused to include a similar clause in the new agreement. The union picketed to enforce its demand, and the company filed unfair labor practice charges against the union. The Board noted that the work to be performed was a service to the union for which the employer had no need. The decision in example (a), above, was distinguished on the ground that setting type could be considered relevant or productive, but checking union cards could not be. Since the steward performed no work for the company, "made work or otherwise," the union violated Section 8(b)(6). To remedy the violation, the Board ordered the union to reimburse the company for wages paid to the steward and for "all reasonable expenditures directly incurred" by the company in its employment of the Teamster steward. See Local 456, Int'l Bhd. of Teamsters (J. R. Stevenson Corp.), 212 NLRB 968 (1974).

See generally Cox, pp. 919–926.

CASE 52—*full payment for minor services is not featherbedding*

The employer operated a number of theaters and occasionally brought in traveling bands to perform. Before the Taft-Hartley Act was passed, the union representing local musicians required the employer to pay members of the local orchestra "stand-by" pay. Although this term suggested that the local musicians would "stand-by", to play in the event of some emergency, in fact they not only did not stand by, they did not even show up. After Section 8(b)(6) was enacted, as a condition of the union's consent to the local appearance of traveling bands, the union asked that local musicians be employed to play "overtures", "intermissions" and "chasers", which are music played when the patrons were leaving the theatre. Was the union seeking payment in the nature of an exaction for work which was not performed?

Ans. No. The union's proposals contemplated the performance of actual services and were not mere "token" or nominal services. Therefore, the union demands were not proscribed by the Act. Only payment for work which is not actually performed, such as "stand-by" pay, was made unlawful by this section of the Act. In this case, however, they did play overtures, intermissions, and chasers, and thus there was no prohibited featherbedding.

See NLRB v. Gamble Enterprises, Inc., 345 U.S. 117, 73 S.Ct. 560, 97 L.Ed. 864 (1953).

LEGAL GEMS—Section 8(g)—Strikes Against Health Care Institutions

1. In 1974 the Act was amended to extend coverage to all private health care institutions, both profit and non-profit.

2. The same unfair labor practices applicable to other employers and unions under the Act are applicable to private health care institutions.

3. With the goal of minimizing the harmful effects of a work stoppage at a health care institution a new unfair labor practice, Section 8(g), was created. It prohibits a labor organization from striking or picketing a health care institution, or engaging in any other concerted refusal to work, without first giving the employer and the Federal Mediation and Conciliation Service a ten day notice of such action.

NOTE—This ten day notice must state the date and time the strike will begin and is in addition to the notice required under

Section 8(d). See Chapter VII, LEGAL GEMS—Duties During Contract Period of the Agreement, above.

4. A strike in violation of the notice requirement of Section 8(g) is an unfair labor practice. It is unprotected activity, and employees who participate in such an unlawful strike may be discharged.

5. Since the obligations of Section 8(g) are intimately related to the good faith bargaining requirement of Section 8(b)(3), a violation of Section 8(g) would probably also constitute a violation of Section 8(b)(3).

X. PICKETING AND BOYCOTTS

LEGAL GEMS—Picketing and Boycotts—Introduction

1. The term "picketing" is not defined in the Act. It was analyzed by an administrative law judge as follows: "The definition of the terms 'picket' and 'picketing' as defined in Black's and Bouvier's law dictionaries do not mention the use of picket signs or placards or the movements of the pickets other than being posted or stationed at a particular place. In NLRB v. Local 182, Int'l Bhd. of Teamsters, Chauffeurs, Warehousemen and Helpers of America (Woodward Motors), 314 F.2d 53, 58 (2nd Cir. 1963), the court quoted Webster's New International Dictionary (2d Ed.) as defining the verb 'picket' as meaning 'to walk or stand in front of a place of employment as a picket,' and the noun as 'a person posted by a labor organization at an approach to the place of work . . . ,' and concluded that any particular movement by the picket was not a necessary ingredient of picketing. In none of these definitions is the patrolling or the carrying of signs considered a requisite component part of picketing. The purpose of picketing in labor disputes is to convey a message which is usually intended to influence the conduct of certain persons to stay away from work or to boycott a product or business, and is frequently accomplished . . . by posting individuals at the approaches to a place of work." United Mine Workers of America, Dist. 12 (Truax-Traer Coal Co.), 177 NLRB 213, 218 (1969).

2. A "boycott" is a concerted refusal to work for, purchase from, or handle the products of an employer. Where the action is directed against the employer directly involved in the labor dispute, it is termed a *primary* boycott. Where the action is directed against other, neutral employers in an attempt to have them cease doing business with the employer with which the union has a dispute, it is known as a *secondary* boycott.

3. The First Amendment, which guarantees freedom of speech and of the press, limits action by the federal government in restricting picketing. The First Amendment has been made applicable to the states through the Fourteenth Amendment Due Process Clause.

4. All picketing may not be prohibited under the constitution, but picketing which violates a valid law or has an illegal object may be prohibited and enjoined.

5. Section 8(b)(7) makes recognition picketing an unfair labor practice where:

    (a) the employer has lawfully recognized another union,

    (b) a valid election has been conducted within one year, or

(c) it continues for an unreasonable length of time without a petition for an election being filed with the NLRB.

6. Section 8(b)(4) is difficult to understand and apply. It may be analyzed by dividing it into parts.

   (a) Section 8(b)(4) prohibits strikes, boycotts and other specified actions by a union to accomplish certain objects.

   (b) Prohibited activity is described in clauses (i) and (ii) as follows:

   (i) forbids a union to engage in a strike, or to induce or encourage a strike, work stoppage, or a refusal to perform services by any employee for one of the prohibited objects listed in subparagraphs (A) through (D).

   (ii) forbids a union to "threaten, coerce or restrain" any employer for one of the prohibited objects listed in subparagraphs (A) through (D).

   (c) Prohibited objectives are listed in subparagraphs (A) through (D). The following paragraphs are lettered to correspond to the same subsection in the Act:

   (A) prohibits unions from engaging in clause (i) or (ii) action to compel an employer or to join any labor or employer organization, or to force an employer to enter into a hot cargo agreement prohibited by Section 8(e).

   e.g. In an attempt to secure for its members certain stevedoring work at an employer's unloading operation, the union pickets to force the employer either to join an employer association with which the union has a contract or to hire a stevedoring firm that is a member of the association. This union activity violates Section 8(b)(4)(ii)(A).

   (B) generally prohibits secondary boycotts and the threat to engage in a secondary boycott by clause (i) or (ii) conduct.

   e.g. Telling an employer that its plant will be picketed if that employer continues to do business with an employer the union has designated as "unfair" is an unlawful threat under Section 8(b)(4)(ii)(B). Asking the employees of that employer not to work on products manufactured by the "unfair" employer which the union is attempting to organize is an unlawful secondary boycott under Section 8(b)(4)(ii)(B).

   (C) prohibits a union from using clause (i) or (ii) conduct to force an employer to recognize or bargain with a labor organization other than the one that is currently certified as the representative of its employees.

PICKETING AND BOYCOTTS

(D) prohibits a union from forcing any employer, by action described in clauses (i) or (ii), to assign certain work to employees in a particular union or trade rather than to employees in another union or trade. The Act establishes a special procedure to resolve such jurisdictional disputes.

(d) A final provision in Section 8(b)(4) provides that publicity other than picketing is permissible to truthfully advise the public that products are produced by an employer with which the union has a primary dispute even where such products are distributed by another employer. However, such publicity is not protected if it has an effect of inducing any persons employed by neutral employers to refuse to handle any goods or not to perform services.

e.g. This provision permits a union to distribute handbills at the stores of neutral food stores asking the public not to buy certain items distributed by a wholesaler with which the union has a primary dispute. It has also been held that peaceful picketing at the stores of a neutral food chain to persuade customers not to buy the products of a struck employer when they traded in those stores was not prohibited by Section 8(b)(4) where the picketing did not "threaten, coerce or restrain" the neutral employer. See CASE 61, below.

NOTE—The contents of this Chapter are arranged in order of increasing complexity. For that reason Section 8(b)(7) is analyzed before Section 8(b)(4). A complicated case involving both sections is included near the end of the Chapter to review the student's understanding of both sections. See CASE 62 and NOTES following, below.

LEGAL GEMS—Constitutionality of State Laws Regulating Picketing

1. The First and Fourteenth Amendments to the Constitution guarantee freedom of speech and of the press. Any law attempting to regulate picketing may not infringe on those rights.

2. A state law banning all picketing at a company without permitting any exceptions violates the union's constitutional right to freedom of speech and of the press. See CASE 53, below.

3. A state may enjoin picketing if the union's actions have an illegal object or violate a valid state law.

e.g. After a union tried unsuccessfully to organize some employees, it began picketing the entrance to the employer's business with a sign reading "The men on this job are not 100% affiliated with the AFL." As a consequence some truck drivers refused to haul goods to and from the company's gravel pit operations. The employer sought an injunction on the grounds that the union was attempting to coerce the employer into forcing its employees to join the union, which would violate the state's labor laws. May the picketing be enjoined? Ans. Yes. Picketing may be enjoined if it violates a valid statute or has an illegal object. Since the union's actions in trying to force employees to join their union against their wishes violated a state statute, the picketing was properly enjoined. See International Bhd. of Teamsters, Chauffeurs, Warehousemen, and Helpers of America, Local 695, AFL v. Vogt, Inc., 354 U.S. 284, 77 S.Ct. 1166, 1 L.Ed.2d 1347 (1957).

4. There is no absolute right to picket either under the common law, or the First and Fourteenth Amendments to the Constitution. See Dorchy v. Kansas, 272 U.S. 306, 47 S.Ct. 86, 71 L.Ed. 248 (1926). See also CASE 54, below.

CASE 53—*broad statute prohibiting all picketing unconstitutional*

The union called a strike against an employer and six to eight men picketed in front of the employer's plant. One of those men, Thornhill, approached an employee who was going to work and told him that they were on strike and did not want anyone to go to work. The employee was not threatened, but he did not report for work. Thornhill was prosecuted for violation of a state statute which prohibited ". . . persons, who, without a just or legal excuse therefor, go near to or loiter about the premises or place of business of any other person, . . . for the purpose . . . of influencing . . . persons not to trade with, . . . or be employed by such persons . . . or who picket . . . for the purpose of . . . interfering with or injuring any lawful business." Did the statute unlawfully restrict freedom of speech and of the press guaranteed by the First Amendment?

Ans. Yes. The statute was invalid on its face. It encompassed every practical way that the facts of a labor dispute could be publicized in the vicinity of the place of business of the employer. It had no exceptions based upon the number of persons involved, the peaceful character of their actions, the nature of their dispute, or the truthfulness of their statements in notifying the public of the dispute. The phrase "without a just or legal excuse" does not effectively restrict the breadth of the regulation. Freedom of speech and of the press includes the right to truthfully discuss publicly all matters of public concern without previous restraint or fear of subsequent punishment. A state can take steps to preserve the peace and protect the lives and property of its residents, but the statute went further and prohibited any activity near the employer's business which sought to publicize the labor dispute. A union cannot be totally prevented from truthfully and peacefully advising the public of its labor dispute with an employer.

See Thornhill v. Alabama, 310 U.S. 88, 60 S.Ct. 736, 84 L.Ed. 1093 (1940).

CASE 54—*right to picket on private property in shopping mall explained*

H was the owner of a large enclosed shopping mall. There were 60 retail stores in the mall leased to different businesses and a large parking area outside the mall. B, a shoe company, leased one of the stores. Most of the stores, including B's, could only be entered from the interior mall. A union which represented B's warehouse employees at another location began an economic strike. The strikers picketed B's warehouse and retail stores carrying signs which read: "B warehouse on strike, AFL–CIO, Local 315." When the strikers attempted to picket in front of B's mall store, H threatened to have them arrested for trespassing. The picketers departed and filed a charge with the NLRB alleging that H violated Section 8(a)(1) by refusing to permit them to picket in front of the entrance to B's store. Should the rights of B's employees and of H to exclude persons from his own property be determined by a constitutional standard under the First Amendment?

Ans. No. The constitutional guarantee of free speech generally restricts only the actions of federal and state governments. An exception was recognized where a town was wholly owned and administered by a private corporation. In that case title to the town was in a private corporation rather than a municipal corporation, and the Court held that fact should not change the constitutional rights of persons in the town. However, to hold that the constitutional guarantee of free speech applied to the shopping mall in this case would be to confiscate part of the owner's private property and disregard the constitutional basis on which the private ownership of property rests. Thus, there is no constitutional basis to require the dedication of private property to public use in the present situation. The rights of the parties depend exclusively upon the provisions of the National Labor Relations Act, as amended. The case was remanded to the Board for a determination of that issue.

See Hudgens v. NLRB, 424 U.S. 507, 96 S.Ct. 1029, 47 L.Ed.2d 196 (1976).

NOTE—On remand the Board held that there was no distinction between a retail store in a shopping mall and a store located on a public sidewalk. There is no reason to insulate one store from the effects of strike activities protected by the Act and not other stores. The Board also held that the picketers should be afforded at least as much protection as nonemployee organizers. (See Chapter V, LEGAL GEMS—Communications Among Employees—No-solicitation and No-distribution Rules, above). The Board concluded that the striking employees had the right to picket immediately in front of B's store in the general walking area used by the invited public in H's mall. See Scott Hudgens, 230 **NLRB** 414 (1977).

LEGAL GEMS—Circumstances Where Recognition Picketing is Prohibited

1. Picketing may be conducted for one or more objects, and may be lawful or unlawful depending on the circumstances.
2. Picketing may be for one of the following purposes:
    (a) recognition of the union,
    (b) to obtain economic benefits for employees,
    (c) to protest unfair labor practices committed by the employer,

LABOR LAW—EMPLOYMENT DISCRIMINATION

(d) to advise the public of a labor dispute with the employer, or

(e) to advise the public that the employees' terms and conditions of employment are inferior to those given by other employers in the area. This is known as "area standards" picketing.

3. Section 8(b)(7) makes it an unfair labor practice for a union to picket with an object of forcing the employer to recognize it or forcing the employees to join the union where:

(a) the employer has lawfully recognized another union,

(b) a valid election has been conducted within one year, or

(c) picketing has been conducted for an unreasonable length of time, not to exceed thirty days, without petitioning for an election EXCEPT a union may picket for the purpose of truthfully advising the public that the employer does not have a contract with or employ members of the union if this does not interfere with pick-ups and deliveries to the employer. See CASE 55, below.

NOTE—Subsections (a), (b), and (c) of GEM 3, above correspond to those sections in the Act and itemize the circumstances where recognition picketing is prohibited.

4. If the union files an unfair labor practice charge instead of a petition for an election within thirty days, as required by 8(b)(7)(C), and the union picketing has two objects, protesting an unfair labor practice and seeking recognition, then the union picketing violates the Act. See CASE 56, below.

5. If the picketing does not have recognition as "an object", it is not limited by 8(b)(7).

e.g. A council of local unions in the building and construction industry asked a contractor to raise its "substandard" wages to those "prevailing" in the area which the unions had negotiated with other contractors. The employer refused and the union commenced picketing with a sign which read, "Houston Building and Construction Trades Council, AFL–CIO protests substandard wages and conditions being paid on this job by Claude Everett Company. Houston Building and Construction Trades Council does not intend by this picket line to induce or encourage the employees of any other employer to engage in a strike or a concerted refusal to work." The picketing continued for more than thirty days and, in fact, induced employees of other employers not to make pick-ups or deliveries or perform other services for the picketed employer. Was the picketing lawful? Ans. Yes. The object of the picketing was to require the employer to conform standards of employment to those prevailing in the area. This is known as *area standards picketing*, and it is not limited by Section 8(b)(7) because it does not seek recognition as "an object". That the picketing stopped pick-ups and deliveries does not make the picketing unlawful because 8(b)(7)(C) is not applicable in this situation. See Houston Building and Construction Trades Council (Claude Everett Construction), 136 NLRB 321 (1962).

CAVEAT—*Area Standards Picketing* is limited to the demand that the employer give his employees an economic package equal to the total cost of what unionized employers paid. If the picketing is for *specific* benefits for employees, such as a welfare and pension plan, rather than for an *overall* economic package, it becomes unlawful recognition picketing. This action is more akin to specific contract demands than to "area standards" enjoyed by employees. Since the picketing is for recognition, it is subject to the limitations of 8(b)(7). See Retail Clerks Int'l Ass'n, Local Union No. 899 (State-Mart, Inc.), 166 NLRB 818 (1967).

6. Section 8(b)(7)(C) also provides for holding an immediate election without regard to the usual pre-election procedures if a representation petition is filed. See Chapter XII, Representation Proceedings, below.

CASE 55—*publicity picketing permitted even if the ultimate object is recognition*

The union picketed the employer's cafeteria for more than thirty days without filing a representation petition with "an object" of securing recognition. "The purpose" of the picketing was to truthfully advise the public that the employer did not have a contract with the union and employed non-union employees. The picketing did not interfere with any pick-ups or deliveries. Is picketing which has recognition as "an object" prohibited even though it has "the purpose" of truthfully advising the public that the employer was non-union?

Ans. No. "An object" of most picketing by a union would have obtaining recognition as an ultimate goal. It is reasonable to conclude that Congress intended to frame in Section 8(b)(7) a general rule to limit recognition picketing in three different situations. It created an exception to permit the comparatively innocuous species of picketing having the immediate purpose of informing the public, even though the union's ultimate objective was recognition. If this statute were construed to prohibit all picketing where *one* of several objects was recognition, then the publicity exception to the rule would have no purpose, because most picketing has eventual recognition as "an object." Therefore, a union may picket indefinitely to inform the public that the employer is non-union without violating the Act if it does not interfere with pick-ups and deliveries.

See Smitley, d/b/a Crown Cafeteria v. NLRB, 327 F.2d 351 (9th Cir. 1964).

NOTE 1—If the picketing discourages the general public from patronizing the picketed establishment, that does not make the picketing illegal. That is frequently the union's objective—to persuade the public not to patronize the picketed business.

NOTE 2—If delivery men from time to time refuse to cross a publicity picket line, this does not make it unlawful. The Board looks to the "actual impact" on the employer's business. The test is whether the picketing disrupted, interfered with, or curtailed pick-ups and deliveries. See Retail Clerks Int'l Ass'n, Local 324 (Barber Bros. Corp.), 138 **NLRB** 478 (1962).

CASE 56—failure to file petition within thirty days is not excused by filing an unfair labor practice charge

Two of the three laborers employed at a construction site signed cards to join the union which demanded recognition. The employer refused to recognize the union and transferred one union member to another job site to destroy the union's majority status. The union began picketing at once for recognition, payment of union scale wages, and to protest the employer's discriminatory transfer of the union supporter. The union signs said only that the company was unfair and the union did not claim that its picketing was informational to bring it within the publicity proviso of Section 8(b)(7). The laborers struck when the picketing began, and the union filed unfair labor practice charges. The charge involving the discriminatory transfer of the employee was settled without the union's consent. The settlement agreement stated that the employer did not admit the commission of any unfair labor practice by signing the settlement agreement. The union's other charges were dismissed because the Board's bargaining order remedy had not been fully developed at that time. See CASE 23, above. The union filed a representation petition, but that was dismissed for two reasons: first, because the jobs would go out of existence in four months and second, the bargaining unit sought was inappropriate. The picketing continued for more than thirty days, and the employer filed a charge against the union. May a union picket for more than thirty days without filing a petition for recognition as required by Section 8(b)(7)(C) when another object of the picketing is to protest the unfair labor practices of the employer?

Ans. No. In the usual situation a representation petition must be filed within thirty days and an expedited election will be conducted. However, when the employer commits an unfair labor practice a fair election may not be possible. In that situation the election petition will be held in abeyance until the unfair labor practice charge is disposed of. If it has no merit it will be promptly dismissed and an election held. If it has merit, the election will not be held until the unfair labor practice has been remedied. In the meantime the innocent union may continue to picket and will be protected if the petition was filed within thirty days. In the present case the union did not file a petition within thirty days of the start of its picketing and "an object" of its picketing was for recognition, so the union violated the Act. If the union had only picketed to protest the unfair labor practice and the failure of the employer to pay union scale wages, the picketing would have been lawful publicity picketing. However, in this case the union also picketed for recognition and was subject to the limitations of Section 8(b)(7)(C).

PICKETING AND BOYCOTTS

See International Hod Carriers, Building and Common Laborers Union, Local 840, AFL–CIO (Blinne Constr. Co.), 135 NLRB 1153 (1962). This case also stands for the principle that Section 8(b)(7)(C) applies to a majority union if it has not been certified. See also GEM 3(c), above.

LEGAL GEMS—Legal Restrictions on Secondary Boycotts

1. The essence of a secondary boycott is the involvement of a neutral employer in a labor dispute which concerns some other employer.

    (a) The neutral employer is called the *secondary* employer.

    (b) The employer who has the dispute with the union is called the *primary* employer. See CASE 61, below.

    (c) A secondary boycott attempts to get the neutral employer to stop dealing with the primary employer with whom the union has a labor dispute.

2. Section 8(b)(4), designed to limit secondary boycotts, makes it an unfair labor practice for a union: (i) "to engage in, or to induce or encourage any individual employed by any person engaged in commerce or in an industry affecting commerce to engage in, a strike or a refusal in the course of his employment to use, manufacture, process, transport, or otherwise handle or work on any goods, articles, materials, or commodities or to perform any services; or (ii) to threaten, coerce, or restrain any person engaged in commerce or in an industry affecting commerce, where in either case an object thereof is:

    (a) forcing or requiring any employer or self-employed person to join any labor or employer organization or to enter into any agreement which is prohibited by Section 8(e);

    (b) forcing or requiring any person to cease using, selling, handling, transporting, or otherwise dealing in the products of any other producer, processor, or manufacturer, or to cease doing business with any other person, or forcing or requiring any other employer to recognize or bargain with a labor organization as the representative of his employees unless such labor organization has been certified as the representative of such employees under the provisions of Section 9: *Provided*, That nothing contained in this clause (b) shall be construed to make unlawful, where not otherwise unlawful, any primary strike or primary picketing;

    (c) forcing or requiring any employer to recognize or bargain with a particular labor organization as the representative of his employees if another labor organization has been certified as the representative of such employees under the provisions of Section 9;

* * *

Provided, That nothing contained in this subsection (b) shall be construed to make unlawful a refusal by any person to enter upon the premises of any employer (other than his own employer), if the employees of such employer are engaged in a strike ratified or approved by a representative of such employees whom such employer is required to recognize under this Act: *Provided further*, That for the purposes of this paragraph (4) only, nothing contained in such paragraph shall be construed to prohibit publicity, other than picketing, for the purpose of truthfully advising the public, including customers and members of a labor organization, that a product or products are produced by an employer with whom the labor organization has a primary dispute and are distributed by another employer, as long as such publicity does not have an effect of inducing any individual employed by any person other than the primary employer in the course of his employment to refuse to pick up, deliver, or transport any goods, or not to perform any services, at the establishment of the employer engaged in such distribution".

3. An outline of these provisions in summary form is as follows: A union may not:

   (i) engage in, or induce individuals to engage in, a strike or refusal to use certain goods, or

   (ii) coerce an employer with the object:

   (a) To force the employer to agree to an unlawful hot cargo clause, see LEGAL GEMS—Section 8(e)—Hot Cargo Clauses Illegal, below.

   (b) To force any person or employer to stop dealing with the picketed employer or force any other employer to recognize a union, *but* this does not make any primary strike or picketing unlawful, see CASE 57, below,

   (c) To force any employer to bargain with a union if another union has been certified.

4. Section 8(b)(4)(ii)(B) does not interfere with the traditional right of a union to picket an employer with whom it has a dispute and if there are incidental secondary effects this does not make the picketing unlawful.

   (a) A union seeking recognition picketed the employer. The union displayed a sign which stated that the employer was "unfair", but no employees participated in the picketing. A customer, with whom the union had no dispute, drove up to the employer's mill in a truck. The pickets formed a line and the truck stopped. The pickets told the truck driver to go back because there was a strike at the mill. Later the truck tried to enter the mill by another entrance and the pickets threw

PICKETING AND BOYCOTTS

stones at it. Was the action of the union in trying to prevent the customer from doing business with the mill a secondary boycott because the more customers the union discouraged from doing business with the struck employer the greater the union's pressure to force recognition of it? Ans. No. The picketing was directed at the employer which operated the mill and its employees in a manner traditional in labor disputes. That was *primary* picketing. The request to honor the picket line did not exceed conduct traditional and permissible in a primary strike. Therefore, this was not an unlawful secondary boycott. The stone throwing may have violated Section 8(b)(1)(A) because it restrained a person from doing business with the employer. (See Chapter IX, LEGAL GEMS—Section 8(b)(1)(A)—Restraint or Coercion of Employees, above). However, that would not convert the picketing to unlawful secondary activity. See NLRB v. International Rice Milling Co., 341 U.S. 665, 71 S.Ct. 961, 95 L.Ed. 1277 (1951).

(b) Company A performs janitorial services at a number of different office buildings and its employees are represented by Union X. Company A also employs window cleaners represented by Union Y, and these employees work at other buildings in the area. Union Y commences an economic strike and pickets Company B from 10:00 p. m. to 6:00 a. m. when the janitorial employees represented by Union X customarily perform their services. No window cleaning services are performed at Company B. The members of Union X honor the picket line of Union Y. Does Union Y's picketing of Company B constitute a secondary boycott? Ans. No. The object is not to get Company B's employees and customers to stop doing business with the primary employer, Company A, but only to have the employees of the primary employer represented by Union X cease work. Therefore, the picketing is still in furtherance of the primary dispute and is not a secondary boycott.

(c) The general contractor, A, was building four high rise apartments and subcontracted the plumbing and heating work to B. B employed both members of the plumbers and members of the pipefitters unions to perform the work. B assigned the work of installing the heating equipment in one building to both the plumbers which violated his contract with the pipefitters. When the pipefitters learned of this they demanded that pipefitters be employed as temporary firemen at the installed heating system until all four heating units were installed and accepted by the owner. That demand was consistent with the contract between the pipefitters and B. B refused and contended that the completed unit would be accepted by A before the other three units were completed and, therefore, no firemen were needed. The pipefitters struck and work on the job ceased. Was the strike a secondary boycott to force B to stop doing business with A? Ans. No. In analyzing the facts the first step is to determine the primary and secondary employers. This can be done by using the "right to control" test in which two questions must be asked: (1) What was the union seeking? (2) Was the person against whom the union directed its action in a position to do anything about it? In the present case the union had a legitimate primary dispute with B. The object of the strike was not to force B to stop doing business with A, but to force B to employ union members in accordance with its contract until the heating units were accepted by A. B was the employer who employed the pipefitters and who was responsible for proper installation and maintenance of the heating units. Therefore, the strike against B was in furtherance of a primary dispute and not a secondary boycott. The secondary effect of the strike—forcing B to cease doing business with A—did not make the strike unlawful. See Beacon Castle Square Bldg. Corp. v. NLRB, 406 F.2d 188 (1st Cir. 1969).

5. A union may not picket a gate of the primary employer which is used exclusively by neutral employers who do work unrelated to the normal business operations of the employer (e. g. construction of a new wing on the plant). See CASE 58, below.

6. Picketing of a neutral employer may be lawful primary action if it meets all the following conditions:

   (a) the picketing is limited to times when the *situs* of the dispute is located on the secondary employer's premises,

   (b) at the time of the picketing the primary employer is engaged in its normal business at the *situs*,

   (c) the picketing is limited to places reasonably close to the location of the *situs*, and

   (d) the picketing discloses clearly that the dispute is with the primary employer.
   See CASE 59, below.

7. Section 303 of the Act permits any person injured in his business or property because of a violation of Section 8(b)(4) to sue the union for compensatory damages in a Federal District Court. Punitive damages may not be recovered. See United Mine Workers of America v. Patton, 211 F.2d 742 (4th Cir. 1954), cert. denied 348 U.S. 824, 75 S.Ct. 38, 99 L.Ed. 649 (1954).

CASE 57—*strike against general contractor to force him to stop doing business with subcontractor is secondary boycott*

G was the general contractor for a commercial building and subcontracted the electrical work to A, which employed non-union electricians. These were the only non-union employees on the project. The representative of a council representing the unionized workers told G that he did not see how the job could progress with A's non-union employees. G said that he would permit A to complete the job. The council posted a picket at the project with a sign which read "This job unfair to Denver Building and Construction Trades Council." No union employees reported for work while the picket sign was displayed. When G ordered A off the job, the picket was removed and the union workers returned to the job. The union contended that it was engaged in a dispute with G to make the project an all union job. Did the union's actions constitute a secondary boycott?

Ans. Yes. The non-union employees were employed by A which had a contract with G. The only way in which the unions could accomplish their objective of having an all union job was for G to stop doing business with A. Section 8(b)(4)(B) makes it an unfair labor practice for a union to strike to try to get one employer to stop doing business with another employer. Since that was *an object* of the picketing, it was unlawful. It was not necessary that the unlawful objective be the *sole* object of the strike, but only that it be *an object*. The picketing was not protected by the free-speech provision (Section 8(c)) because the picket sign was used as a signal to the trades to cease work. The free-speech provision cannot protect a sign which is a signal for an unlawful work stoppage.

See NLRB v. Denver Bldg. & Constr. Trades Council, 341 U.S. 675, 71 S.Ct. 943, 95 L.Ed. 1284 (1951).

CASE 58—*picketing prohibited at gate reserved for neutral employers*

General Electric Co. (GE) manufactured various appliances on a 1,000 acre site. There were five entrance gates to the plant. One gate was for the exclusive use of independent contractors who performed some construction work, repair work, and others who did maintenance work. GE employed approximately 10,500 employees of which 7,600 production and maintenance employees were represented by the union. The union called a strike because of some unsettled grievances and picketed all plant gates, including the gate reserved for the independent contractors. May a union be prohibited from picketing a gate reserved solely for independent contractors at the employer's premises when it has a dispute with the employer?

Ans. Yes, if three conditions are met: (1) it is a separate gate marked and set apart from other gates, (2) the work done by the men who used the gate must be unrelated to the normal operations of the employer, and (3) the work must be of a kind that would not, if done when the plant were engaged in its regular operations, necessitate curtailing those operations. It does not matter if the gate is established solely to limit the effect of picketing due to labor disputes. The key to the problem is the work being done by the employees who use the reserved gate. If there were a separate gate for regular plant deliveries, picketing that gate would be lawful because it is traditional primary activity of appealing to neutral employees who aid the primary employer's everyday operations. In the present case some maintenance work was done by an independent contractor, and some by bargaining unit employees. The case was remanded for a determination of the type and extent of maintenance work done by that independent contractor. If the maintenance work was insubstantial the court indicated that it could be treated as *de minimis*, but if the contractor performed conventional maintenance work necessary to the normal operations of the plant the picketing would be permissible.

See Local 761, Int'l Union of Electrical, Radio and Machine Workers, AFL–CIO v. NLRB, 366 U.S. 667, 81 S.Ct. 1285, 6 L.Ed.2d 592 (1961).

NOTE—The employer had a railroad spur coming into its plant, which was used exclusively by railroad employees. The railroad right-of-way was owned by the railroad. The union began an economic strike against the employer and massed pickets on the spur track by the gate to the employer's premises attempting to prevent the railroad from bringing empty box cars to the plant and removing filled box cars. Did the picketing violate Section 8(b)(4)(B)? Ans. No. The proviso to Section 8(b)(4)(B) protects primary picketing at a gate reserved for neutral delivery men furnishing day-to-day service essential to the employer's normal operations. Although the gate was on the railroad's property, this was adjacent to the employer's property and the delivery related to the employer's normal business operations, so the picketing was no more unlawful than if it occurred on the property of the primary employer. See United Steelworkers of America v. NLRB (Carrier Corp.), 376 U.S. 492, 84 S.Ct. 899, 11 L.Ed.2d 863 (1964).

CASE 59—*picketing of neutral employer permitted when primary employer is working there*

A Greek-owned shipping company contracted with Company A to haul gypsum in its ship *Phopho*. This meant the replacement of the American crew with a Greek crew. *Phopho* was taken to a ship yard of Company B to be converted. Company B agreed that the Greek company could put its crew on the ship for training two weeks before the conversion was completed. When the union which represented the American crew learned of this, it demanded recognition for the Greek crew. The demand was refused and the union picketed the entrance to the ship yard, and requested B's employees not to work on the *Phopho*. Was that unlawful secondary picketing?

Ans. No. The *situs* of the dispute was the ship *Phopho* because it was where the crew worked. Picketing of the *situs* of a dispute is traditionally recognized as primary picketing even though it encouraged neutral persons to cease doing business with the picketed employer. When the *situs* is ambulatory, it may come to rest at the premises of another employer. When that occurs the right of the union to picket the site of its dispute must be balanced against the right of the neutral (secondary) employer to be free from picketing in a controversy in which it is not directly involved. The primary picketing must meet the following conditions to be lawful: (1) The picketing must be limited to times when the *situs* of the dispute is located on the secondary employer's premises; (2) at the time of the picketing the primary employer must be engaged in its normal business at the *situs*; (3) the picketing must be limited to places reasonably close to the location of the *situs*; and (4) the picketing must disclose that the dispute is only with the primary employer. When these criteria were applied to the present case, it was found: (1) *Phopho* was at B's ship yard during the entire period of the picketing; (2) the Greek crew was engaged in its normal work aboard the *Phopho*—getting the ship ready for its voyage by cleaning it, loading stores, etc.; (3) the picketing was done as close to the *Phopho* as possible; and (4) the union showed by its picket signs and requests to employees that its dispute was solely with the owner of the *Phopho*. Therefore, the picketing of the neutral employer was lawful.

See Sailor's Union of the Pacific (Moore Dry Dock Co.), 92 NLRB 547 (1950).

LEGAL GEMS—Secondary Boycotts—Ally Doctrine

1. Secondary boycotts were made an unfair labor practice so that neutral employers would not become involved in labor disputes that they could not resolve. The "ally doctrine" is an exception to the secondary boycott provisions of the Act.

2. An employer who performs struck work for or assists a struck employer in some way is considered his "ally".

3. Under the "ally doctrine" the ally is considered a primary employer for the purpose of the secondary boycott provisions of the Act because such an employer has ceased to be neutral.

4. When a struck employer subcontracts work to another employer and such work would normally be performed by the striking employees, the subcontractor is considered an ally of the struck employer and may be picketed just as the primary employer.

   e.g. Employer A is engaged in the business of supplying engineering services for business. Employer B, a company completely independent of A, performs some work for A. The employees of A commenced an economic strike and A increased the business which it gave to B. The union picketed B with signs stating that B was a "Scab shop" for A. Was this an unlawful secondary boycott? Ans. No. Employer B did work, which, but for the strike of Employer A's employees, would have been done by Employer A. The economic effect upon A's employees was the same which would flow from A hiring strike breakers to work on its own premises. The conduct of the union in inducing B's employees to refuse to handle the struck work is not different in kind from its conduct in inducing A's employees to strike. Since the union could lawfully induce the employees of A to strike, it could also lawfully induce the employees of its "ally" B to strike. See Douds v. Metropolitan Federation of Architects, Engineers, Chemists & Technicians, 75 F.Supp. 672 (S.D.N.Y.1948).

   NOTE—If Employer B had not increased the work performed for Employer A during the strike, Employer B would still be considered a neutral, secondary employer and could not be

LABOR LAW—EMPLOYMENT DISCRIMINATION

picketed. It was only when B performed struck work that it became an ally.

5. Where there is common ownership *and* control of two companies, they are considered a single employer. Thus, employees on strike at one company may picket both companies.

NOTE—The mere fact that there is common ownership of two companies does not make them a single employer or allies. There must be an appreciable integration of operations and management. Whether the companies have a common labor relations policy is always an important factor. See Miami Newspaper Pressmen's Local 46 (Knight Newspapers, Inc.), 138 NLRB 1346 (1962), enforced, 322 F.2d 405 (D.C.Cir. 1963); American Federation of Television and Radio Artists (Hearst Corp.), 185 NLRB 593 (1970), enforced 462 F.2d 887 (D.C.Cir. 1972).

LEGAL GEMS—Other Elements of Secondary Boycott

1. Section 8(b)(4)(i) prohibits inducement of individuals. This includes not only employees but also supervisors. See CASE 60, below.

2. The publicity proviso to Section 8(b)(4) permits publicity other than picketing to truthfully advise the public that a product is "produced by an employer with whom the labor organization has a primary dispute and [is] distributed by another employer."

3. The picketing must "threaten, coerce, or restrain" before it is prohibited in spite of the apparently clear language of the proviso. See CASE 61, below.

4. The word "produced" in the proviso includes anyone who enhances the economic value of the product ultimately sold. See NOTE after CASE 60, below.

NOTE 1—The first step in analyzing any secondary boycott situation is to determine who is the primary employer and who is the secondary employer. The student may find it helpful to draw a diagram when reading cases to give him a picture of the parties and their actions.

NOTE 2—At this point the student should be able to identify and analyze cases where a single issue is presented. However, this area of the law is difficult because the problems which occur often involve many of the principles explained above. Therefore, the authors have included a complicated example to help the student "pull together" the various rules of this Chapter. An understanding of the analysis of this CASE is a good indication that the student has grasped most problems in this area. See CASE 62, below.

PICKETING AND BOYCOTTS

CASE 60—*request to neutral employers not to handle certain goods is lawful*

Servette, a wholesale distributor of specialty food products, sold its products to food chains. The union called a strike against Servette, and union representatives approached managers of super markets and asked them to discontinue handling the merchandise supplied by Servette, against whom they were on strike. The union representatives warned the managers that if they continued selling the products, the union would distribute handbills to the public in front of their stores asking the public not to buy named items distributed by Servette. The union distributed handbills at stores that continued to sell the employer's merchandise. Did the union's actions constitute an unlawful secondary boycott violating Section 8(b)(4)(i) and (ii)(B)?

Ans. No. Section 8(b)(4)(i)(B) prohibits the inducement of individuals to engage in a strike. The term "individual" is more inclusive than the term employee. Although the store managers are supervisors and not employees as defined in the Act, supervisors are included in the broader term "individual". If the union had asked managers not to perform their managerial duties in order to force their employers to cease doing business with Servette, they would have violated the Act. However, the union only asked the managers to make a managerial decision not to handle certain goods. That request was permissible. Likewise, 8(b)(4)(ii)(B) does not condemn the mere request that certain action be taken. The inducement must "threaten, coerce or restrain" to violate the Act. The "threat" of the union was to distribute handbills to the public. The proviso to 8(b)(4) permits a union to truthfully advise the public by publicity other than picketing that a product produced by one employer with whom the union has a primary dispute and distributed by any other employer as long as it does not interfere with pick-ups and deliveries. Although the particular employer in question was not involved in the physical process of creating the products, such a narrow interpretation of the word "produced" is not warranted. The word "produced", viewed in the light of congressional use of the term in other statutes and the legislative history of the publicity proviso, includes a wholesale distributor of products which were made by someone else. The union told the managers that they would do something which they had a right to do, and, therefore, the union did not unlawfully "threaten, coerce or restrain" any employer.

See NLRB v. Servette, Inc., 377 U.S. 46, 84 S.Ct. 1098, 12 L.Ed.2d 121 (1964).

NOTE—The union called a strike against a TV station and asked businesses not to advertise on that station. The union also distributed handbills in front of stores which handled products advertised on the struck station. The handbills advised the public of the union's dispute with the station and asked customers of the stores not to buy the products produced by the advertisers on the television station. The union's actions did not cause a work stoppage at any of the stores. The Board held that the TV station was a "producer" within the meaning of the publicity proviso to Section 8(b)(4). The Board defined "producer" as "anyone who enhances the economic value of the product ultimately sold or consumed". By the addition of its advertising services to the product involved, the TV station became a producer within the meaning of the statute. Therefore, the publicity proviso protected the union's actions, and there was no unlawful secondary boycott. See American Federation of TV & Radio Artists (Great Western Broadcasting Corp. d/b/a KXTV), 150 NLRB 467 (1964).

CASE 61—*peaceful publicity picketing which specifies struck product permitted at business of a neutral employer*

The union called a strike against firms which sold Washington State apples to a chain of supermarkets. Pickets were placed at those supermarkets which sold the apples. The pickets carried signs and distributed handbills asking the public not to buy Washington State apples. The publicity proviso to Section 8(b)(4) permitted the union to publicize its dispute with publicity "other than picketing". Did the union violate the secondary boycott ban by picketing the neutral supermarkets urging customers not to buy a specified struck product?

Ans. No. Only picketing which threatens, coerces or restrains the secondary or neutral employer, in this case, the supermarket, is proscribed by 8(b)(4). The Supreme Court has followed a policy of not attributing to Congress an intent to prohibit peaceful picketing unless there is a clear congressional intent to do so. The Court found that Congress did not intend to proscribe all consumer picketing at the businesses of neutral employers. Such a broad ban on peaceful picketing might violate the First Amendment. The Court stated the following principle to regulate public picketing at a neutral employer: "When consumer picketing is employed only to persuade customers not to buy the struck product, the union's appeal is closely confined to the primary dispute. The site of the appeal is expanded to include the premises of the secondary employer, but if the appeal succeeds, the secondary employer's purchases from the struck firms are decreased only because the public has diminished its purchases of the struck product. On the other hand, when consumer picketing is employed to persuade customers not to trade at all with the secondary employer, the latter stops buying the struck product, not because of a falling demand, but in response to pressure designed to inflict injury on his business generally. In such case, the union does more than merely follow the struck product; it creates a separate dispute with the secondary employer." Since the union clearly identified the product of the primary employer, the picketing did not "threaten, coerce or restrain" the employer and did not constitute a secondary boycott. This is known as the *Tree Fruits* doctrine.

See NLRB v. Fruit and Vegetable Packers, Local 760, 377 U.S. 58, 84 S.Ct. 1063, 12 L.Ed.2d 129 (1964).

NOTE—The union picketed six gasoline service stations asking customers to boycott Bay brand gasoline. Bay gasoline was produced at a refinery where the union had a dispute. In a three to two decision the Board refused to apply the *Tree Fruits* doctrine because Bay gasoline was the mainstay of the businesses of the neutral employers. If the picketing were successful some stations might be forced out of business or squeezed into a position wherein another brand of gasoline would have to be carried. Due to the economic importance of gasoline sales to the stations' operations, the

Board majority held the one-product picketing to be tantamount to inducing customers not to patronize the stations at all. Thus, the picketing had an illegal object of having the station owners curtail or cease doing business with the refinery. The predictability of such an impact on the stations rendered the picketing unlawful. The dissenting opinion asserted that the *Tree Fruits* doctrine should be applied. They viewed the consumer product picketing as a lawful appeal for public support of the primary dispute with the refinery of Bay gasoline. See Local 14055, United Steelworkers of America, AFL–CIO (Dow Chem. Co.), 211 NLRB 649 (1974), enforcement denied 524 F.2d 853 (D.C.Cir. 1975), judgment vacated and case remanded to NLRB for reconsideration in light of intervening circumstances 429 U.S. 807, 97 S.Ct. 43, 50 L.Ed.2d 68 (1976). Upon reconsideration by the Board the charge was dismissed. The Board held that the case had been rendered moot by the dissolution of Local 14055 and the fact that no other labor organization had succeeded to its status as collective bargaining representative of the employees in the bargaining unit formerly represented by Local 14055. See Local 14055, United Steelworkers of America, AFL–CIO (Dow Chem. Co.), 229 NLRB 302 (1977).

CASE 62—*defenses to charge of unlawful secondary activity analyzed*

Employer A was erecting family residences at a large site. A awarded a contract for rough carpentry work at the job site to S. Contracts for other work were awarded to about 16 other contractors. When construction was in progress a representative from the Carpenters Union told A that the employees of S were not represented by the Carpenters. He told A of the advantages of having S sign a collective bargaining agreement with the Carpenters, and warned A that if S did not, there would be informational picketing at the job site. A had no employees in the carpentry trade and no contract with the carpenters Union at that time. The next day a Carpenters representative asked S to sign up his men with the union. He told S of the advantages of becoming a union employer and offered membership to S's employees with a reduced initiation fee. When S refused, the representative said that if it were up to him he "would picket the area." On September 15 the union began picketing all entrances to the job with signs reading: "Picket, Protest—Unfair; Doing work under the Jurisdiction of Carpenters; does not employ workmen under the terms of a collective bargaining agreement with Carpenters Union; workmen and deliverymen are not requested to honor this picket; do not talk to picket." On September 19 A posted a sign at one entrance limiting its use to employees of S. Signs were posted at other entrances stating that they were reserved for contractors other than S, and those contractors were named. The union was notified of the entrance reserved for S, but picketing continued at all entrances until October 11, when picketing was limited to S's reserved gate. All picketing ceased December 28, after it had been enjoined by a state court. On certain days during the picketing, employees of neutral contractors refused to enter the job site, but there were no work stoppages after October 11. A filed a charge against the carpenters alleging that the picketing was conducted with an object of inducing employees of A and neutral subcontractors to strike to force A to cease

LABOR LAW—EMPLOYMENT DISCRIMINATION

doing business with S, or to force subcontractors to cease doing business with A, in order to unionize S in violation of Section 8(b)(4)(ii)(B). It was also alleged that the picketing threatened and was later conducted to coerce Employer A to cease doing business with S, and to coerce the subcontractors to cease doing business with A, in violation of Section 8(b)(4)(ii)(B). In defense the Carpenters contended: (a) A was a primary employer, so all picketing was lawful. (b) If A were not a primary employer it was not neutral, but an ally of S, because A purchased materials which were installed by S's employees, and because A permitted those materials to be delivered through gates reserved for neutral contractors. (c) The reserved gate doctrine should not apply because S used gates reserved for other employers on two occasions, and many neutral employers used the gate reserved for S and his employees. (d) If S were the primary employer, picketing was permitted at all gates used by S. Were any of the union's defenses valid?

Ans. No. (a) A is not a primary employer. When a subcontractor and a union have a primary dispute, the general contractor is a secondary employer. The union's dispute was with S, and the mere fact that S performed work for A does not make A a primary employer. See CASE 57, above. (b) A is not an ally of S because A purchased the materials which were installed by S at the job site. Such a relationship, without more, does not render A an ally of S. The gate used by those suppliers does not change that result. (c) The Carpenters had a primary dispute with S; they wanted to organize S's employees. In furtherance of that dispute the union told A that the alternative to unionizing S would be "informational picketing." That threat to picket was coercive within the meaning of 8(b)(4)(ii)(B) as to A because it applied to the entire job without any distinction between primary and neutral employers and employees. However, since the threat was not made to any other neutral employer, the statement did not unlawfully coerce the other neutral employers. The credible evidence offered by the union showed that after an entrance was reserved for S and his employees, S used a gate reserved for other contractors once before normal working hours, and once during working hours. The use of the gate during non-working hours was innocuous, and, therefore, did not cause the gates reserved for neutral employers to lose their protected status. The other incident was isolated, and did not render the gate subject to picketing. Since the gates reserved for neutral employers were not used in a manner to subject them to picketing, the picketing constituted an unfair labor practice. The union offered evidence that some neutral employers used the gate reserved for S many times. However, that does not authorize the union to picket gates reserved for the neutral employers and their employees. The picketing of gates reserved for contractors other than S amounted to inducement and encouragement of employees of neutral employers to strike in violation of 8(b)(4)(ii)(B). In addition, an object of the picketing of the gates reserved for neutral employers and their employees was to pressure A, a neutral, to cease doing business with S. Since the pressured employers, A and the other neutrals, could not accede to the union's wishes of unionizing S's employees, the union's activities were secondary. That is, the union took action against A and the other neutrals because of its effect on S. This violated 8(b)(4)(ii)(B). (d) The Carpenters contended that if it was determined that their dispute was with S, they were privileged to picket all gates prior to September 20, and to picket the gate reserved for S thereafter. However, such picketing must conform to the Moore Dry Dock standards.

See CASE 59, above. One of the Moore Dry Dock criteria is that the picketing clearly establish that the dispute is with the primary employer. In this case the union never made clear that its dispute was with S. S was not named on the picket signs, or otherwise, as the employer with which the Carpenters had a dispute. Thus, such picketing violated 8(b)(4)(i) and (ii)(B).

> See United Bhd. of Carpenters and Joiners of America, AFL–CIO, Local No. 639 (American Modulars Corp.), 203 NLRB 1112 (1973).

NOTE 1—Although the picket signs read: ". . . workmen and deliverymen are not requested to honor this picket," this is no defense. The Board looked to the object of the picketing and whether its effect was to induce or encourage proscribed activities rather than limiting itself to the wording on the signs.

NOTE 2—The statement to A concerning the possibility of informational picketing at the job site unless S became unionized constituted a threat within the meaning of Section 8(b)(4)(ii)(B). This statement, by its breadth, contemplated picketing of the entire job site and anyone working there, whether connected with the primary or neutral persons or employers. As such, it went beyond the mere giving notice of prospective picketing against a subcontractor to the general contractor. See Construction, Bldg. Material and Miscellaneous Drivers Local Union No. 83, Int'l Bhd. of Teamsters (Marshall and Haas), 133 NLRB 1144, 1146 (1961).

NOTE 3—The above analysis does not dispose of all possible union violations. Since the picketing continued for more than 30 days without a representation petition being filed, it must be determined whether the picketing violated Section 8(b)(7)(C). If *an* object of the picketing was to force S's employees to join the Carpenters Union or to force S to recognize and bargain with the union, the picketing violated 8(b)(7)(C). It is only necessary that one of the objectives of the picketing be to force an employer to recognize or bargain with a union. That the carpenters were seeking to organize S's employees is shown by: (a) The conversation between the union representative and A in which the union representative spoke of the advantages of employing union labor and his desire to have S sign up with the union. (b) The statement of another union representative that unless there were union people on the job the union would have to advertise. (c) The admission of a union representative that his purpose in going to the job site was to have S recognize the union or have a union contractor do the work. (d) The conversation between the union agent and S in which the union agent said that it would allow S's employees to join the union at a special rate, the discussion of union benefits, and the statement that S would not be permitted to build at that site. Relying on the above evidence the Board held that the Carpenters violated 8(b)(7)(C) by picketing for more than 30 days without petitioning the NLRB for an election. See United Bhd. of Carpenters and Joiners of America, Local No. 639, AFL–CIO (American Modulars Corp.), 206 NLRB 18 (1973).

LABOR LAW—EMPLOYMENT DISCRIMINATION

LEGAL GEMS—Section 8(e)—Hot Cargo Clauses Unlawful

1. Hot Cargo does *not* refer to the temperature of some product.

2. Hot Cargo refers to goods produced or handled by an employer which the union considers "unfair." This may occur where:

    (a) employees of the employer are on strike,

    (b) employees of the employer are not represented by a particular union, or

    (c) the union considers the wages or working conditions of the employer substandard.

3. Section 8(e) makes it an unfair labor practice for an employer and a union to sign a contract whereby the "employer ceases or refrains or agrees to cease or refrain from handling, using, selling, transporting or otherwise dealing in any of the products of any other employer or to cease doing business with any other person, and any contract or agreement entered into heretofore or hereafter containing such an agreement shall be to such extent unenforceable and void: *Provided*, That nothing in this subsection (e) shall apply to an agreement between a labor organization and an employer in the construction industry relating to the contracting or subcontracting of work to be done at the site of the construction, alteration, painting, or repair of a building, structure or other work."

4. Simply stated, Section 8(e) prohibits agreements, express or implied, written or oral, between an employer and a union whereby the employer agrees not to handle or use the goods of someone else, which is "hot cargo."

    e.g. The following three contract clauses were considered by the court: (a) A clause permitted the union to reopen the whole contract for renegotiation and terminate it if agreement was not reached within ten days if the employer handled any non-union work. The Court *held* that the employer's agreement that he will deal with non-union employers only at the risk of giving up all benefits under the contract, amounts to an implied promise not to deal with such employers and violates Section 8(e); (b) The employer agreed not to perform struck work, but he was permitted to continue performing work ordinarily done for the struck employer. The Court *held* that clause was lawful because performing struck work would make the employer an "ally" and subject him to action just as though he were the primary employer because an "ally" is not considered "any other employer" within the meaning of the secondary boycott provisions of the Act; (c) A clause required the employer, which operated several plants, if there were a strike at one of its plants, not to handle the work of *his own* struck plant at another of his own plants. The Court held that the clause was lawful because Section

PICKETING AND BOYCOTTS

8(e) referred only to handling the work of "any other employer". The Court also found that a strike to obtain clauses violative of Section 8(e) violated the union's duty to bargain in good faith, Section 8(b)(3). See NLRB v. Amalgamated Lithographers of America, 309 F.2d 31 (9th Cir. 1962).

CAVEAT—The construction industry proviso contained in Section 8(e) applies only to contracting at the job site where the agreement arises from a collective bargaining relationship. It is not applicable to products manufactured off the job site and delivered to the site. See CASE 3, and NOTE 2 following, above.

5. It is an unfair labor practice for both employers and unions to make an agreement with a hot cargo clause. Of course, only the union commits the unfair labor practice if the union's attempt to secure a hot cargo clause is not successful.

6. A union may demand clauses to recapture, preserve or expand bargaining unit work if the work is fairly claimable by bargaining unit employees. The fact that such clauses produce incidental secondary effects, such as interfering with the business of neutral employers, does not make them illegal. See CASE 63, below.

7. A clause which reserves work traditionally performed by bargaining unit employees to them is lawful. This is known as a work preservation clause.

e.g. The collective bargaining agreement between a contractor and the Carpenters union provided that carpenters would not be required to handle any doors which had been fitted before delivery to the job site. The purpose of the clause was to preserve work traditionally performed by carpenters at the job site, which was the finishing of doors. When the contractor had prefabricated doors delivered to the job site the union struck to enforce the applicable contract clause. Did the clause violate Section 8(e)? Ans. No. The clause was an attempt to preserve work for craftsmen which they had traditionally performed at the job site. The legislative history of Section 8(e) does not show any intention to make such activity unlawful. The clause in this case regulates labor relations between the contracting employer and its own employees by preserving their traditional work. There is no evidence that the clause was directed against a secondary employer. Therefore, picketing to enforce the clause was lawful. See National Woodwork Manufacturers Ass'n v. NLRB, 386 U.S. 612, 87 S.Ct. 1250, 18 L.Ed.2d 357 (1967).

NOTE—A clause whereby an employer agreed not to use prefabricated products unless they were produced by union employees would violate Section 8(e). This is so because it would have an object of affecting the labor relations of a secondary employer. It is not necessary to have an actual dispute between the union and the secondary employer for conduct to constitute a violation of Section 8(e).

8. A clause may limit subcontracting to employers who give their employees a *total* economic package the same or greater than bargaining unit employees enjoy. See **CASE 63**, below.

   (a) The subcontract may not specify the specific benefits that their workers must enjoy, but must be limited to the total value of economic benefits.

   (b) Subcontracting may not be limited to companies which employ members of a particular union, because that would discriminate against employees for exercising their rights guaranteed in Section 7 of the Act.

CASE 63—*union may recapture lost work*

The union represented truck drivers employed by Armour, Swift and other Chicago packing companies. For many years city drivers made deliveries in the Chicago area which originated at packing houses of those companies. Only occasional deliveries were made by over-the-road truck drivers when meat was shipped in from outside that area. During the term of the contract the larger companies moved their slaughtering operations out of the Chicago area. This resulted in Chicago deliveries being made by over-the-road truck drivers rather than by the city drivers. Because of the loss of a substantial amount of work, the union proposed in contract negotiations that all Chicago deliveries be made from a distribution facility. This would require employers to divide their deliveries into two stages: the incoming products would be delivered to the distribution facility by the interstate carrier and then they would be delivered locally by city drivers. In connection with the distribution clause, the union also proposed that if the employers were required to subcontract any of the Chicago deliveries that work would only be given to companies whose drivers enjoyed the same or greater wages and other benefits as provided in the current contract between the employer and the union. Each contract proposal must be considered separately: (a) Did the distribution proposal, which would have required employers to stop doing some business with interstate carriers, violate Section 8(e)? (b) Did the clause restricting to whom the employer may and may not subcontract violate Section 8 (e)?

Ans. (a) No. (b) No. (a) The union was attempting to recapture work lost through a change in the employer's method of distribution. It is work which the members of the bargaining unit were qualified to perform. Deliveries within the Chicago area regardless of origin can be considered the work of bargaining unit employees. It is closely allied or identical to work performed for many years, and bargaining about it is mandatory. A union is permitted to bargain about the expansion of employment opportunities within the bargaining unit. The bargaining demand by the union that all city deliveries be made by bargaining unit employees did not violate the Act. (b) The second clause in issue gives the union a veto over who may receive the employer's subcontracts if any are required. This clause seeks to preserve bargaining unit work by preventing the employer from subcontracting to "cheap labor". This is permissible and does not violate Section 8(e). Subcontracting may be limited to employers who offer their employees a *total* economic package the same or greater than bargaining unit employees enjoy. However, a subcontracting clause where the employer agreed to subcontract to a company which employed members of a specific union is unlawful because it encouraged a boycott of companies whose employees were not represented by that particular union. Since Section 7 gives employees the right to refrain from engaging in union activities, the clause would be a reprisal for relying on a statutory right and would be unlawful. In this case the union sought to recapture bargaining unit work which had been lost and to prevent the employer from subcontracting it to companies which employed "cheap labor". This activity is permitted under the Act.

See Meat & Highway Drivers, Local 710 v. NLRB, 335 F.2d 709 (D.C.Cir. 1964).

LEGAL GEMS—Sections 8(b)(4)(ii)(D) and 10(k)—Jurisdictional Disputes

1. A jurisdictional dispute occurs when more than one union claims that a particular job should be assigned to it rather than to another union.

   CAVEAT—A jurisdictional dispute requires two competing claims for certain work. If an employer and only one union or craft have a dispute over a work assignment these sections of the Act do not apply. In such a situation the employer or union may seek arbitration of the dispute, if permitted by their collective bargaining agreement, or either party may file an AC or UC petition with the Board. See Chapter XII, LEGAL GEMS—The Appropriate Bargaining Unit, below.

2. Section 8(b)(4)(D) prohibits a union from engaging in a work stoppage, or threatening to do so, in order to force the employer to assign work to a particular union, unless the employer is failing to conform to an order or certification of the Board.

3. If a charge is filed alleging a jurisdictional dispute, the parties are given ten days to settle their dispute voluntarily.

4. Section 10(k) provides that if the parties do not have an agreed upon method of settling their dispute or do not settle their dispute within ten days, the Board can hear the dispute and make an affirmative assignment of the disputed work.

   NOTE 1—No unfair labor practice finding is made in a hearing to assign work involved in a jurisdictional dispute. Only the actual work dispute is resolved.

LABOR LAW—EMPLOYMENT DISCRIMINATION

NOTE 2—All parties must agree to be bound by the voluntary method of settling the dispute. If only the unions agree to abide by the decision, the employer may insist that the NLRB make the award in a Section 10(k) proceeding. That fact is important because many unions have agreed to be bound by decisions of the National Joint Board for Settlement of Jurisdictional Disputes, established by the AFL-CIO. Some employers believe that the Joint Board gives insufficient consideration to the employer's assignment of the work and economy of the employer's operations in rendering decisions and refuse to be bound by its decisions. See NLRB v. Plasterers' Local 79, 404 U.S. 116, 92 S.Ct. 360, 30 L.Ed.2d 312 (1971).

5. The Board requires that there be reasonable cause to believe that Section 8(b)(4)(ii)(D) has been violated before a hearing is conducted to resolve the dispute.

6. A hearing held under Section 10(k) only determines which union must be assigned the disputed work. It does not resolve the unfair labor practice charge.

7. The Board makes a work assignment based on all relevant factors, such as the practice in the industry, skills of workers involved, contracts between the parties, certification by the Board, the employer's assignment and the efficient operation of the employer's business. See CASE 64, below, and NOTE following.

8. The Board may obtain an injunction to prevent any work stoppage while the dispute is being resolved.

9. Section 10(k) provides in part that "Upon compliance by the parties to the dispute with the decision of the Board or upon such voluntary adjustment such charge shall be dismissed."

10. If the parties do not comply with the Board determination or voluntary adjustment, an unfair labor practice complaint is issued against the offending union. The Board will enter a cease and desist order and seek Court enforcement.

NOTE—A 10(k) hearing and determination by the Board is not a prerequisite for issuance of an unfair labor practice complaint. The complaint may issue if one of the unions does not comply with the determination as a result of the parties' voluntary adjustment of the dispute (e. g. submission of the parties to an arbitrator). See Wood, Wire and Metal Lathers Int'l Union (Acoustical Contractors Ass'n), 119 NLRB 1345 (1958). See also, Cohen, "The NLRB and Section 10(k): A Study of the Reluctant Dragon", 14 Lab.L.J. 905 (1963); O'Donoghue, "Jurisdictional Disputes in the Construction Industry Since CBS", 52 Geo.L.J. 314 (1964); and Atleson, "The NLRB and Jurisdictional Disputes: The Aftermath of CBS", 53 Geo.L.J. 93 (1964).

PICKETING AND BOYCOTTS

11. In addition to the usual cease and desist order and posting of a Notice, the following remedies are available:
    (a) After an unfair labor practice complaint has been issued, the NLRB may seek to enjoin any work stoppage by seeking an injunction under Section 10(1).
    (b) An employer which has suffered damages because of an unlawful work stoppage may sue the offending union for damages under Section 303.

CASE 64—board must consider all relevant factors in resolving jurisdictional disputes

Union A represented television "technicians" and Union B represented "stage employees" at CBS. Both unions claimed that they should be assigned the work of providing electric lighting for TV shows. Neither union was given that work by its collective bargaining agreements with the company or by its certification. At a planned telecast from a hotel CBS assigned the remote lighting work to Union B, and Union A refused to operate cameras, forcing cancellation of the show. CBS filed a charge against Union A alleging that its actions violated 8(b)(4)(D). At a hearing the Board found that Union A was not entitled to the work because it had no right to it under its certification or its collective bargaining agreement with the employer. The Board refused to consider other criteria, such as the employer's prior practices and the custom of the industry, and also refused to make an affirmative award of the work between the employees represented by the two competing unions. When Union A refused to comply with the Board's decision the present action was instituted. May the Board limit its determination of a jurisdictional dispute to legal considerations such as contract terms and the wording of the union's certification?

Ans. No. It is the Board's duty to make an award of the work involved binding on both unions as to which is entitled to the disputed work. Although no standards are set forth in the Act to make such determinations, the Board may establish appropriate criteria based on its expertise and knowledge of the standards used by arbitrators, unions and employers. Since the Board construed Section 10(k) too narrowly and did not consider relevant factors such as the employer's past practices, and custom in the industry, the Board could not find that Union A committed an unfair labor practice for failing to abide by the Board's decision.

See NLRB v. Radio & Television Broadcast Engineers Union, Local 1212, IBEW (CBS), 364 U.S. 573, 81 S.Ct. 330, 5 L.Ed.2d 302 (1961).

NOTE 1—The Board has stated that the following criteria will be used in making an award: "The Board will consider all relevant factors in determining who is entitled to the work in dispute, e. g., the skills and work involved, certifications by the Board, company and industry practice, agreements between unions and between employers and unions, awards of arbitrators, joint boards and the AFL–CIO in the same or related cases, the assignment made by the employer, and the efficient operation of the employer's business." International Association of Machinists (Jones Construction Co.), 135 NLRB 1402 (1962).

LABOR LAW—EMPLOYMENT DISCRIMINATION

NOTE 2—If the normal criteria are not applicable and other factors are balanced, controlling weight in making the work assignment may be given to an agreement between the two unions involved even though the employer was not contractually bound by that agreement. See Local No. 68, Wood, Wire & Metal Lathers Union, 142 NLRB 1073 (1963).

NOTE 3—There is no direct court review of a 10(k) decision. If a union refuses to comply with the Board's award of the work, an unfair labor practice complaint is issued against the union charging a violation of Section 8(b)(4)(D). It is only after the Board finds an 8(b)(4)(D) violation that a court may review the 10(k) determination. When a dispute reaches the court it determines: (a) whether the Board's findings of fact are supported by substantial evidence on the record considered as a whole, and (b) whether the Board's legal conclusions are arbitrary and capricious in the light of the facts. The Board's decision must evaluate the relevant factors, explain why some are more important than others, and reconcile its award with past awards of a similar nature. Failure to do so is grounds to deny enforcement of the unfair labor practice cease and desist order because a court cannot determine whether the Board's decision is arbitrary or capricious in such circumstances. See NLRB v. International Longshoremen's & Warehousemen's Union, Local 50, 504 F.2d 1209 (9th Cir. 1974), cert. denied 420 U.S. 973, 95 S.Ct. 1393, 43 L.Ed.2d 652 (1975).

XI. OTHER RIGHTS OF EMPLOYEES

LEGAL GEMS—Other Rights of Employees—Introduction

1. Unfair labor practices under the National Labor Relations Act, and the rights of employees related thereto have been analyzed in previous Chapters of this Review.

2. In addition to the rights which are administered by the NLRB, an employee may also bring suit directly against his employer or union in a state or federal court in certain situations.

3. In such situations an employee may sue:

    (a) directly based upon the collective bargaining agreement,

    (b) upon rights afforded him under the Landrum-Griffin Act, or

    (c) under other labor laws. See Chapter XIII, Other Laws Governing Labor Relations, below.

4. The Landrum-Griffin Act was enacted in 1959 to guarantee certain rights to union members:

    (a) Title I establishes a Bill of Rights for union members.

    (b) Titles II and III provide for financial reports of unions.

    (c) Title IV deals with the election of union officers.

    (d) Title V deals with the fiduciary responsibility of union officers.

5. In most situations federal labor laws preempt state laws. For that reason labor law is generally thought of as a "federal law" subject. However, an employee may also have rights under state laws.

LEGAL GEMS—Employee's Right to Sue on His Own Behalf

1. Courts permit an employee to sue his employer for breach of a collective bargaining agreement when his individual rights are involved, based on one of the following theories:

    (a) the collective bargaining contract is incorporated in each individual employee's employment contract with the company when he is hired,

    (b) the employee is a third party beneficiary of the collective bargaining agreement, or

    (c) the collective bargaining agreement is like a trust with the union holding the employer's promises in trust for the benefit of the individual employee. See Jenkins v. William Schluderberg—T. J. Kurtle Co., 217 Md. 556, 144 A.2d 88 (1958).

2. Before bringing suit based upon a right conferred on the employee in the collective bargaining agreement, the employee must normally exhaust his contract remedies because the contract is the source of his right.

3. If the contractual grievance procedure is followed, it is final and binding on all parties absent evidence of bad faith or discrimination. See CASE 65, below.

4. A union owes the duty of fair representation to all employees in the bargaining unit and may not discriminate against any group of employees. However, a union is given wide latitude in its representation of employees.

   e.g. The union and employer agreed that all World War II veterans would be given seniority credit for time spent in the military service. This gave more seniority to veterans than to some employees who had actually been employed for a longer period of time because it applied to persons who had not been employed at the company before entering military service. Suit was brought to have that seniority provision declared invalid. Did the union breach its duty of fair representation? Ans. No. "Inevitably differences arise in the manner and degree to which the terms of any negotiated agreement may affect individual employees and classes of employees. The mere existence of such differences does not make them invalid. The complete satisfaction of all who are represented is hardly to be expected. A wide range of reasonableness must be allowed a statutory bargaining representative in servicing the unit it represents, subject always to complete good faith and honesty of purpose in the exercise of its discretion." Variations in seniority may reasonably include consideration of the nature of work performed, the fitness, age or family responsibilities of employees, injuries received in employment and time devoted to public service whether civil or military, voluntary or involuntary. Thus, the union did not violate its duty of fair representation. See Ford Motor Co. v. Huffman, 345 U.S. 330, 73 S.Ct. 681, 97 L.Ed. 1048 (1953).

5. An employee may sue in a federal or state court to enforce an individual right under the collective bargaining agreement. See CASE 66, below.

6. The union may commit an unfair labor practice if it refuses to process an employee's grievance (see CASES 42 and 43, above), but that does not limit court jurisdiction because there is no federal preemption. See CASE 67, below. For further analysis of this problem, see Lewis, "Fair Representation in Grievance Administration: Vaca v. Sipes", 1967 Sup.Ct.Rev. 81.

OTHER RIGHTS OF EMPLOYEES

CASE 65—*bargaining agent must represent all employees fairly*

The Brotherhood which represented railroad engineers and firemen proposed to amend its existing collective bargaining agreement with the railroad so that only white firemen could be promoted to serve as engineers and only "promotable" men could be employed as firemen. The effect of this proposal would be to ultimately exclude all Negro firemen from service. The parties entered into an agreement which provided that not more than 50 percent of the firemen in each class of service in each seniority district should be Negroes, and that until that percentage was reached, all new jobs should be filled by white men only. The railroad was prevented from employing Negroes in seniority districts in which no Negroes were then employed. The agreement reserved the right of the Brotherhood to negotiate further restrictions on the employment of Negro firemen. Three months later the Brotherhood entered into a supplemental agreement with the railroad further controlling the seniority rights of the Negro firemen and restricting their employment. No notice or opportunity to be heard was given to the Negro firemen with respect to these agreements, which were put into effect before their existence was disclosed to the Negro firemen. Negro employees were required to perform less desirable jobs because of the discriminatory provisions of the collective bargaining agreement. They brought the present suit against the railroad and the Brotherhood for damages and to rescind the discriminatory contract provisions. Does the collective bargaining agent of employees have plenary authority to negotiate terms and conditions of employment for bargaining unit employees without regard to the protection of minorities from discrimination or unfair treatment?

Ans. No. Since Negroes were excluded from membership in the Brotherhood, the authority to act for them is not derived from their consent but wholly from the Railway Labor Act. Congress did not intend to confer plenary power on unions in passing the Act to sacrifice the rights of minority groups without imposing on the union a duty to protect the minority. The Act permits the union to act as the exclusive bargaining representative of employees. Members of a minority group cannot select another union to represent them and must act through their collective bargaining agent. Negroes are therefore deprived of a right they would otherwise have: The right to choose a representative of their own or bargain individually. The exclusive bargaining representative must represent all employees in the bargaining unit, at least to the extent of not discriminating against some minority. Otherwise, the minority would be left with no means to protect its interests. The exercise of a power to act in behalf of others involves the assumption toward them of a duty to exercise the power in their interest. A union must protect equally the interest of unit employees just as the Constitution imposes upon a legislature the duty to give equal protection to the interests of those for whom it legislates.

See Steele v. Louisville & Nashville Railroad Co., 323 U.S. 192, 65 S.Ct. 226, 89 L.Ed. 173 (1944).

LABOR LAW—EMPLOYMENT DISCRIMINATION

CASE 66—*employees may sue union under section 301 for a violation of duty under contract*

Employers A and B transported new automobiles from a Ford assembly plant to various cities. Due to a decline in business Ford notified A and B that it would only use the services of one of the trucking companies. After considering the matter A and B decided to exchange certain ICC operating authorities. This resulted in A continuing its activities in that area and transporting automobiles for Ford. B obtained routes in a more northern area from A in exchange. B laid off some of its local drivers. These drivers filed a grievance claiming that their seniority should be dovetailed with that of A's employees because A and B had consolidated their businesses within the meaning of the provisions of their collective bargaining agreement. The employees of A and B were represented by the same union with substantially the same contract with each employer. The grievance was processed according to the "final and binding" contract procedure, and an employer-union panel decided that the seniority of the employees should be dovetailed. B was the older company and its drivers had more seniority than A's drivers. The decision resulted in the layoff of a number of A's drivers, who sued in a state court to enjoin enforcement of the decision of the grievance panel. They claimed that the union breached its duty of fair representation to them by espousing the cause of a rival group of drivers after assuring them that it would protect their rights. Two issues are presented: (a) May an employee sue under Section 301 if he is deprived of rights under a collective bargaining agreement? (b) Did the union violate its duty to represent fairly A's employees?

Ans. (a) Yes. (b) No. (a) This is a suit under Section 301 because it alleges that the union permitted the employer to lay off drivers in violation of the collective bargaining agreement which covered them. The fact that this allegation might also constitute an unfair labor practice does not deprive the court of jurisdiction of a suit under Section 301. (b) A collective bargaining agent does not breach its duty of fair representation in taking a good faith position contrary to that of some individuals whom it represents nor in supporting the position of one group of employees against that of another. The court reasoned, "just as a union must be free to sift out wholly frivolous grievances which would only clog the grievance process, so it must be free to take a position on the not-so-frivolous disputes. Nor should it be neutralized when the issue is chiefly between two sets of employees. Conflict between employees represented by the same union is a recurring fact To remove or gag the union in these cases would surely weaken the collective bargaining and grievance processes." In the present case the union took its position honestly and in good faith without hostility or arbitrary discrimination. Instead of showing that the union took its position in bad faith, the evidence disclosed that the union, by choosing to dovetail seniority lists, acted upon relevant considerations. The union did not violate its duty of fair representation because: (1) there was no proof of dishonesty or bad faith by the union; (2) although the union favored one group of employees over another, its decision was based on relevant considerations which were not capricious or arbitrary; and (3) the disadvantaged group of employees was given the opportunity to state its position before the grievance committee and did not request time to obtain further representation when they learned that the union would support the other group of employees. Therefore, A's employees may not upset the decision of the grievance committee.

See Humphrey v. Moore, 375 U.S. 335, 84 S.Ct. 363, 11 L.Ed.2d 370 (1964).

CASE 67—*no federal preemption of employee's right to sue union for arbitrary and capricious conduct under contract*

An employee was discharged because the company doctor concluded that he was unable to perform required heavy work due to high blood pressure. The employee's family doctor and another doctor certified that he was physically able to perform his job. The union processed his grievance up to arbitration. The union then sent the employee to another doctor to obtain additional medical evidence regarding his ability to work. The new doctor concluded that the employee was not able to perform his job and the union refused to arbitrate the grievance. The employee sued the union in a state court for damages for its arbitrary and capricious failure to arbitrate the grievance. Two issues were presented to the court: (a) May suit be brought in a state or federal court based on the union's breach of its duty of fair representation even though that is also an unfair labor practice? (b) May an employee sue a union for damages if, acting in good faith, it fails to process a meritorious grievance to arbitration?

Ans. (a) Yes. (b) No. (a) The breach of its duty of fair representation by a union can constitute an unfair labor practice. See CASES 42 and 43, above. It is also established that Congress intended the NLRB to have exclusive jurisdiction over unfair labor practices in order to avoid conflicting rules of substantive law in labor relations, and because of the desirability of having an administrative agency develop such rules. However, if it were held that the NLRB had exclusive jurisdiction in this field, an employee could not secure an impartial review of his charge because the NLRB's decision not to institute unfair labor practice proceedings is not reviewable by the courts. Therefore, the court would lose its jurisdiction to curb arbitrary conduct by a union as in CASE 65, above, if the preemption doctrine were applied. The existence of even a small group of cases in which the Board would be unable or unwilling to remedy a union's breach of duty would frustrate the basic purposes of the fair representation doctrine. Thus, it cannot be assumed that Congress intended to oust courts of jurisdiction in this area. Furthermore, the problem could arise in a Section 301 suit by an employee against his employer over a breach of contract and the arbitrary failure of the union to process his grievance. An employee must be permitted to sue both the employer and the union in such a situation or else the employer could defend by showing that the employee did not exhaust the contract grievance procedure. The fact that the employee's cause of action may arguably be an unfair labor practice does not prevent him from suing as there is no federal preemption in this situation. (b) A breach of the statutory duty of fair representation occurs only when a union's conduct toward a member of the collective bargaining unit is arbitrary, discriminatory or in bad faith. A union may not arbitrarily ignore a meritorious grievance or process it in a perfunctory fashion. However, the individual employee does not have an *absolute* right to have his grievance taken to arbitration

LABOR LAW—EMPLOYMENT DISCRIMINATION

regardless of the provisions of the applicable collective bargaining agreement. The employer and the union are expected to endeavor in good faith to settle the grievance short of arbitration. Frivolous grievances can be ended and both sides can resolve contract interpretations. The decision of a union that a grievance lacks sufficient merit to justify arbitration cannot be termed arbitrary or capricious because a judge or jury later may conclude that the grievance was meritorious. Otherwise, a union would have little incentive to settle grievances before arbitration and collective bargaining would be impaired. In order for an employee to maintain an action against his union, he must show that the union acted in an arbitrary or discriminatory manner or in bad faith. It is not sufficient to show merely that his grievance was meritorious.

See Vaca v. Sipes, 386 U.S. 171, 87 S.Ct. 903, 17 L.Ed.2d 842 (1967).

LEGAL GEMS—Rights Under Landrum-Griffin Act

1. The Labor-Management Reporting and Disclosure Act of 1959, popularly known as the Landrum-Griffin Act, was passed "to eliminate or prevent improper practices on the part of labor organizations, employers, labor relations consultants, and their officers and representatives which distort and defeat the policies of the Labor Management Relations Act, 1947, as amended, and the Railway Labor Act. . . ." Section 2(c).

2. Title I of the Act established a Bill of Rights for union members which contains the following guarantees:

"Sec. 101(a)(1) EQUAL RIGHTS.—Every member of a labor organization shall have equal rights and privileges within such organization to nominate candidates, to vote in elections or referendums of the labor organization, to attend membership meetings, and to participate in the deliberations and voting upon the business of such meetings, subject to reasonable rules and regulations in such organization's constitution and by-laws.

"(2) FREEDOM OF SPEECH AND ASSEMBLY.—Every member of any labor organization shall have the right to meet and assemble freely with other members; and to express any views, arguments, or opinions; and to express at meetings of the labor organization his views, upon candidates in an election of the labor organization or upon any business properly before the meeting, subject to the organization's established and reasonable rules pertaining to the conduct of meetings: *Provided*, That nothing herein shall be construed to impair the right of a labor organization to adopt and enforce reasonable rules as to the responsibility of every member toward the organization as an institution and to his refraining from conduct that would interfere with its performance of its legal or contractual obligations.

"(3) DUES, INITIATION FEES, AND ASSESSMENTS. . . . [T]he rates of dues and initiation fees payable by members of any organization . . . shall not be increased, and no general or special assessment shall be levied upon such members, except—

(A) in the case of a local labor organization,

   (i) by majority vote by secret ballot of the members in good standing . . . after reasonable notice . . . or

   (ii) by majority vote of the members in good standing voting in a membership referendum conducted by secret ballot; or

(B) in the case of a labor organization, other than a local labor organization . . .

   (i) by majority vote of the delegates voting at a regular convention . . . or

   (ii) by majority vote of the members in good standing of such labor organization voting in a membership referendum conducted by secret ballot, or

   (iii) by majority vote of the members of the . . . governing body . . . *Provided*, That such action on the part of the . . . governing body shall be effective only until the next regular convention.

   . . .

"(4) PROTECTION OF THE RIGHT TO SUE.—No labor organization shall limit the right of any member thereof to institute an action in any court, or in a proceeding before any administrative agency, . . . or to petition any legislature or to communicate with any legislator: *Provided*, That any such member may be required to exhaust reasonable hearing procedures (but not to exceed a four-month lapse of time) . . . . [See CASE 70, below].

"(5) SAFEGUARDS AGAINST IMPROPER DISCIPLINARY ACTION.—No member of any labor organization may be fined, suspended, expelled, or otherwise disciplined except for non-payment of dues by such organization or by any officer thereof unless such member has been

(A) served with written specific charges;

(B) given a reasonable time to prepare his defense; and

(C) afforded a full and fair hearing."

3. The right of union members to freedom of speech and freedom of assembly has *only* two exceptions:

   (a) a member must not interfere with the union's performance of its legal obligations, and

LABOR LAW—EMPLOYMENT DISCRIMINATION

(b) a member must obey reasonable rules regulating his responsibility toward the union as an institution.

e.g. During a union election campaign one candidate accused his opponent, who was the president, of mishandling union funds. Thereafter, the president brought charges within the union alleging that he had been libeled. The member was found guilty at a union trial and removed from his office of financial secretary and prohibited from attending union meetings or participating in any union affairs for five years. Did the union's action infringe upon the member's rights guaranteed in the Act? Ans. Yes. The legislative history of Section 101(a)(2) shows that Congress intended only two exceptions to that Section. The accusation did not interfere with the union's legal rights or obligations, and the disclosure of monies paid to the union president would actually help honest management of the union. Freedom of expression would be stifled if those in power could claim that any charge against them was libelous, and then proceed to discipline those responsible on a finding that the charge was false. If the statements were libelous the union president had a civil remedy, but that did not affect the member's rights under the Act. A member is privileged to make even untrue statements under the Act without subjecting himself to union discipline. See Salzhandler v. Caputo, 316 F.2d 445 (2d Cir. 1963).

4. Requirements of Section 101(a)(5) do not apply to union officers. Otherwise, a wrong doing officer could continue in office while the due process provisions were complied with. However, an officer may not be removed from office for engaging in intra-union activity, since that right is guaranteed in Section 101(a)(1)(2). See CASE 68, below.

5. Titles II and III of the Act provide for financial reports of unions and trusteeships and make those reports available to the public.

6. Title IV of the Act sets up a statutory scheme providing for the following:

(a) the election of union officers,

(b) fixing the terms during which they may hold office,

(c) requiring that elections be by secret ballot,

(d) regulating the handling of campaign literature,

(e) requiring a reasonable opportunity for the nomination of candidates,

e.g. A union had a bylaw which limited eligibility for major elective offices to union members who hold or have previously held elective office. Section 401(e) provides that

OTHER RIGHTS OF EMPLOYEES

"every member in good standing shall be eligible to be a candidate and to hold office (subject to . . . reasonable qualifications uniformly imposed . . . ." Is the bylaw valid? Ans. No. The bylaw was not valid because it unduly restricted candidacy qualifications by rendering 93 percent of the union's members ineligible. In addition, it was impossible to be elected to minor union positions unless the candidate was nominated by the incumbent party. Since application of the bylaw might have affected the result of the election which was challenged, the Court directed that a new election be held under the supervision of the Secretary of Labor, and enjoined enforcement of the bylaw. See Wirtz v. Hotel, Motel and Club Employees Union, Local 6, 391 U.S. 492, 88 S.Ct. 1743, 20 L.Ed.2d 763 (1968).

(f) authorizing unions to fix reasonable qualifications uniformly imposed for candidates, and

(g) attempting to guarantee fair union elections in which all the members are allowed to participate.

7. Section 402 of Title IV sets up the exclusive method for members to vindicate their rights by challenging elections for union officers after they have been held by:

   (a) exhausting all remedies available within the union up to three months,

   (b) filing a complaint with the Secretary of Labor, who,

   (c) may, after investigating the violation alleged, bring suit in a United States District Court to attack the validity of the election. See CASE 69, below.

8. The refusal of the Secretary of Labor to institute proceedings against a union for alleged election irregularities is subject to limited judicial review.

   e.g. A union member who was defeated in a union election filed a complaint with the Secretary of Labor. After an investigation the complaint was dismissed. The member sought court review of that decision. The Court noted that the Act relies on the special knowledge and discretion of the Secretary of Labor for the determination of both the probable violation and its probable effect on the election. Therefore, the reviewing court is not authorized to substitute its judgment for the decision of the Secretary not to bring suit. A court should only determine whether the Secretary exercised his discretion in a manner that is neither arbitrary nor capricious. For the court to do this, the Secretary must issue a statement of reasons for the decision and the essential facts upon which the Secretary's inferences are based. The reviewing court should confine itself to examining the reasons statement and deter-

LABOR LAW—EMPLOYMENT DISCRIMINATION

mining whether the statement, without more, shows that the Secretary's decision was so irrational as to be arbitrary and capricious. Court review does not extend to an adversary trial of a complaining union member's challenges to the factual basis for the decision. See Dunlop v. Bachowski, 421 U.S. 560, 95 S.Ct. 1851, 44 L.Ed.2d 377 (1975).

9. Section 101(a)(4) provides that a union member "may be required" to exhaust internal union remedies before bringing suit. Thus, the exhaustion provision gives some discretion to the courts and is not required in all cases. See CASE 70, below. See also Boyle, "The Labor Bill of Rights and Doctrine of Exhaustion of Remedies—A Marriage of Convenience", 16 Hastings L.J. 590 (1965); O'Donoghue, "Protection of a Union Member's Right to Sue under the Landrum-Griffin Act", 14 Catholic U.L.Rev. 215 (1965).

NOTE—Title V of the Act establishes standards for the fiduciary responsibility of union officers. See LEGAL GEMS—Responsibility of Union Officers, below.

CASE 68—*union officers may be summarily removed from office*

After a union election, union officers who supported an unsuccessful candidate were summarily discharged. They brought suit in District Court based on Section 101(a)(5) which provides in pertinent part that no member may be "fined, suspended, expelled, or otherwise disciplined" without due process, and Section 101(a)(1) and (2) which give members the right to engage in intra-union political activity. The union moved to dismiss. Two issues were presented: (a) Does Section 101(a)(5) include removal from office in the phrase "otherwise disciplined"? (b) Does the right of members to engage in intra-union political activity apply to appointed officers?

Ans. (a) No. (b) Yes. (a) Congress did not intend to bar summary removal of officials suspected of malfeasance and the means chosen to accomplish that purpose was to exclude from the due process requirements of the Act removal from union office. Otherwise, wrong doing officials could remain in control while the time consuming due process requirements were met. Therefore, Section 101(a)(5) only applies to suspension from *membership* in the union and does not relate to suspension or removal from union *office*. (b) There is no indication in the legislative history that Congress did not intend the guarantees of equal political rights and freedom of speech and assembly to apply to union officers. To permit reprisals against officer-members for exercising political rights guaranteed in the Act would inhibit the exercise by officers of rights important to effective democracy in union government. Since officers are union members as much as any other union members, their rights are the same as other members. Therefore, the union violated the Act by removing the appointed officers for engaging in intra-union activity.

See Grand Lodge of Machinists v. King, 335 F.2d 340 (9th Cir.), cert. denied 379 U.S. 920, 85 S.Ct. 274, 13 L.Ed.2d 334 (1964).

OTHER RIGHTS OF EMPLOYEES

CASE 69—*member may not sue for Title IV violation*

The union constitution provided that no member would be eligible for office until he had been a member for five years and has served 180 days of seatime in each of two of the preceding three years on ships covered by collective bargaining agreements with the union. A by-law of the union deprived members of nominating any one but themselves for office. Several members filed suit against the union alleging that the above requirements violated their equal rights guaranteed in Section 101(a)(1). They asked that the union be enjoined from holding an election until its election procedures were revised to provide for fair nomination and eligibility requirements. Does the court have jurisdiction to entertain this suit?

Ans. No. Title IV of the Act sets standards for eligibility and qualifications for candidates and provides that the Secretary of Labor shall enforce that section and individual members do not have standing to sue under that section of the Act. Individual members have the right to sue for a violation of Section 101 (a)(1). However, the equal rights language of that section is not broad enough to hold that members have a right to nominate any one without regard to valid union rules. Although some members were not permitted to run for office, that was because of a non-discriminatory application of union rules. If those rules violated Title IV, that would have no bearing on the present suit under Title I because the Act established different methods to enforce Title I and Title IV. A possible violation of Title IV cannot be combined with an alleged Title I violation. Therefore, the suit was dismissed.

See Calhoon v. Harvey, 379 U.S. 134, 85 S.Ct. 292, 13 L.Ed.2d 190 (1964).

CASE 70—*no absolute duty to exhaust internal union remedies prior to suit*

P was a professional entertainer and a member of AGVA, a union representing most performers. P failed to perform at a resort hotel as scheduled, and the matter was taken to arbitration. It was concluded that P breached his contract with the hotel. AGVA notified P that unless he complied with the award, P would be placed on the union's "unfair" list. P did not comply and he was placed on the union's "unfair" list. That action deprived P of employment opportunities, and P filed suit against AGVA to have his name removed from the list. P contended that the union took disciplinary action against him without a hearing as required by Section 101(a)(5). The defense was that P failed to exhaust his internal union remedies before filing suit. Is the defense valid?

Ans. No. Section 101(a)(4) does not impose an absolute duty to exhaust union remedies before applying to federal courts for relief. It states only that exhaustion "may be required." The Congressional purpose was to preserve the doctrine of exhaustion as it had been developed by courts and to encourage unions to establish honest and democratic procedures. However, there are many broad exceptions to the general rule requiring exhaustion. In the present case it is not necessary to determine whether this situation comes within an exception because P's internal union remedies were uncertain. Considering that fact, and the fact that the violation of federal law is clear and undisputed, P should not be required to exhaust his union remedies. Since placing P's name on the "unfair" list was disciplinary action, and P was not given a union hearing to determine whether such action should be taken, the union was ordered to remove P's name from its "unfair" list.

> See Detroy v. American Guild of Variety Artists, 286 F.2d 75 (2nd Cir. 1961), cert. denied 366 U.S. 929, 81 S.Ct. 1650, 6 L.Ed.2d 388 (1961).

LEGAL GEMS—Responsibility of Union Officers

1. Title V of the Landrum-Griffin Act deals with the fiduciary responsibility of union officers.

2. A union officer accused of wrong doing may not use union funds to defend himself. See Highway Truck Drivers and Helpers Local 107 v. Cohen, 182 F.Supp. 608 (E.D.Pa.), affirmed 284 F.2d 164 (3d Cir. 1960).

3. A union constitutional provision or resolution passed by members permitting the use of union funds to defend an accused officer is inconsistent with the purposes of the Act and is void as contrary to public policy. See Highway Truck Drivers and Helpers Local 107 v. Cohen, 215 F.Supp. 938 (E.D.Pa.1963), affirmed 334 F.2d 378 (3d Cir. 1964).

4. If the accused union officer is exonerated from any wrong doing, "or perhaps even where his actions were based on a reasonable judgment as to appropriate procedures and do not evidence bad faith," he may be reimbursed by the union for his legal expenses. See Holdeman v. Sheldon, 204 F.Supp. 890 (S.D.N.Y.), affirmed 311 F.2d 2 (2d Cir. 1962).

5. Title V, Section 504(a) prohibits a person from holding union office or acting as a labor relations consultant for five years after conviction of certain named felonies, a violation of narcotics laws, or a violation of Title II or III of the Act.

NOTE—Section 504(a) also prohibited members of the Communist Party from holding union office or acting as a labor relations consultant for five years after termination of such membership. That Section was held unconstitutional under Article I, Section 9(3) which prohibits bills of attainder. A bill of attainder is a legislative act which inflicts punishment without a judicial trial upon an individual who is either named or described by certain conduct which, because it is past conduct, operates only as a designation of particular persons.

> e.g. Section 504(a) made it a crime for anyone who had been a Communist Party member within the past five years to serve as an officer or as an employee of a labor union. The purpose of the statute was to prevent political agitators from obtaining control of unions. D was convicted under the statute. He appealed, contending that the Section under which he was convicted was unconstitu-

tional. Should the conviction be upheld? **Ans. No.** The statute disqualified all Communist Party members regardless of their past conduct or whether they advocated any unlawful action. It punished all Communist Party members and was void as a bill of attainder. The Court rejected the argument that it was not a bill of attainder because the prohibition against holding such positions was not a punishment. See United States v. Brown, 381 U.S. 437, 85 S.Ct. 1707, 14 L.Ed.2d 484 (1965). See also Smith's Review, Constitutional Law, Chapter II, LEGAL GEMS—Bill of Attainder and Ex Post Facto clauses.

See generally Cox, pp. 1290–1302.

LEGAL GEMS—Rights of Union Members under State Law

1. The general rule is that federal labor laws preempt state jurisdiction over matters arguably covered by federal law. There are exceptions to that rule, especially where:

(a) there is a substantial state interest in the regulation of the conduct at issue, and

(b) the state interest does not threaten undue interference with the federal regulatory scheme.

See CASE 71, below.

e.g. P, a union officer, filed suit against the union alleging: (a) the union discriminated against him in employment referrals because of P's intraunion political activities, and (b) intentional and outrageous conduct of other union officers caused him emotional distress resulting in bodily injury. The Court said that the allegations of discrimination in hiring hall referrals were properly dismissed because they would form the basis for unfair labor practice charges before the NLRB. However, the claims of intentional infliction of emotional distress are not preempted by federal law. The state has a substantial interest in protecting its citizens from torts such as the intentional infliction of emotional distress. The abusive conduct with which the tort action is concerned occurred in a context of federally prohibited discrimination and there is a potential interference with the federal scheme of regulation. "Viewed, however, in light of the discrete concerns of the federal scheme and the state tort law, that potential for interference is insufficient to counterbalance the legitimate and substantial interest of the State in protecting its citizens. If the charges in P's complaint were filed with the Board, the focus of any unfair labor practice proceeding would be on whether the statements or conduct on the part of union officials discriminated or threatened discrimination against him in employment referrals for reasons other than failure to pay union dues. Whether the statements or conduct of the respondents also caused P severe emotional distress and physical injury would play no role in the Board's disposition of the case, and the Board could not award P damages for P's pain, suffering, or medical expenses. Conversely, the state court tort action can be adjudicated without resolution of the 'merits' of the underlying labor dispute." Thus, P may maintain suit against the union for the tort they committed. See Farmer v. United Bhd. of Carpenters, Local 25, 430 U.S. 290, 97 S.Ct. 1056, 51 L.Ed.2d 338 (1977).

NOTE—Where the union's duty of fair representation is involved, an employee may bring suit against the employer and union after exhausting contract remedies. This is so because it cannot be fairly inferred that Congress intended exclusive jurisdiction to lie with the NLRB. Since the decision of the Board's General Counsel not to prosecute an unfair labor practice charge is not subject to judicial review, the employee would be without a remedy were the rule otherwise. Thus, an employee may bring suit against the employer under Section 301 of the Act based on breach of the collective bargaining agreement and against the union for breach of its duty of fair representation to provide a complete remedy to the employee. See CASE 67, above.

2. Section 103 of the Landrum-Griffin Act permits state courts to continue their traditional jurisdiction over the activities of unions with respect to members.

3. Union membership is a valuable right which is protected by the states.

4. Most state courts require that a union member exhaust his internal union remedies before invoking the state court for relief. See Falsetti v. Local 2026, United Mine Workers of America, 400 Pa. 145, 161 A.2d 882 (1960).

5. Courts have held that a union may expel a member for conduct which is antagonistic to the continued existence of the union as collective bargaining agent.

   e.g. A company spy, dual unionism, violating work rules, working below the union wage scale, and engaging in an unauthorized strike.

6. Unions may not interfere with the personal rights of members, such as voting or campaigning in an election.

OTHER RIGHTS OF EMPLOYEES

e.g. A union member was expelled because he campaigned for a right to work law, contrary to the policy of the union which opposed the law. The court held that "where the political activity of the member is not patently in conflict with the union's best interests, the union should not be permitted to use its power over the individual to curb the advocacy of his political views." The member was ordered reinstated. The court reasoned that it was in the public interest to have a subject such as voluntary unionism discussed because its long-range effects are debatable. See Mitchell v. International Ass'n of Machinists, 196 Cal.App.2d 796, 16 Cal.Rptr. 813 (1961).

7. Section 14(b) of the Taft-Hartley Act permits states to prohibit union security agreements which are otherwise valid under Section 8(a)(3). Such state laws are known as right to work laws.

NOTE—The federal government has placed restrictions on the use of union and company funds with respect to political contributions. While that subject is beyond the scope of a course in labor law, the Supreme Court has held that the use of union dues obtained by a union security clause for political purposes is prohibited in some circumstances. See CASE 72 and NOTE following, below.

CASE 71—*state court jurisdiction preempted by federal labor law*

A collective bargaining agreement contained a union security clause which required employees to become and remain members of the union "as a condition precedent to continued employment." P, an employee, paid his dues directly to the union rather than have them deducted from his wages by the company. P failed to pay his union dues in October, and on November 2 the union suspended P from membership and requested his discharge. The employer complied. The union refused P's tender of dues a few days later, and P filed suit against the union in state court. The union's constitution provided that "where a member allows his arrearage . . . to run into the second month before paying the same, he shall be debarred from benefits for one month after payment. Where a member allows his arrearage . . . to run over the last day of the second month without payment, he does thereby suspend himself from membership . . . ." P contended that since he was less than two months behind in the payment of dues, he could not be suspended. He merely ceased to be a member in good standing. Since the union shop clause only required that employees "remain members," the union improperly obtained his discharge. P's contention was accepted by the state courts, and he was awarded damages. The union appealed to the United States Supreme Court contending that the NLRB had exclusive jurisdiction because the actions of the union were arguably protected by Section 7 or prohibited by Section 8(b)(1)(A) and (2). Is the union's contention valid?

Ans. Yes. In establishing a uniform national labor law, Congress gave the task of primary interpretation and application of its rules to the NLRB. The purpose of this federal preemption of state regulation was to avoid conflicting regulation of the same conduct. Thus, any complaint based upon employee, union, or employer conduct arguably protected or prohibited by the Taft-Hartley Act must first be heard by the NLRB. There are exceptions to this original jurisdiction of the Board: (a) when state interests in regulating the wrongful conduct are great, such as when violence is involved, (b) where Congress has authorized other tribunals to hear the charge, or (c) where the matter is only of peripheral federal concern. Where those exceptions are not present, neither federal nor state courts have original jurisdiction to regulate conduct arguably subject to NLRB regulation. In the present case the union's alleged wrongful conduct was arguably prohibited by Sections 8(b)(1)(A) and (2). Since none of the above exceptions is applicable, P is limited to his remedy before the NLRB. The judgment of the state court in P's favor was reversed.

See Amalgamated Ass'n of Street, Electric Ry. and Motor Coach Employees v. Lockridge, 403 U.S. 274, 91 S.Ct. 1909, 29 L.Ed.2d 473 (1971).

CASE 72—*expenditure of union funds for political purposes limited*

Employees of a railroad were required to join and remain union members as a condition of employment. That union shop clause was specifically authorized by the Railway Labor Act. The union used part of the members' dues to make political contributions. Some employees brought suit in state court against the union for improper expenditure of union funds. Does a union subject to the Railway Labor Act have unlimited power to spend dues received under a union shop clause when members object?

Ans. No. Congress authorized the union shop so that all employees could be required to pay the costs of collective bargaining and the administration of the contract. Although the Act does not regulate union expenditures, in the present case the union expended funds for a use which is clearly outside the reasons accepted by Congress to justify union shop agreements. The interests of employees who are required to pay union dues and who object to the expenditure of funds for political purposes must be protected. Thus, the expenditure of the funds of employees who objected was improper. In remanding the case for the lower court to consider the proper remedy, the United States Supreme Court stated that the union shop clause itself was not unlawful. Further, it would be improper to enjoin all political contributions by the union because many union members might favor such action. One possible remedy would be to refund part of the union dues which represent political contributions to employees who have affirmatively made known their objections to the union.

See International Ass'n of Machinists v. Street, 367 U.S. 740, 81 S.Ct. 1784, 6 L.Ed.2d 1141 (1961).

NOTE—A union and three officers were convicted of violating 18 U.S.C.A. § 610 which prohibited unions from making contributions in connection with a federal election. The union appealed, contending that the funds were voluntarily donated by members. The Court held that Section 610 did not apply to contributions from voluntarily financed union political funds. However, a union's political funds must be segregated from union dues and assessments. Solicitation of voluntary political contributions by union officials is permissible if conducted under circumstances plainly indicating that donations are for a political purpose, and that those solicited may decline to contribute without reprisal. The Court reversed the conviction and remanded the case to the trial court because the jury was not properly instructed concerning the voluntariness of the contributions. See Pipefitters Local Union No. 562 v. United States, 407 U.S. 385, 92 S.Ct. 2247, 33 L.Ed.2d 11 (1972).

XII. REPRESENTATION PROCEEDINGS

LEGAL GEMS—Representation Proceedings—Introduction

1. The right of representation is authority to bargain for a group of employees in an appropriate bargaining unit.

2. The term "appropriate bargaining unit" refers to a group of employees who have a similar community of interest which is appropriate for bargaining.

    e.g. all production and maintenance employees or all office clerical employees.

3. The representation right may be obtained in the following ways:
    (a) *voluntary* recognition by the employer,

    (b) *involuntary* recognition, as a remedy for employer substantial unfair labor practices, and

    (c) in an NLRB conducted election.

4. This Chapter focuses upon NLRB conducted elections and rules relating thereto. Examples of permissible and impermissible employer conduct before an NLRB election are given in CHART III and CHART IV, below.

    See generally Chapter I, CHART II, Types of Petitions Which May Be Filed, above.

CHART III

PERMISSIBLE EMPLOYER CONDUCT BEFORE AN NLRB ELECTION

Examples of what supervisors may do before an election in urging employees to vote against union representation

1. Tell employees that if a majority of them select the union, the company will have to deal with it on all their daily problems involving wages, hours and other conditions of employment. Tell them that the company would prefer to continue dealing with them directly on such matters.
2. Tell employees that supervisors are always willing to discuss with them any subject of interest to them.
3. Tell employees about the benefits they presently enjoy, all of which may have been obtained without union representation.
4. Tell employees how their wages, benefits and working conditions compare favorably with other companies in the area.
5. Tell employees some of the disadvantages of belonging to a union, such as the expense of dues and initiation fees, fines, strike assessments, and membership rules restricting their personal freedom. Quote from the specific union's constitution and bylaws granting to the union power to impose punishment and discipline against its members.
6. Tell employees that in negotiating with the union the company does not have to agree to all the union's terms, and certainly not to any terms which are not in the economic interest of the business.
7. Tell employees management's opinion of union policies and of the leaders of the organizing union, even in uncomplimentary terms. This information should be factually correct.
8. Tell employees about any untrue or misleading statements made by the union organizers.
9. Tell employees that merely signing a union authorization card or application for membership does not mean that they must vote for the union in an election. If the situation warrants, advise them that the union may use the signed authorization cards to obtain bargaining rights without an NLRB election.

[C473]

LABOR LAW—EMPLOYMENT DISCRIMINATION

CHART IV

IMPERMISSIBLE EMPLOYER CONDUCT BEFORE AN NLRB ELECTION

Examples of what supervisors may _not_ do before an NLRB election

1. Promise or grant employees a pay increase, promotion, benefit or special favor if they refuse to join the union or promise to vote against it. Customary wage increases must be granted as scheduled.
2. Threaten loss of jobs, reduction of income, discontinuance of privileges or benefits presently enjoyed to influence employees in the exercise of their right to support the union.
3. Threaten or actually discharge, discipline or lay off an employee because of pro-union activities.
4. Threaten, through a third party, any of the foregoing acts of interference.
5. Threaten to close or move the plant, or to reduce operations if the union wins the election.
6. Spy on union meetings or act in a way which would indicate to the employees that they are being watched to determine whether or not they are participating in union activities.
7. Discriminate against employees who are supporting the union.
8. Ask employees for their opinion about the union.
9. Ask employees if they signed a union card or how they intend to vote in the election.
10. State that the employer will not deal with the union.
11. Help employees to withdraw their cards authorizing the union to represent them.

[C442]

LEGAL GEMS—NLRB Election Procedure

1. A document, called a petition, can be filed with the NLRB asking for an election. There are several types of petitions:

    (a) CERTIFICATION OF REPRESENTATIVE—RC—The petitioner desires to be certified as the representative of a group of the employees (bargaining unit) described in the petition.

    (b) DECERTIFICATION—RD—Filed by an employee or union acting for the employee, and it asserts that the currently recognized union no longer represents the employees.

    (c) REPRESENTATION (EMPLOYER PETITION)—RM— One or more individuals or labor organizations have presented

REPRESENTATION PROCEEDINGS

a claim to the employer to be recognized. The employer may also question the continued majority of an incumbent union with this Petition.

(d) WITHDRAWAL OF UNION SHOP AUTHORITY—UD— Filed by an employee and it asserts that the employees in a bargaining unit covered by a collective bargaining agreement desire to have the union security clause in that contract rescinded.

NOTE—The labels, RC, RD, RM, and UD are the shorthand descriptions of the various kinds of petitions.

2. After the petition is filed the Board determines:
   (a) whether the employer meets any of the jurisdictional standards established by the Board, See **CASE 4**, and **NOTE** following, above,
   (b) if there is a "showing of interest" supporting the petition,
   (c) if a question concerning representation exists, and
   (d) what is the appropriate unit.

3. If the parties reach agreement on these issues, they set a date, time, and place for the election and sign an appropriate agreement.

4. If the parties cannot agree on some issue, a non-adversary, investigatory hearing is held before a hearing officer, where the employer and union present evidence on their position. The hearing officer rules on the admissibility evidence, and the regional director determines the issues in a written decision.

NOTE—"The only function of a hearing officer is to produce a full presentation of factual material so that the Board will be in a position to decide all issues upon an adequate record." Monticello Charm Tred Mills, Inc., 80 NLRB 378 (1948). See also Sections 101.20(c) and 101.21(b), NLRB Rules and Regulations and Statements of Procedure, Series 8, as amended.

5. A party may request review of the regional director's decision by the Board, but this review (like certiorari to the Supreme Court) need not be granted.

6. At the election the employer and union(s) are entitled to an observer, who checks off the names of voters and assists the Board agent in conducting the election.

7. An observer may challenge the vote of any person whom he believes is not eligible to vote. In such an event the ballot is placed in a challenge envelope.

   (a) When challenged ballots are determinative of the result, the determination as to whether or not they are to be counted rests with the Regional Director in the first instance, subject to possible appeal to the Board.

LABOR LAW—EMPLOYMENT DISCRIMINATION

    (b) If the challenges are not determinative they are not resolved, and the certification is based on the tally of unchallenged ballots.

8. After the secret ballot election has been conducted the ballots are counted and a Tally of Ballots issued and served on the parties.

9. Parties have five business days after issuance of the Tally of Ballots to file objections to the election.

    (a) If no objections are filed the results are certified.

    (b) If objections are filed, they are investigated. A hearing may be held to receive evidence pertaining to the objections. The Regional Director or Board will then rule on the objections and either order a rerun election or overrule the objections and certify the results of the election.

10. A union must receive a majority of valid votes cast to be certified. A tie vote with only two choices on the ballot means that the union loses the election.

11. If there are three or more choices on the ballot and no party receives a majority, a run-off election is conducted between the two choices receiving the most votes.

12. The Board will only conduct one valid election in a period of a year in the same bargaining unit.

13. If a majority of employees in a UD election vote to rescind the union security clause in the contract, neither the employer nor the union may thereafter enforce it.

    See generally Chapter I, **CHART II**, Types of Petitions Which May Be Filed, above.

LEGAL GEMS—Showing of Interest

1. An RC, RD, or UD petition must be accompanied by signed and dated authorizations of 30 percent of the employees in the appropriate unit indicating that they want an election.

2. No particular wording or form is required and the wording of authorizations is liberally construed.

3. An authorization is usually in the form of a "card", but may take any form, so long as it is written.

4. A petition filed by an employer must be supported by some objective evidence that it has reasonable grounds for believing that an incumbent union has lost its majority status. See United States Gypsum Co., 157 NLRB 652 (1966). If there is no incumbent union a demand for recognition is sufficient.

REPRESENTATION PROCEEDINGS

LEGAL GEMS—Questions Concerning Representation—Contract Bar

1. A question concerning representation means that there is a question as to whether or not one or more unions represent a majority of employees in an appropriate unit.

2. A question concerning representation may not be raised during the term of a collective bargaining agreement up to three years. This is known as a *contract bar*.

CAVEAT—If the contracting union has become defunct (i. e., it is unable or unwilling to represent the employees in the bargaining unit), its contract with the employer will not bar a representation election. See Container Corp., 61 NLRB 823 (1945). Likewise, if there is a schism in the contracting union (a division of the union into factions resulting in one group leaving the union), the contract will not bar an election, nor will the contract bind the winning union, if any, after the election. See Hershey Chocolate Corp., 121 NLRB 901 (1958).

3. A contract which will not bar a representation election will not bind the parties after the election if a new union is certified. See American Seating Co., 106 NLRB 250 (1953). A petition may be filed by a rival union in the thirty day period from ninety to sixty days before the expiration of a collective bargaining contract, or after the contract expires if a new contract has not been signed.

4. The incumbent union and the employer are given a sixty day insulated period prior to the expiration of the contract to negotiate a new contract without representation claims from rival unions.

5. A contract renewed or extended prior to the sixty-day insulated period is considered a *premature extension* and will not bar an election petition during the ninety- to sixty-day period of the original contract.

See generally Cox, pp. 284–294; Smith, pp. 224–227.

LEGAL GEMS—The Appropriate Bargaining Unit

1. There is no *one* appropriate bargaining unit of employees. The Board determines whether a proposed or existing unit is *an* appropriate unit based upon many factors including the extent of organization, work and skills of the employees involved, their community of interest, working conditions, and history of bargaining. See CASES 73 and 74, below.

NOTE—The act excludes supervisors and guards from bargaining units and it prohibits the grouping of professional employees with non-professional employees without their voting to be included in such a unit. See Sections 2(3) and 9(b) of the Act.

LABOR LAW—EMPLOYMENT DISCRIMINATION

2. Besides the usual situation in which the Board determines the appropriate bargaining unit, the employees themselves are sometimes permitted to determine the bargaining unit in what is known as a Globe election. See Globe Machine and Stamping Co., 3 NLRB 294 (1937).

   (a) Union A sought a unit of office clerical employees at the employer's Oakland general office and at its Emoryville terminal. Union B sought a unit of office clerical employees at only the Emoryville terminal. The Board found that the following factors showed that the larger unit was appropriate: the skills and duties of all employees were similar, wage rates were comparable, there was some interchange of employees, the two offices were located only three miles apart, and both groups were subject to the same ultimate supervision. On the other hand, there were factors which supported the appropriateness of separate units: the terminal office was concerned with the movement of freight, but the general office dealt with administrative and clerical duties for all the employer's terminals, each group of employees had different immediate supervision and working hours were different. Thus, the factors supporting either single units or a two office unit were balanced, and there was no history of collective bargaining. The Board ordered a Globe-type election: (a) employees at the Oakland office may vote for Union A or Union B, if it has a sufficient showing of interest for the larger unit, or for neither union; (b) employees at the Emoryville office may vote for Union A, Union B, or no union. If the employees at both offices select the same union to represent them, then the overall unit will be found appropriate. If the employees at each office select different unions to represent them, then separate units will be found appropriate. See Pacific Intermountain Express Co., 105 NLRB 480 (1953).

   (b) Section 9(b)(1) of the Taft-Hartley Act provides that professional employees may not be included in a unit of employees who are not professionals unless a majority of the professional employees vote to be included in such a unit. A Globe election may be used to determine the desires of the professional employees. If a majority of the professional employees vote to be represented by the union representing another group of employees at the plant, the professionals will be "globed" into the other unit.

3. A bargaining unit may be multi-employer or single employer, multi-plant or single plant, plant-wide or merely a craft or a department within a plant.

4. Race, sex and size are irrelevant to unit determinations, except that a unit must consist of at least two employees.

5. After a bargaining unit has been established either the union or employer may file one of the following petitions:

   (a) **AMENDMENT OF CERTIFICATION—AC**—The petitioner seeks to amend an existing certification to reflect changed circumstances, such as changes in the name or affiliation of the labor organization involved or in the name or location of the employer involved.

   (b) **UNIT CLARIFICATION—UC**—The petitioner seeks a determination as to whether certain classifications of employees should or should not be included within the bargaining unit.

   NOTE—The labels AC and UC are the shorthand descriptions of these two kinds of petitions.

6. A UC petition is appropriate to determine:

   (a) the unit placement of employees in a *new classification*, or

   (b) whether employees come within an *existing classification* in which there has been a substantial change in job content.

   e.g. The union is certified to represent all production and maintenance employees. Subsequently, a question arises as to whether one or more employees are plant clerical employees. Plant clerical employees are normally included in the production and maintenance unit, but office clerical employees are normally excluded from the production and maintenance unit. A UC petition may be filed to determine the placement of the clerical employees in question.

7. A UC petition is not appropriate where it would upset the provisions in a collective bargaining agreement or a past practice of the parties. The past practice of the parties does not have to be negotiated. It may be shown by acquiescence, by silence, or even acquiescence because of a mistaken belief as to the duties of the employees involved.

   See generally Cox, pp. 294–327.

CASE 73—*company wide units—extent of organization considered*

In Quaker City Life Ins. Co., 134 NLRB 960 (1961) the Board reversed its policy of finding only state-wide or company-wide units of insurance agents appropriate for bargaining "absent, unusual circumstances". In finding smaller units appropriate the Board invariably found that the petitioned for unit of insurance agents was appropriate for collective bargaining. In Metropolitan Life Ins. Co. v. NLRB, 327 F.2d 906 (1st Cir. 1964) the Court of Appeals noted this fact and concluded that the Board must have made the extent of the union's organization the controlling factor in determining the bargaining unit. That would contravene Section 9(c)(5) which prohibits such determination. Does the Act prohibit the consideration of the extent of union organization already achieved among the employees of the employer in determining the appropriate collective bargaining unit?

Ans. No. Section 9(c)(5) does not prohibit the Board from considering the extent of organization as one factor in determining the collective bargaining units. However, it must not be the controlling factor in the unit determination. In this case the Board did not articulate the reasons for its decision, and therefore, it was not possible to conclude how much weight was given by the Board to the extent of union organization. The case was remanded to the Board for an explanation of the basis of its unit determination.

See NLRB v. Metropolitan Life Ins. Co., 380 U.S. 438, 85 S.Ct. 1061, 13 L.Ed.2d 951 (1965).

NOTE—Upon remand the Board re-affirmed its holding that each of "the individual district offices is a separate administrative entity through which the employer conducts its business operations, and therefore is inherently appropriate for purposes of collective bargaining." See Metropolitan Life Ins. Co., 156 NLRB 1408 (1966).

CASE 74—*severance of a craft unit—factors considered*

The International Brotherhood of Electrical Workers filed a timely petition for a unit of twelve instrument mechanics who had been represented for a number of years by another union along with 250 production and maintenance employees. The employer opposed severance of the mechanics contending that the integration of their functions with the entire production process of purification and manufacture of uranium and the long bargaining history as a single unit demonstrate that the single overall unit should be continued. Should the group of skilled instrument mechanics be severed from the existing production and maintenance unit?

Ans. No. All relevant factors in each industry are considered in determining whether a particular craft will be severed from an established unit. Specifically, these factors include: (a) skills of the craft or departments; (b) history of bargaining, including whether that has produced stability in labor relations and the effect of a change in that relationship; (c) the extent to which the craft group has maintained a separate identity while in the larger unit; (d) the history and pattern of bargaining in the industry involved; (e) the integration of the group sought in the employer's production process; and (f) the qualifications of the union seeking the group, including its experience in representing similar groups of employees. Applying those factors to the present case, the Board denied severance of the instrument mechanics emphasizing their long inclusion in the larger unit, their community of interest with those employees, and their close work with the employer's production processes. The Board also noted that the bargaining interests of mechanics had not been neglected in negotiations by the incumbent union, and the petitioning union had not traditionally represented mechanics.

See Mallinckrodt Chem. Works, 162 NLRB 387 (1966).

NOTE—This decision reversed American Potash & Chem. Corp., 107 NLRB 1418 (1954) which had permitted severance if: (a) the employees involved

REPRESENTATION PROCEEDINGS

were a true craft or a departmental group and (b) the union seeking to carve out the craft or department traditionally represented the group involved. The Board in reversing the *Potash* case concluded that by considering only those criteria which favored severance of the craft or department it was not discharging its statutory responsibility. Therefore, the Board determined to consider all relevant factors, including the interest of other employees whose unity of association would be broken by severance and whose collective strength would thereby be weakened.

LEGAL GEMS—Judicial Review of Representation Cases

1. There is no direct judicial review of representation cases under the Act.

2. Judicial Review must be obtained through court review of an unfair labor practice finding.

    e.g. An employer who believes that the Board erred in its unit determination can refuse to bargain with the union if it is certified after an election. Since the Board will not consider its representation decision in a subsequent unfair labor practice case, it will find the employer guilty of refusing to bargain. The employer can then obtain court review of the representation decision because an element of a refusal to bargain finding is that the union must represent a majority of employees in an appropriate unit.

3. If the Board acts contrary to the wording of the Act in rendering its unit determination, Federal courts have original jurisdiction to set aside the Board determination. See **CASE 75**, below.

CASE 75—*original court review when board violates statute*

Union A petitioned for a unit of non-supervisory professional employees. Union B intervened and contended that a bargaining unit of professional employees should include five other classifications performing technical work. After a hearing the Board found that while the five additional classifications were not professional employees, some of those employees should be included in the unit of professional employees because they "share a close community of employment interests with [the professional employees, and their inclusion would not] destroy the predominantly professional character of such a unit." Subsequently, an election was conducted and Union A was certified. Since Union A only wanted to represent the professional employees, it filed suit against the NLRB alleging that the Board had exceeded its statutory authority by including non-professional employees in a unit of professional employees without their consent as required by Section 9(b)(1) of the Act. Does the District Court have original jurisdiction over a suit against the Board to vacate a determination in excess of its statutory authority even though the Act contains provisions for court review available only through unfair labor practice proceedings?

Ans. Yes. This is not a suit to "review" as that term is used in the Act, but it is an action to invalidate an order in excess of the Board's statutory powers. Congress gave professional employees a "right" not to be included in a unit of non-professional employees without their consent. Congress must have intended that there be some means to protect and enforce that right. The general jurisdiction of Federal Courts is sufficient to remedy a decision of the Board in excess of its statutory powers. Therefore, the court had jurisdiction to set aside the Board's unit determination, the election, and the union's certification.

See Leedom v. Kyne, 338 U.S. 184, 79 S.Ct. 180, 3 L.Ed.2d 210 (1958).

NOTE 1—The *Leedom* decision, CASE 75, above, involved only a legal question—the proper interpretation of a statute. Its application is limited to such situations. Where there is a factual issue such as whether the evidence showed that employees are independent contractors, the court will not take original jurisdiction. See Boire v. Greyhound Corp., 376 U.S. 473, 84 S.Ct. 894, 11 L.Ed.2d 849 (1964).

NOTE 2—If the union in the *Leedom* case refused to represent the technical employees, court review might have been obtained through unfair labor practice proceedings in this manner: The employer could file a refusal to bargain charge against the union charging a violation of Section 8(b)(3), or the technical employees could charge that the union refused to represent them in violation of Section 8(b)(1)(A). The Board would not review its representation decision in the unfair labor practice decision and would find the violation alleged. The union could petition the court to review unfair labor practice findings based on these charges and that would bring the issue of the appropriate unit determination before the court. See Chapter IV, Procedure and Remedies, above. See also CASE 76, below.

LEGAL GEMS—Setting Aside an Election

1. Conduct by an employer or union which constitutes an unfair labor practice is normally sufficient to set aside an election if it could have affected the outcome.

2. Some conduct which does not violate the Act is, nevertheless, sufficient to set aside an election.

    (a) Employers and unions are both prohibited from making election speeches *on company time* to mass assemblies of employees within 24 hours of a scheduled election. This is known as the Peerless Plywood or Twenty-four Hour Rule, and it prohibits such "captive audience" meetings. The Board reasons that such speeches tend to interfere with that "sober and thoughtful choice which a free election is designed to reflect". Peerless Plywood Co., 107 NLRB 427 (1953).

    (b) This rule does not apply to meeting *before* or *after* working hours where attendance is VOLUNTARY and employees are not paid for their time.

REPRESENTATION PROCEEDINGS

(c) The employer must submit an eligibility list containing the names and addresses of all eligible voters to enable the union to inform the electorate of the issues and investigate the eligibility of voters previously unknown to them. Failure to comply with this rule is grounds to set aside an election. See Excelsior Underwear, Inc., 156 NLRB 126 (1966).

NOTE—In a court test of the rule in GEM 2, above, the Supreme Court held that it was within the Board's discretion to encourage an informed electorate by allowing unions the right of access to employees that management already possesses. That determination may be made for each individual case without following the usual rule making procedures of the Administrative Procedure Act. See CASE 78, below.

(d) Other conduct which interferes with the free choice of employees may be grounds for setting aside an election.

e.g. After a petition for an election had been filed, the union announced that it would waive initiation fees for all employees who signed union "recognition slips" before the election. The Supreme Court concluded that this interfered with employees' freedom of choice in the election because: (a) An employee who signs the slip indicates to other employees that he supports the union, and this can be used by the union in its election campaign. This has the effect of permitting the union to buy endorsements and paint a false portrait of employee support during the election campaign. (b) An employee who signed a slip may feel morally obligated to vote for the union. (c) The "recognition slips" could be used by the union to demand bargaining rights without an election. (d) The failure to sign a slip may seem ominous to those who oppose the union fearing a wrathful union regime if the union is successful. See CASE 76, below.

3. A misrepresentation by an employer or union to employees is grounds to set aside an election if:

   (a) it concerns an important matter,

   (b) it is a substantial departure from the truth,

   (c) the other party does not have the opportunity to make an effective reply, and

   (d) the misrepresentation—whether intentional or not—may reasonably be expected to have an impact on the election. See CASE 77, below.

   See generally CHART III and CHART IV, above.

LABOR LAW—EMPLOYMENT DISCRIMINATION

CASE 76—*influencing employees by unfair means invalidates election*

Prior to an NLRB election the union distributed "recognition slips" to employees. An employee who signed a slip before the election became a member of the union without having to pay an initiation fee. If a majority of employees voted for the union, then employees who did not sign slips would be required to pay the usual union initiation fee if the employer agreed to a union shop clause in its contract with the union. The union won the election by a vote of 22 to 20. The employer filed objections to the election because of the distribution of "recognition slips." The Board concluded that the union had a valid interest in waiving the initiation fee before the election because employees otherwise sympathetic to the union might be reluctant to pay money to the union before it had done anything for them. Waiver of the initiation fee would remove that obstacle. The Board found against the employer and certified the union. However, the employer refused to bargain, and the union filed an unfair labor practice charge against the employer. The employer sought court review of the Board finding of an 8(a)(5) and (1) violation, contending that the election was invalid because of the distribution of the "recognition slips." Should the Board's position be upheld?

Ans. No. If payment of an initiation fee were an obstacle to organization, the union could waive it for all employees who joined after the election as well as before. Limiting the waiver to employees who joined before the election serves the additional purpose of affecting the union organizational campaign and the election. "Whatever his true intentions, an employee who signs a recognition slip prior to an election is indicating to other workers that he supports the union. His outward manifestation of support must often serve as a useful campaign tool in the union's hands to convince other employees to vote for the union, if only because many employees respect their coworkers' views on the unionization issue. By permitting the union to offer to waive an initiation fee for those employees signing a recognition slip prior to the election, the Board allows the union to buy endorsements and paint a false portrait of employee support during its election campaign. . . . In addition, while it is correct that the employee who signs a recognition slip is not legally bound to vote for the union and has not promised to do so in any formal sense, certainly there may be some employees who would feel obliged to carry through on their stated intention to support the union. And on the facts of this case, the change of just one vote would have resulted in a 21–21 election rather than a 22–20 election." The union would not have been certified if the vote were tied, and would have had to wait one year before another election. Since the union should not have been certified, the employer did not violate the Act by refusing to bargain with the union.

See NLRB v. Savair Mfg. Co., 414 U.S. 270, 94 S.Ct. 495, 38 L.Ed.2d 495 (1973).

NOTE—An employer may not grant benefits to employees prior to an election even though they are permanent and unconditional. In such a situation employees are "not likely to miss the inference that the source of benefits now conferred is also the source from which future benefits must flow and which may dry up if it is not obliged." Thus, the granting of benefits before an election by an employer would invalidate the results of the election. See CASE 5, above.

REPRESENTATION PROCEEDINGS

CASE 77—false election campaign statements may cause election to be set aside

The day before an election at Company A the union distributed a circular to employees which purported to compare wage rates of various job classifications at Company A with other plants in the industry. The handbills did not take into account an incentive pay plan at Company A. Further, while the plants used for comparison were in the same general industry as the employer, they were not truly comparable as to the type of operations and degree of skill required for the jobs involved. This resulted in an overstatement of the wages of "comparable" employees. Do these facts interfere with full and complete freedom of employees in selecting a bargaining representative in the election held the next day?

Ans. Yes. The Board said "We believe that an election should be set aside only where there has been a misrepresentation or other similar campaign trickery, which involves a substantial departure from the truth, at a time which prevents the other party or parties from making an effective reply, so that the misrepresentation, whether deliberate or not, may reasonably be expected to have a significant impact on the election". Here the handbill concerned a matter of utmost concern to the employees—wages—and its distribution in the afternoon before the election did not give the employer a chance to make an effective reply. Company A rates were grossly understated and those of other plants were exaggerated. The omission of further information concerning plant and jobs compared compounds the misrepresentation. Thus, the union exceeded the bounds of fair and lawful electioneering and interfered with the free choice of employees.

See Hollywood Ceramics Co., 140 NLRB 221 (1962).

NOTE—In Shopping Kart Food Market, 228 NLRB 1311 (1977), the Board overruled CASE 77, above, stating that it would not continue to set aside elections based upon false or misleading campaign statements. After a change of Board membership the Shopping Kart decision was overruled and the standard of review stated in CASE 77, was readopted. Thus, CASE 77, above, continues to be the law applicable to NLRB elections. See General Knit of California, Inc., 239 NLRB No. 101 (1978).

LEGAL GEMS—Rule Making Authority of the NLRB

1. The establishment of representation election procedures has required the NLRB to make a number of rules for the guidance of the parties and to assure fair elections.

2. In exercising its rule making authority the NLRB is subject to Section 533 of the Administrative Procedure Act (APA) which sets forth the following requirements:

    (a) publication of notice in the Federal Register, along with a statement of the basis for the rule and its purpose,

    (b) providing an opportunity for persons to present their views on the proposed rule, and

LABOR LAW—EMPLOYMENT DISCRIMINATION

    (c) after establishment of the rule as provided in the APA, it must then be published in the Federal Register and made effective in not less than thirty days.

See CASE 78, below.

    CAVEAT—In addition to the rule making procedures enunciated in the APA, an agency may also make rules through adjudication of cases. This is the procedure usually followed by the NLRB. See CASE 79, below.

3. A rule (or regulation) promulgated under APA procedures must be published in the Federal Register in order to have binding effect on the public, unless it can be shown that the person charged had actual knowledge of it. See APA Section 552(a)(1).

4. A trial type hearing is not required for rule making by the Administrative Procedure Act.

5. The Federal Register is published every working day by the Federal Government and it contains:

    (a) all Presidential proclamations, orders, and other documents,

    (b) amendments to the Code of Federal Regulations,

    (c) notices of proposed rule changes required by Section 553 of the Act, see GEM 2, above, and

    (d) statements of agency organization, procedure and rules required by Section 552 of the Act.

CASE 78—*failure to follow APA rule making requirements invalidates rule*

Two unions filed objections to an NLRB election on the ground that the employer failed to furnish the union with the names and addresses of eligible voters before the election. In considering the matter the Board "invited certain interested parties" to file briefs and participate in oral argument on the issue of whether employers should be required to furnish names and addresses of employees. However, Section 553 of the APA required specific rule making procedures which were not followed. Various employer groups and unions did file briefs as *amici curiae*. Thereafter, the Board made its decision and ordered that for all elections agreed to or ordered subsequent to thirty days from the date of its decision, the employer must furnish the participating union(s) with the names and addresses of eligible voters. Pursuant to that rule, in a later case, the Board ordered an employer to submit the names and addresses of eligible voters for use by the two unions in their election campaign. Although the employer refused to comply the Board conducted the election and a majority of employees voted against being represented by either union. The Board set aside the election because the employer did not furnish the names and addresses of employees and ordered a new election. A subpoena was issued for the names and addresses, but the employer refused to obey it. The Board now seeks to enforce its subpoena. May a substantial regulation be promulgated in an adjudicatory proceeding if the rule making provisions of the APA are not met?

REPRESENTATION PROCEEDINGS

Ans. No. The National Labor Relations Act authorized the Board to make rules and regulations to carry out the provisions of the Act as prescribed by the APA. The APA requires publication in the Federal Register of the notice of the proposed rule making an opportunity to be heard, a statement in the rule of its basis and purposes and publication of the rule in the Federal Register as adopted. Those requirements were not followed: The Board only gave notice to selected organizations, whereas notice in the Federal Register would have been general in character, and the "rule" was never published in the Federal Register. The procedures for rule making stated by Congress in the APA may not be avoided by making rules in the course of adjudicatory proceedings as the Board did in the present case. There is no doubt that the promulgation of a disclosure rule would be within the discretion of the agency. It would be a valid legislative rule if the procedures of the APA had been followed. Congress granted the Board wide discretion in establishing election procedures for employees. It is within that discretion to require disclosure thereby encouraging an informed employee electorate and allowing unions the same access to employees that the employer already possesses. It is for the Board and not the court to balance those and other factors and establish a policy consistent with its responsibility under the Act. Besides announcing rules of general applicability an agency can also make rules on a case by case basis as it sets up elections. In the present case the employer was specifically directed to submit the names and addresses when the election was ordered. It is because of that specific order and not because of the "rule" that the employer must furnish the list.

See NLRB v. Wyman-Gordon Co., 394 U.S. 759, 89 S.Ct. 1426, 22 L.Ed.2d 709 (1969).

NOTE—Only four Justices subscribed to the plurality opinion in CASE 78, above. The reasoning of three Justices who joined in a concurring opinion is instructive. Most administrative agencies are granted two functions: (1) the power to make rules having the effect of laws, and (2) the power to hear and adjudicate controversies. The APA specifies a required procedure by which an agency may exercise its rule making power, (Sec. 553) and a different procedure for the exercise of its adjudicatory power (Sec. 554). Although the Board did not comply with the requirements of the statute regarding rule making, the procedural safeguards required for adjudication were satisfied. In that adjudicatory proceeding the unions argued that the election should be set aside because the employer did not give them the names and addresses of employees. In its opinion the Board explained that although it agreed with the unions as to the disclosure requirement, it did not believe that the election should be set aside in that case because the employer relied on past precedent in refusing to divulge the requested information. In an adjudicatory proceeding it is not uncommon for one party to advocate a "new" requirement. If the "new" theory is accepted, the agency can apply it retroactively or prospectively. In the present case the agency decided, based on considerations and fairness, to apply the rule prospectively only. An agency should not be required to either make the adjudicatory decision retroactive or initiate a new rule making proceeding. Therefore, it was proper to announce a prospective rule in rendering its decision and the agency should not be required to restate its election rule every time it directs an election.

CASE 79—*agency has discretion to make rules either through adjudication or rule making procedures*

A union filed a petition with the National Labor Relations Board seeking to represent the employees classified as buyers at X company. X performed research and development work in the design and fabrication of aerospace products. X opposed the petition on the grounds that: (a) the buyers were managerial employees, and, in accordance with the Board's decisions of long standing, were not covered by the Act, and (b) the authority of the buyers to commit X's credit, select vendors, and negotiate purchase prices would create a potential conflict of interest as the buyers might favor union contractors. The Board found that managerial employees were covered by the Act and that the possible conflict of interest was "unsupported conjecture." Where the Board departs from a long standing interpretation of the Act, may this be done by decision rather than invoking rule making procedures?

Ans. Yes. The Board is not precluded from announcing new principles in an adjudicative proceeding. The choice of whether to use the rule making procedures of the APA or an adjudicative proceeding to make a new rule lies within the Board's decision. Although there may be situations where the Board's reliance on adjudication would amount to an abuse of discretion or a violation of the Act, nothing in the present case would justify such a conclusion. The duties of the buyers will vary widely depending on the company and the industry. It would be difficult to formulate any generalized standard for all buyers. Thus, the Board has good reason to proceed in a case-by-case manner. Although employers have relied on past decisions of the Board excluding buyers from bargaining groups, no adverse consequences would result from such reliance in the present case. No new liability, fines or damages is imposed. An agency has the discretion to make a new rule either through an adjudicatory proceeding or through rule making proceedings. The Board did not abuse that discretion in the present case, so its rule is valid.

See NLRB v. Bell Aerospace Co., Div. of Textron, Inc., 416 U.S. 267, 94 S.Ct. 1757, 40 L.Ed.2d 134 (1974).

NOTE—CASE 79, above, is also important for its holding that the Board may not bring managerial employees within the protection of the Act. The Court noted that: (a) early decisions of the Board excluded managerial employees from units of rank and file employees, (b) the legislative history of the Taft-Hartley Act indicated an intent to exclude them, and (c) the consistent construction of the Act by the Board and courts for more than twenty years was that managerial employees were excluded from the coverage of the Act. Thus, the Court rejected the Board's finding that managerial employees were covered by the Act unless there was a conflict of interest.

XIII. OTHER LAWS GOVERNING LABOR RELATIONS

LEGAL GEMS—Other Laws Governing Labor Relations

INTRODUCTORY NOTE—The purpose of this Chapter is to give the student an outline of the more important laws which apply to employers and unions and affect labor relations other than those discussed above. This Chapter outlines the principal labor laws to alert the students to various rights of employees and the obligations of employers and labor organizations.

1. The United States Constitution does not prohibit employment discrimination, as such, by private individuals, employers or unions unless it involves "state action".

    (a) Where the federal government discriminates, the Due Process Clause of the Fifth Amendment is usually the basis of the suit.

    (b) Where a state government discriminates, the Equal Protection Clause of the Fourteenth Amendment is usually the basis of a claim for relief.

    See generally Smith's Review, Constitutional Law, Chapter X, Fifth Amendment—Rights of Persons and Chapter XVII, Fourteenth Amendment—Limitations on the State. See also Chapter XVI, Thirteenth Amendment—Slavery and Involuntary Servitude and Chapter XVIII, Right of Citizens to Vote.

2. The previous Chapters of this Review have analyzed early labor laws, the National Labor Relations Act, as amended, and the Labor-Management Reporting and Disclosure Act. This Chapter outlines the basic provisions of the following laws:

    (a) Title VII of the Civil Rights Act, as amended by the Equal Employment Opportunity Act,

    (b) Fair Labor Standards Act,

    (c) Equal Pay Act,

    (d) Age Discrimination in Employment Act,

    (e) Walsh-Healey Public Contracts Act,

    (f) Davis-Bacon Act,

    (g) Service Contract Act,

    (h) Executive Order No. 11246,

    (i) Occupational Safety and Health Act, and

    (j) Consumer Credit Protection Act.

LABOR LAW—EMPLOYMENT DISCRIMINATION

3. A plan to reorganize and consolidate the administration of federal civil rights programs became law on May 5, 1978. That plan was implemented by Executive Order No. 12067 in June 1978. The reorganization involves the following changes:

   (a) The Equal Employment Opportunity Coordinating Council was abolished and its functions were transferred to the EEOC, effective July 1, 1978.

   (b) The Office of Federal Contract Compliance of the Department of Labor received authority for federal contract compliance which was previously exercised by eleven government compliance agencies monitoring government contracts, effective October 8, 1978.

   (c) The EEOC received authority for equal opportunity in federal employment from the United States Civil Service Commission, effective January 1, 1979.

   (d) The EEOC received authority to enforce the Equal Pay Act and the Age Discrimination in Employment Act from the Wage and Hour Division of the Department of Labor, effective July 1, 1979.

4. Most of the laws which are discussed in this Chapter cover employers whose operations affect interstate commerce. The jurisdictional standard to be applied under each Act varies somewhat depending on the wording of the statute and the regulations of the governmental agency which administers the Act.

5. By contrast, some laws are applicable to employers by virtue of the fact that they have a contract with an agency of the federal government.

   e.g. By contracting with the federal government an employer agrees to comply with Executive Order No. 11246.

6. In any given situation the initial issue to resolve is the basis of the government's jurisdiction over the employer or union involved. Only then should conduct be analyzed to determine whether there is a violation.

LEGAL GEMS—Civil Rights Act—Equal Employment Opportunity Act—Introduction

1. Title VII of the Civil Rights Act of 1964, as amended by the Equal Employment Opportunity Act of 1972, 42 U.S.C.A. § 2000 et seq., prohibits discrimination based on race, color, religion, sex, and national origin in hiring and in all terms and conditions of employment by employers, employment agencies, and labor unions.

2. Title VII established the Equal Employment Opportunity Commission (EEOC) to administer the Act.

OTHER LAWS GOVERNING LABOR RELATIONS

3. The EEOC is composed of five members who are appointed by the President. The following offices are the principal operating units within the Commission:

   (a) Compliance, which includes the Conciliation Division,

   (b) General Counsel,

   (c) Office of Technical Assistance,

   (d) Office of Research,

   (e) State and Community Affairs,

   (f) Legislative Affairs, and

   (g) Public Affairs.

4. The EEOC has jurisdiction over:

   (a) employers with fifteen (15) or more employees for at least twenty or more calendar weeks in the year in an industry affecting commerce,

   (b) employment agencies which regularly secure employees for employers covered by the Act,

   (c) state and local employment agencies receiving federal assistance, and

   (d) labor unions engaged in an industry affecting commerce with fifteen (15) or more members or which operate a hiring hall.

5. Certain categories of employers are excluded from coverage of the Act, at least in part. These include:

   (a) religious organizations, with respect to employment of persons connected with religious activities, and

   (b) educational institutions with religious affiliation, on the basis of religion with regard to all their employees.

   See §§ 702, 703(e)(2).

   NOTE—Enterprises which are not covered by federal law may be subject to similar state laws.

6. The Act gives the Court power to order any equitable relief deemed appropriate to remedy the unlawful employment practice. This may include either a court order or an injunction requiring:

   (a) reinstatement or hiring of employees,

   (b) back pay,

   (c) elimination of the discriminatory employment practice, and

   (d) reasonable attorney's fees and costs.

7. An award of back pay is appropriate where there is an aggrieved class of employees, just as it is where there is only one discriminatee. This is so even though unnamed class members did not file charges with the EEOC and the employer acted in good faith. See Albemarle Paper Co. v. Moody, 422 U.S. 405, 95 S.Ct. 2362, 45 L.Ed.

LABOR LAW—EMPLOYMENT DISCRIMINATION

2d 280 (1975); Oatis v. Crown Zellerbach Corp., 398 F.2d 496 (5th Cir. 1968).

8. The general rule is that punitive damages are not allowed in suits for unlawful discrimination.

   (a) Section 706(g) of the Civil Rights Act of 1964 provides for "other equitable relief," but that does not include damages which are a legal (as distinguished from equitable) remedy.

   (b) The Civil Rights Act of 1866 does not provide for relief through damages or otherwise.

   NOTE—In one case back pay damages were awarded a female plaintiff. She was the victim of the defendant union's maintenance of two sex-segregated locals, which constituted an unlawful employment practice. The damages awarded to the plaintiff were calculated to restore her to her rightful economic place because of the discrimination against her. See Evans v. Sheraton Park Hotel, 503 F.2d 177 (D.C.Cir. 1974).

9. Attorney fees are awarded in suits brought under Section 706(k) of the Civil Rights Act as follows:

   (a) The prevailing plaintiff should ordinarily recover an attorney's fee unless special circumstances would render such an award unjust. See Albemarle Paper Co. v. Moody, 422 U.S. 405, 95 S.Ct. 2362, 45 L.Ed.2d 280 (1975); Newman v. Piggie Park Enterprises, 390 U.S. 400, 88 S.Ct. 964, 19 L.Ed.2d 1263 (1968).

   (b) The prevailing defendant should be awarded an attorney's fee only when the plaintiff's action is shown to have been frivolous, unreasonable, or without foundation, even though not brought in subjective bad faith. See Christiansburg Garment Co. v. EEOC, 434 U.S. 412, 98 S.Ct. 694, 54 L.Ed.2d 648 (1978).

LEGAL GEMS—Title VII—General Types of Discrimination Prohibited

1. Unlawful employment practices are specifically set forth in Section 703 of the Act. It provides:

   "(a) It shall be an unlawful employment practice for an employer

   "(1) to fail or refuse to hire or to discharge any individual, or otherwise to discriminate against any individual with respect to his compensation, terms, conditions, or privileges of employment, because of such individual's race, color, religion, sex, or national origin; or

   "(2) to limit, segregate, or classify his employees or applicants for employment in any way which would deprive or tend to deprive any individual of employment opportunities or otherwise adversely affect his status as an employee, be-

OTHER LAWS GOVERNING LABOR RELATIONS

cause of such individual's race, color, religion, sex, or national origin.

"(b) It shall be an unlawful employment practice for an employment agency to fail or refuse to refer for employment, or otherwise to discriminate against, any individual because of his race, color, religion, sex, or national origin, or to classify or refer for employment any individual on the basis of his race, color, religion, sex, or national origin.

"(c) It shall be an unlawful employment practice for a labor organization—

"(1) to exclude or to expel from its membership, or otherwise to discriminate against any individual because of his race, color, religion, sex, or national origin;

"(2) to limit, segregate, or classify its membership or applicants for membership, or to classify or fail or refuse to refer for employment any individual, in any way which would deprive or tend to deprive any individual of employment opportunities, or would limit such employment opportunities or otherwise adversely affect his status as an employee or as an applicant for employment, because of such individual's race, color, religion, sex, or national origin; or

"(3) to cause or attempt to cause an employer to discriminate against any individual in violation of this section."

2. Discrimination based upon race, color, religion, sex, or national origin by an employer, or union is also prohibited in any apprenticeship or other training program. See Section 703(d).

3. Title VII prohibits discrimination based on race, color, religion, sex or national origin in all terms, conditions, and privileges of employment. For example, employees are entitled to be free from unlawful discrimination with regard to:

(a) recruitment,

(b) classified advertising,

(c) job description,

(d) hire,

(e) utilization of physical facilities,

(f) transfer,

(g) promotion,

(h) discharge,

(i) wages and salaries,

(j) seniority,

(k) testing,

LABOR LAW—EMPLOYMENT DISCRIMINATION

(l) insurance coverage,

(m) pension and retirement benefits,

(n) referral to jobs,

(o) union membership, and

(p) causing or attempting to cause another to discriminate.

4. In addition, it is unlawful for an employer, employment agency or union to retaliate against any person for:

(a) filing a charge,

(b) participating in an EEOC investigation or hearing, or

(c) opposing any prohibited employment practice.

See Section 704(a).

5. Section 704(b) makes it an unlawful employment practice for an employer, employment agency, or union to print or publish any notice or advertisement regarding employment, referral for employment, or membership in a labor organization which indicates any preference, limitation or discrimination based on race, color, religion, sex, or national origin unless "religion, sex, or national origin is a bona fide occupational qualification for employment."

e.g. Newspaper advertisements for employment may not specify "male" or "female".

6. The exception to the non-discrimination provisions of Title VII for bona fide occupational qualifications is narrow and must be "reasonably necessary" to the business enterprise.

(a) The legislative history of the Act lists three examples:

(i) the preference of a French restaurant for a French cook,

(ii) employing men for a professional baseball team, and

(iii) employing a salesperson of a particular religion to sell religious articles.

(b) The United States Supreme Court has held that in certain situations prison guards may be limited to men. This was so because of the peculiarly hostile environment at the prison involved. See Dothard v. Rawlinson, 433 U.S. 321, 97 S.Ct. 2720, 53 L.Ed.2d 786 (1977).

LEGAL GEMS—Title VII—Specific Discriminatory Acts Prohibited

1. Tests administered to employees or prospective employees must be:

(a) necessary for safe and efficient operation of the employer's business,

(b) job related and shown to bear a significant relation to successful job performance, and

(c) the only reasonable method of employee selection.

OTHER LAWS GOVERNING LABOR RELATIONS

NOTE—Where the *effect* of a test is discriminatory, it is unlawful even though the test is fair in form. See CASE 80, above.

2. Where there has been discrimination against a protected class of persons, merely changing seniority and promotion procedures so that they are neutral on their face may perpetuate the discrimination. Such seniority and promotion procedures may be unlawful. See CASE 83, below.

3. When the Civil Rights Act was enacted, there were numerous state laws designed to protect the health and safety of female employees. These so called "protective statutes" limited the employment of women:

    (a) in certain hazardous occupations,

    (b) where they were required to lift more than a specified weight,

    (c) to a certain number of hours per day or per week, or

    (d) during certain hours of the night.

4. Where state "protective statutes" operate to discriminate against women, the statutes are void under Title VII.

    e.g. An employer refused to permit female employees to bid on jobs which required the employee to lift more than 35 pounds. This rule was adopted because of a state law. Certain female employees brought suit against their employer on the grounds that they were discriminated against because of their sex by being deprived of the opportunity to bid on certain jobs. The Court said that the weight limit was arbitrary, and the broad limitation involved the use of class stereotypes in which sex was the stereotyping factor. Individuals must be considered on the basis of individual capacities and not on the basis of any characteristics generally applicable to the group. The Court ordered the employer to "notify all of its workers that each of them who desires to do so will be afforded a reasonable opportunity to demonstrate his or her ability to perform more strenuous jobs on a regular basis. Each employee who is able to so demonstrate must be permitted to bid on and fill any position to which his or her seniority may entitle him or her." Thus, the refusal to permit women to bid on jobs that required lifting more than 35 pounds constituted unlawful sex discrimination. See Bowe v. Colgate-Palmolive Co., 416 F.2d 711 (7th Cir. 1969).

5. While Title VII prohibits discrimination against certain classes, discrimination against a sub-class within such a class is also unlawful.

    (a) An employer had a policy of not hiring women with pre-school age children, but it hired men with pre-school age children. A woman who was refused employment on that basis brought suit under Title VII. The lower courts found no unlawful sex discrimination because 75% to 80% of those hired to fill the job applied for were women. The United States Supreme Court reversed. It said that Section 703(a) required that persons of like qualifications be given equal employment opportunities irrespective of sex unless sex is a bona fide occupational qualification reasonably necessary to the normal operation of a business. Since there was no evidence that women with preschool age children were less able to perform the job than men with pre-school age children, the employment policy violated the Act. See Phillips v. Martin Marietta Corp., 400 U.S. 542, 91 S.Ct. 496, 27 L.Ed.2d 613 (1971).

(b) Female employees filed suit against their employer under Title VII alleging that the employer's disability insurance plan discriminated on the basis of sex because disabilities arising from pregnancy were excluded. The employer contended that the same sickness and accident plan was provided for all employees, and, therefore, there was no discrimination. The Court held that there was no unlawful discrimination in the absence of evidence that the exclusion of pregnancy disability was a pretext for discriminating against women. The plan did not exclude anyone from eligibility because of sex, but merely removed one physical condition, pregnancy, from the list of compensable disabilities. The employer's insurance package covered some risks and excluded others. The same insurance "package" was offered to all employees. There was no risk from which men were protected and women were not; there was no risk from which women were protected and men were not. That the "package" did not include all risks did not render it unlawful. Although pregnancy-related disabilities constitute an additional risk unique to women, the failure to compensate them for this risk did not destroy parity of benefits to men and women under the plan. "To hold otherwise would endanger the commonsense notion that an employer who had no disability benefits program at all does not violate Title VII even though the 'underinclusion' of risks impacts, as a result of pregnancy-related disabilities, more heavily on one gender than upon the other. Just as there is no facial gender based discrimination in that case, [where the employer has no benefits plan] so, too, there is none here." The suit was dismissed. See General Electric Co. v. Gilbert, 429 U.S. 125, 97 S.Ct. 401, 50 L.Ed.2d 343 (1977), petition for rehearing denied 429 U.S. 1079, 97 S.Ct. 825, 50 L.Ed.2d 800 (1977).

NOTE 1—In a subsequent case the Court held that an employer's policy of denying employees returning from pregnancy leave their accumulated seniority while on leave deprived them of employment opportunities because of their sex in violation of Title VII. The Court explained that the em-

OTHER LAWS GOVERNING LABOR RELATIONS

ployer's policy was more than the mere refusal to extend a benefit to women as in General Electric v. Gilbert, but it imposed on women a substantial burden which men need not suffer. Therefore, it violated Title VII. See Nashville Gas Co. v. Satty, 434 U.S. 136, 98 S.Ct. 347, 54 L.Ed.2d 356 (1977).

NOTE 2—In 1978 Congress amended the Act to specifically prohibit discrimination because of pregnancy. The effect of the amendment was to nullify the holding in General Electric v. Gilbert, above.

6. The term "religion" is defined to include "all aspects of religious observance and practice, as well as belief." Discrimination because of religion is prohibited "unless an employer demonstrates that he is unable to reasonably accommodate to an employee's or prospective employee's religious observance or practice without undue hardship on the conduct of the employer's business." Section 701 (j).

e.g. A collective bargaining agreement gave employees a choice of job and shift assignments based upon seniority. X voluntarily transferred to a department that operated 24 hours a day throughout the year. X's religious beliefs prohibited him from working on Saturdays. The employer was unwilling to permit X to work only four days per week because that would impair operations, either on X's job or the job from which another employee was temporarily transferred to perform X's work. The union was not willing to violate the seniority system by changing the work assignment of an employee with more seniority. X was discharged for refusing Saturday work. X filed suit against the employer and the union. The Court recognized that the employer and union were required to make "reasonable accommodations" to the religious needs of employees, but upheld the discharge because: (a) the seniority system itself was a significant accommodation to the needs of employees, (b) the parties who had agreed to the seniority system were not obligated to deny shift and job preference to one employee to accommodate the religious beliefs of another, (c) Title VII, § 703(h) specifically provides that the operation of a bona fide seniority system cannot be an unlawful employment practice, and (d) to require the employer to bear more than a de minimis cost to give X Saturdays off would place an undue hardship on the employer. Thus, there was no unlawful discrimination against X because of his religion and his suit was dismissed. See Trans World Airlines, Inc. v. Hardison, 432 U.S. 63, 97 S.Ct. 2264, 53 L.Ed.2d 113 (1977).

NOTE—Although not stated as a reason for its decision in Trans World Airlines, Inc. v. Hardison, above, the Court may have

LABOR LAW—EMPLOYMENT DISCRIMINATION

considered the fact that X voluntarily transferred to the job in question. When X transferred he knew that he would be required to work on Saturday because he did not have the required bidding seniority to select that day off. However, X chose to transfer and then asked his employer and union to accommodate his religious beliefs by permitting him to take Saturday off. This fact may have led the court to take a less sympathetic view of his situation than it would have if the transfer were involuntary.

7. The effect of the statutory provision in **GEM 6**, above, is to place the burden of going forward with evidence on the employer to demonstrate that accommodation of the religious practices of an employee will produce undue hardship.

8. The term "national origin" refers to the country where a person was born or the country from which his or her ancestors came.

e.g. An employer refused to hire a citizen of Mexico based on its policy of employing only citizens of the United States. X sued the employer under Title VII contending that she had been discriminated against because of her national origin. The Court said that "it would be unlawful for an employer to discriminate against aliens because of race, color, religion, sex, or national origin—for example, by hiring aliens of Anglo-Saxon background but refusing to hire those of Mexican or Spanish ancestry. Aliens are protected from illegal discrimination under the Act, but nothing in the Act makes it illegal to discriminate on the basis of citizenship or alienage." However, a citizenship requirement would be unlawful if it were used to disguise what is in fact national origin discrimination. In this case 96% of the employees at the plant involved were of Mexican ancestry. Thus, it is clear that the employer did not use the citizenship requirement as a pretext to discriminate because of national origin. The suit was dismissed. See Espinoza v. Farah Mfg. Co., 414 U.S. 86, 94 S.Ct. 334, 38 L.Ed.2d 287 (1973).

CASE 80—*only job related tests permissible for employees*

The employer was organized into five operating departments. Prior to passage of the Civil Rights Act, Negroes were only employed in the labor department which consisted of the lowest paid jobs. When the Act was passed the employer abandoned its policy of restricting Negroes to the labor department. However, the company retained its policy of requiring a high school education for employment in other departments. The employer also permitted its employees to transfer from the labor department if they made satisfactory scores, which was the national median for high school graduates, on two professionally prepared aptitude tests. New employees were required to pass both tests and have a high school education. Suit was brought by Negroes in the labor department charging the employer with racial discrimination under the Act. The Court of Appeals held that in the absence of a discriminatory purpose the employer's requirements were valid. Is it necessary to show a discriminatory motivation to prohibit testing or educational requirement?

Ans. No. "The Act proscribes not only overt discrimination but also practices which are fair in form, but discriminatory in operation. The touchstone is business necessity. If an employment practice which operates to exclude Negroes cannot be shown to be related to job performance, the practice is prohibited." The employer's "good intent or absence of discriminatory intent does not redeem employment procedures" that prevent minority employees from obtaining jobs through the use of tests which are not job related. The Court noted that neither the requirement of a high school education nor the passing of the aptitude test had any demonstrable relationship to the successful performance of the jobs for which they were used. Company contended: (a) the requirements were instituted based on its judgment that they would improve the overall quality of its work force, and (b) that the Act permitted use of "any professionally developed ability test" that is not "designed, intended or used to discriminate." The Court rejected those arguments by stating that the employer must show that the tests were job related to be valid. Since the employer in the present case denied jobs and transfers to Negroes because of requirements which were not job related, the employer violated the Act.

See Griggs v. Duke Power Co., 401 U.S. 424, 91 S.Ct. 849, 28 L.Ed.2d 158 (1971).

NOTE 1—The rule in the CASE above applies to all tests whether they affect initial employment, promotion, or transfer. For the requirements for test validation, see Guidelines on Employee Selection Procedures, 29 C.F.R. §§ 1607.1–1607.14.

NOTE 2—Company X had a policy of discharging any employee whose wages were garnished twice within a twelve-month period. This policy affected a disproportionate number of black employees. X was unable to show a business necessity for the rule, that is, that the garnishment policy fostered employee productivity and there was no alternative policy that would accomplish the same goal with a lesser racial impact. Does the rule violate Title VII of the Civil Rights Act? Ans. Yes. Although the garnishment rule was facially neutral it had a disproportionate impact on blacks. The application of CASE 80, above, is not limited to required qualifications for particular jobs or to employment policies which perpetuate prior racial discriminatory practices. It encompasses "all artificial, arbitrary, and unnecessary racial barriers to employment." Since the practical effect of the policy was to discriminate against blacks and there was no business necessity for the policy, it constituted a violation of Title VII of the Civil Rights Act. The Court rejected the employer's contention that only those facially neutral employment practices which had the effect of perpetuating prior discriminatory racial practices violate the Act. The case was remanded for a new trial. See Wallace v. Debron Corp., 494 F.2d 674

LABOR LAW—EMPLOYMENT DISCRIMINATION

(8th Cir. 1974). See also Legal Gems—Consumer Protection Act, below.

LEGAL GEMS—Title VII—Procedure for Instituting Suit

1. Cases are initiated under the Act by filing a charge with the EEOC.
   (a) The individual who believes that he or she is the victim of discrimination may file a charge.
   (b) A union or other organization may file a charge on behalf of the alleged discriminatee to keep the real charging party anonymous.
   (c) One of the EEOC's five Commissioners may file a charge.
   NOTE 1—The purpose of a Commissioner's charge is to permit the charging party to remain anonymous. The person or group writes a charge to one of the Commissioners and requests that a charge be filed. The Commissioner may, at his discretion, file a charge, which must be within the 180 day period.
   NOTE 2—The procedure described in NOTE 1, above, should be contrasted to NLRB procedures under which the Board cannot initiate charges itself.

2. A charge must be filed within 180 days after the alleged discrimination.
   (a) If the state has a fair employment practices commission with authority to provide relief in cases of employment discrimination, the charge must be filed with the appropriate state agency *before* the charge is filed with the EEOC.
   NOTE—Where a charge was received by the EEOC before state remedies were exhausted, it was proper to refer it to the appropriate state agency directly without formal filing. If the state agency declines to take action the Commission may then file the charge and take appropriate action itself. Thus, state proceedings may be initiated by the EEOC on behalf of the complainant. To require a second "filing" by the aggrieved party after termination of state proceedings would only add an unnecessary procedural technicality. See Love v. Pullman Co., 404 U.S. 522, 92 S.Ct. 616, 30 L.Ed.2d 679 (1972).
   (b) Where a charge is filed with the state agency, the charge must be filed with the EEOC within 300 days of the alleged discrimination or within thirty days after receiving notice that the state agency has terminated proceedings, whichever is earlier.

3. After a charge has been filed it is investigated, and the Commission determines whether there is reasonable cause to believe that the charge is meritorious.

OTHER LAWS GOVERNING LABOR RELATIONS

4. If the charge appears to be meritorious, the EEOC attempts to eliminate the unlawful practice through conciliation.

5. Court action may be initiated by the private party who filed the charge if:

    (a) 180 days have elapsed after the charge has been filed,

    (b) the charging party has received notice from the EEOC that the charge has been dismissed or that the agency has not filed suit, and

    (c) the EEOC has not signed a conciliation agreement with the charged party.

NOTE—The notice referred to above from the EEOC is known as a right to sue letter, and there is a ninety day time limit on the commencement of suit by the alleged discriminatee after such letter is received. Thereafter, the right to sue by the charging party is extinguished. See 43 U.S.C.A. § 2000e-5(f)(1).

6. The 180 day period is not a limitation on the EEOC for filing suit. See Occidental Life Ins. Co. v. EEOC, 432 U.S. 355, 97 S.Ct. 2447, 53 L.Ed.2d 402 (1977).

7. The Commission may institute suit at any time, provided:

    (a) at least thirty days have elapsed from the filing of the charge, and

    (b) the Commission shall have failed to obtain an acceptable conciliation agreement.

NOTE—There is a ninety day period when the charging party and the Commission have concurrent rights to bring suit. See EEOC v. Cleveland Mills Co., 502 F.2d 153 (4th Cir. 1974), cert. denied 420 U.S. 946, 95 S.Ct. 1328, 43 L.Ed.2d 425 (1975).

CAVEAT—When the Commission brings suit it is not on behalf of the charging party, but to further the public interest. Although a charge must be filed with the EEOC before it can institute suit, the Commission is not limited to the wording of the charge and may expand the discrimination alleged or the individuals affected by the discriminatory practices. See EEOC v. Huttig Sash & Door Co., 511 F.2d 453 (5th Cir. 1975).

8. If a charge is litigated, suit must be filed with the appropriate United States District Court by the charging party, the EEOC, or, in a few special situations, the Attorney General. By contrast, charges filed with the NLRB are prosecuted by that agency and initially adjudicated in an administrative hearing before an administrative law judge.

9. The Act provides for expedited handling of court cases. When suit is filed, Section 706(f)(5) calls for immediate appointment of a judge to hear and decide the case. Should 120 days elapse with

LABOR LAW—EMPLOYMENT DISCRIMINATION

the matter not scheduled for trial, the judge may appoint a master to hear the case and make findings of fact and conclusions of law.

10. The trial of a Title VII case proceeds as the normal civil action. The plaintiff has the burden of establishing a prima facie case of discrimination by a preponderance of the evidence. At that time the burden of going forward shifts to the defendant to show a legitimate nondiscriminatory reason for the action taken. The plaintiff then has the opportunity to rebut the defense to show it was pretextual. See CASE 81, below.

CAVEAT—The proof required to establish a violation is different depending upon which of the following theories is used:
   (a) disparate impact, where a practice is neutral on its face but has a discriminatory impact, no unlawful intent need be shown, and

   (b) disparate treatment, where there is an intent to discriminate, the unlawful intent must be shown.

11. An employee may pursue his claim under Title VII even though it has been arbitrated under the collective bargaining agreement between his employer and his union and the issue resolved against him.

e.g. X was discharged and filed a grievance under the collective bargaining agreement between his employer and union. The contract contained a non-discrimination clause, and X contended that he had been discharged because of his race. The union processed X's grievance through arbitration, but the discharge was upheld. X filed a charge with the EEOC and subsequently X sued his employer on the ground that he was unlawfully discharged because of his race. The employer moved to dismiss the suit on the ground that X's claim had been submitted to an arbitrator and resolved adversely to X. The Court said that the rights of an employee under a collective bargaining agreement and under the Act were independent of each other. Therefore, an employee may obtain a trial de novo in federal court even though his claim had been determined by an arbitrator. The arbitration decision is admissible at the trial and may be given whatever weight the Court deems appropriate. See Alexander v. Gardner-Denver Co., 415 U.S. 36, 94 S.Ct. 1011, 39 L.Ed.2d 147 (1974).

CASE 81—*Title VII suit—plaintiff has burden of proof*

A number of employees were laid off as part of a general reduction in the employer's work force. X, one of those laid-off employees, was a Negro and a long time activist in the civil rights movement. After his layoff, X protested his termination and the general hiring practices of the employer, claiming that they were racially motivated. As part of this protest, X, and other members of CORE

(Congress of Racial Equality), illegally stalled their cars on main roads leading to the employer's plant, for the purpose of blocking access to it at the time of the morning shift change. This tied up traffic and prevented many employees from reporting to work. X was arrested for obstructing traffic. He pleaded guilty and was fined. On another occasion, X participated in a civil rights demonstration by ACTION, a civil rights organization. This latter incident resulted in a chain and padlock being placed on the front door of one of the employer's buildings, preventing its occupants from leaving. Three weeks after the layoff the company advertised for mechanics, which was X's trade. The company refused to recall X because he participated in the "stall in" and "lock in". X filed charges with the Equal Employment Opportunity Commission, claiming that he was not rehired because of his race and his involvement in the civil rights movement. The Commission found reasonable cause to believe that the employer refused to rehire Green because of his civil rights activities, but it made no finding concerning the charge of racial bias. X filed suit against the company alleging discrimination on both counts. The District Court dismissed the suit insofar as it alleged racial discrimination, on the grounds that the Commission had failed to make a determination concerning reasonable cause to believe that the company's actions were racially motivated. It also found that the company's refusal to recall X was based solely on his participation in the illegal demonstrations, not on his legitimate civil rights activities, and dismissed that aspect of the suit. Was that ruling correct?

Ans. No. There are only two prerequisites to filing suit in the District Court: (a) the filing of a timely charge with the EEOC, and (b) receiving and acting upon the commission's statutory notice of the right to sue. That the Commission failed to rule on one allegation in the charge did not bar a suit based upon that allegation. Therefore, the case was remanded for a new trial on the question of whether the employer discriminated against X because of his race.

The Court next considered another issue which involved the shifting of the burden of going forward with evidence at trial. On that issue it said: "The complainant in a Title VII trial, must carry the initial burden under the statute of establishing a prima facie case of racial discrimination. This may be done by showing: (i) that he belongs to a racial minority; (ii) that he applied and was qualified for a job for which the employer was seeking applicants; (iii) that, despite his qualifications he was rejected; and (iv) that, after his rejection, the position remained open and the employer continued to seek applicants from persons of complainant's qualifications." In the present case, the Court found that X established these elements and so the burden of going forward with evidence shifted, at that point, to the employer to show some legitimate, nondiscriminatory reason for rejecting X. The employer offered evidence that X's unlawful conduct against it was the cause for his rejection. That was sufficient to discharge the employer's burden at that stage and to meet X's prima facie case of discrimination. "Nothing in Title VII compels an employer to absolve and rehire one who has engaged in such deliberate, unlawful activity against it. . . . While Title VII does not, without more, compel rehiring of respondent, neither does it permit petitioner to use respondent's conduct as a pretext" for discriminating against him. When the new trial is conducted, X must be afforded an opportunity to show that the company's stated reasons for rejecting him were a pretext to cover up its discriminatory motivations. The Court noted that: "Especially relevant to such a showing would be evidence that white employees involved in acts against petitioner of comparable seriousness to the stall in, were nevertheless retained or rehired. Petitioner may justifiably refuse to rehire one who was engaged in unlawful, disruptive acts against it, but only if this criterion is applied alike to members of all races." For the above reasons, the case was remanded for a new trial to permit X to rebut the employer's defense which X had not been permitted to do in the original hearing of the case because of a ruling by the trial judge.

    See McDonnell Douglas Corp. v. Green, 411 U.S. 792, 93 S.Ct. 1817, 36 L.Ed.2d 668 (1973). See also Smith's Review, Evidence, Chapter III, Burden of Proof, Presumptions and Inferences.

NOTE 1—Three black bricklayers brought suit against an employer for discrimination under Title VII. They applied for work at the job site and were qualified. They were not hired and the positions remained open for some time thereafter. Those facts established a prima facie case under the rule in CASE 81, above, even as to one of the persons bringing suit who was subsequently hired. The prima facie case raises an inference of discrimination because, if those facts were not otherwise explained, it is more likely than not that the employer based hiring practices on an impermissible consideration such as race. To dispel the adverse inference the employer need only show a legitimate nondiscriminatory reason for the rejection of the applicant. The employer explained the necessity of employing only highly skilled fire-bricklayers in performing its work on blast furnaces in steel mills with firebrick. For that reason only persons known to be skilled or recommended as skilled in this type of work were hired. Bricklayers were hired only for a particular job. Statistics offered by the employer showed that only 5.7 percent of the bricklayers in the relevant labor force were minority group members, but 13.3 percent of the man-days on this job were worked by black bricklayers. The lower court did not give sufficient consideration to the statistics offered by the employer and found a Title VII violation because the employment system used did not consider the qualifications of the largest number of minority applicants. That was error. Statistics showing the racial mix of the work force should be considered in determining an employer's motivation. Further, Title VII "does not impose a duty to adopt a hiring procedure that maximizes hiring of minority employees." The case was remanded for consideration of the employer's defenses. See Furnco Constr. Corp. v. Waters, 438 U.S. 567, 98 S.Ct. 2943, 57 L.Ed. 2d 957 (1978).

NOTE 2—In a later case, the Court explained that there was a difference between showing a legitimate nondiscriminatory reason for the action taken and showing the absence of a discriminatory motive. It is only necessary to show a legitimate nondiscriminatory reason to meet the employee's prima facie case of discrimination. The employer is not required to prove the absence of any discriminatory motive. See Board of Trustees of Keene State College v. Sweeney, — U.S. —, 99 S.Ct. 295, 58 L.Ed.2d 216 (1978).

OTHER LAWS GOVERNING LABOR RELATIONS

LEGAL GEMS—Class Actions Under Title VII

1. The charging party may sue not only to remedy the alleged discrimination himself, but also to remedy the discrimination against all other employees similarly affected. This is known as a class action.

2. A class action may be brought under Title VII if the following requirements are met:

   (a) the class action meets the requirements of Rule 23, Federal Rules of Civil Procedure,

   (b) the plaintiff has standing to raise the issues in the complaint, which is, the plaintiff has been aggrieved, and

   (c) the issues were raised in a charge before the EEOC.

   See Oatis v. Crown Zellerbach Corp., 398 F.2d 496 (5th Cir. 1968).

3. It is not necessary for each member of the class to file a charge with the EEOC in order for them to join in the class action and share in a remedial back pay order.

CAVEAT—A class action should be distinguished from actions in the public interest brought by the EEOC. Class suits serve different ends than public interest suits. A suit in the public interest by the EEOC is governed by a desire to achieve broad public goals and the need to harmonize public policies that may be in conflict. Class actions seek to vindicate the rights of specific individuals, the class members. See Bryan v. Pittsburgh Plate Glass Co., 494 F.2d 799 (3rd Cir. 1974), cert. denied 419 U.S. 900, 95 S.Ct. 184, 42 L.Ed.2d 146 (1974), reh. denied 420 U.S. 913, 95 S.Ct. 836, 42 L.Ed.2d 844 (1975).

LEGAL GEMS—Preliminary Injunctive Relief

1. Section 706(f)(2) of Title VII empowers the EEOC to seek a preliminary injunction where "prompt judicial action is necessary to carry out the purpose of this Act."

2. An action for a preliminary injunction, that is, a temporary restraining order effective until the decision is rendered on the merits of the case, may be brought by the Commission at any time after a charge is filed.

3. Traditionally, courts consider the following factors in deciding whether to grant or deny a preliminary injunction:

   (a) the probability of ultimate success after a trial on the merits,

   (b) whether there will be irreparable injury if the injunction is not granted,

LABOR LAW—EMPLOYMENT DISCRIMINATION

    (c) the potential hardships between the parties which may result from granting or withholding injunctive relief, and

    (d) the public interest.

4. The party seeking the injunction must present sufficient evidence to show the likelihood of success on the merits. It is not necessary to prove the case with absolute certainty. See Pride v. Community School Bd., 482 F.2d 257 (2d Cir. 1973); EEOC v. Tufts Institution of Learning, 421 F.Supp. 152 (D.C.Mass.1975); Garza v. Texas Educational Foundation, Inc., 565 F.2d 909 (5th Cir. 1978).

5. Some courts have said that the traditional requirement of irreparable injury need not be established by the EEOC to obtain an injunction. Those courts reason that irreparable injury should be presumed from the fact that the statute has been violated, and the Commission is entrusted with enforcement of the Act. See United States v. Hayes Int'l Corp., 415 F.2d 1038 (5th Cir. 1969); EEOC v. Pacific Press Pub. Ass'n, 535 F.2d 1182 (9th Cir. 1976).

    NOTE—The alleged discriminatee may suffer irreparable injury if preliminary relief is not granted, and that fact may be shown. In granting such a preliminary injunction one court stated: "Unless preliminary injunctive relief is granted, it is certainly possible that qualified women will not be promoted. . . . Positions in the interim would be filled and thus unavailable to qualified women even if they succeeded in later obtaining permanent injunctive relief. While back pay might offer some relief, the relief would obviously be inadequate since Title VII prohibits discrimination not only with respect to compensation, but also with respect to 'terms, conditions, or privileges of employment' . . . . Discrimination with respect to terms, conditions or privileges of employment may be difficult, if not impossible, to compensate with money damages." Leisner v. New York Tel. Co., 358 F.Supp. 359, 369 (S.D.N.Y.1973).

6. In exercising its discretion to grant preliminary relief, the court balances the equities between the parties and the possible injuries to them which may result from granting or withholding injunctive relief. See Johnson v. University of Pittsburgh, 359 F.Supp. 1002 (W.D.Pa.1973); EEOC v. Liberty Mutual Ins. Co., 346 F.Supp. 675 (N.D.Ga.1972).

    e.g. In considering whether to order an employer to reinstate an employee, the court will weigh the hardship on the alleged discriminatee against the potential hardship or harm to the employer.

7. Courts consider whether relief is in the public interest. Courts are more likely to grant relief to further the public interest than would be done if only private interest were involved. See EEOC

OTHER LAWS GOVERNING LABOR RELATIONS

v. Tufts Institution of Learning, 421 F.Supp 152 (D.C.Mass.1975); Gulf King Shrimp Co. v. Wirtz, 407 F.2d 508 (5th Cir. 1969).

LEGAL GEMS—EEOC Reporting Requirements

1. Certain organizations are required to keep records and submit reports to assist the EEOC in administering Title VII.

2. All employers with 100 or more employees are required to submit information annually to the EEOC listing the number of employees in specified job categories by race, sex and national origin. The form is known as EEO-1, and it is also used by the OFCC.

3. Labor organizations with 100 or more members must file information on Form EEO-3. The form asks whether the union membership includes specified minority groups and women, and the reason for exclusion of such persons where it exists.

4. The statistical information regarding the make up of an employer's work force and union's membership may be used to establish a prima facie case of discrimination when it is compared to the minority representation in the area.

5. The prima facie case based on statistics may be rebutted by showing non-discriminatory hiring after becoming subject to the Act or that hiring practices were justified by some legitimate purpose such as safety or efficiency. See Senter v. General Motors Corp., 532 F.2d 511 (6th Cir.), cert. denied 429 U.S. 870, 97 S.Ct. 182, 50 L.Ed.2d 150 (1976). See also Hazelwood School Dist. v. United States, 433 U.S. 299, 97 S.Ct. 2736, 53 L.Ed.2d 768 (1977); Furnco Constr. Corp. v. Waters, 438 U.S. 567, 98 S.Ct. 2943, 57 L.Ed.2d 957 (1978).

CAVEAT—Although statistics are not conclusive, they are a very useful and important method of establishing a prima facie case. As one court said: "In the problem of racial discrimination, statistics often tell much, and courts listen." Alabama v. United States, 304 F.2d 583, 586 (5th Cir. 1962).

LEGAL GEMS—Fair Labor Standards Act

1. The Fair Labor Standards Act, 29 U.S.C.A. § 201 et seq., was enacted in 1938. It has been amended on numerous occasions since that date, usually to expand coverage and increase the minimum wage.

    e.g. In 1974 coverage was expanded to include most employees of the federal government, including the United States Postal Service.

2. The principal provisions of the Act include:

    (a) the payment of a specified minimum wage,

(b) overtime payment for more than forty (40) hours of work in any work week at a rate of one and one-half times the employee's regular wage rate, and

(c) the prohibition of child labor.

NOTE 1—The provisions outlined above are administered by the Wage and Hour Division of the Department of Labor.

NOTE 2—The Act also prohibits sex discrimination in the payment of wages. That provision is now administered by the EEOC. See LEGAL GEMS—Equal Pay Act, below.

3. In addition to the compensation due employees, the Act permits employees to recover:

   (a) reasonable attorney fees and costs, and

   (b) liquidated damages of 100 percent where the violation is wilful.

4. Wilfulness is not determined by the good faith of an employer, but by whether the employer knew or should have known that compensation was due employees under the Act.

   (a) Liquidated damages may be imposed unless an employer can show not only that the violation was in good faith, but also that there were reasonable grounds to believe that it was not violating the Act. See Reid v. Day & Zimmerman, 73 F.Supp. 892 (D.C.Iowa 1947).

   (b) Reliance on the opinion of counsel does not prevent assessment of liquidated damages where the attorney's opinion was contrary to the view of the Wage and Hour Division of the Department of Labor. See Gustafson v. Fred Wolferman, 73 F.Supp. 186 (D.C.Mo.1947).

5. The provisions of the Act may be enforced by suit in "any court of competent jurisdiction," federal, state, or municipal, by the Secretary of Labor or by the alleged discriminatee.

6. Class actions are not permitted under the Act as they are for suits under Title VII of the Civil Rights Act. For members of a class to recover, they must "opt in" the suit filed by another employee. That means they must authorize suit to be brought for them in writing.

7. The statute of limitations for bringing suit is:

   (a) two years for non-wilful violations, and

   (b) three years for wilful violations.

8. Criminal penalties may be imposed for wilful violations, including the failure to keep records of hours worked. Criminal penalties are enforced by the Justice Department. See 29 U.S.C.A. § 216.

OTHER LAWS GOVERNING LABOR RELATIONS

LEGAL GEMS—Equal Pay Act

1. The Equal Pay Act of 1963, 29 U.S.C.A. § 206(d), is an Amendment to the Fair Labor Standards Act. It was enacted to equalize pay to men and women performing the same job and requires that equal work be rewarded by equal wages.

2. The Act prohibits employers from discriminating on the basis of sex in the payment of wages. It also prohibits unions from causing or attempting to cause an employer to discriminate in violation of the Act.

3. To establish a prima facie case under the Act the Secretary of Labor, who administers the Act, must show that an employer pays different wages to employees of opposite sexes for "equal work on jobs the performance of which requires equal skill, effort, and responsibility, and which are performed under similar working conditions." The Secretary has the burden of proof on this issue.

4. The Act establishes four exceptions to the general rule. Different payments to employees of opposite sexes is permitted where it is made pursuant to:

    (a) a seniority system,

    (b) a merit system,

    (c) a system which measures earnings by quantity or quality of production, or

    (d) a differential based on any other factor other than sex.

5. The burden of proof to show that the wage differential is justified under one of the exceptions above falls on the party charged because the exceptions are considered to be affirmative defenses.

6. Working conditions which would justify a higher base rate encompass:

    (a) surroundings, which measure such elements as toxic chemicals or fumes regularly encountered by the employee, and

    (b) hazards, which consider physical dangers encountered and their frequency.

7. The time of day worked cannot be considered a working condition sufficient to justify a higher base rate for a particular job. However, a night shift differential is permissible because it is applicable to all employees on a shift. See CASE 82, below.

8. To remedy a violation of the Equal Pay Act, the wages of the higher paid employee may not be reduced.

9. The Act has been administered by the EEOC since July 1, 1979. Formerly it was administered by the Wage and Hour Division of the Department of Labor.

LABOR LAW—EMPLOYMENT DISCRIMINATION

CASE 82—unequal base rates for the same work on different shifts unlawful

When the Equal Pay Act was enacted, a company employed only men on its night shift as inspectors to comply with state law. In order to obtain men to do this job they gave them a higher base rate than inspectors on the day shift who were females. The higher night base rate was in addition to a separate night shift differential. In order to bring itself into compliance with the Act the company permitted women to bid on night shift inspector jobs. Those who bid for the job successfully were given the higher base rate that the men were receiving in addition to the night shift differential. An action was brought against the company by the Secretary of Labor alleging that the higher base rate for night shift inspectors violated the Act. Is the contention valid?

Ans. Yes. The Court said that inspection work done on the night shift did not justify a higher base rate for those inspectors because the work itself was the same as the day shift, and the shift on which work was performed was insufficient reason in itself. Even though women were permitted to bid for the job of inspecting on the night shift, and those women received the higher base rate, the inspectors on the day shift, who were all females, continued to receive a lower base rate. Thus, the day shift inspectors were discriminated against in violation of the Equal Pay Act. The employer contended that the violation was cured when a later collective bargaining agreement provided equal base rates for inspectors on the day and night shifts. However, the new contract continued the unequal base rates for inspectors employed before the effective date of the contract. Those were known as red circle rates. (See Chapter II, above for definition.) The Court concluded that the red circle rates perpetuated the effect of the company's past conduct and were, therefore, unlawful.

See Corning Glass Works v. Brennan, 417 U.S. 188, 94 S.Ct. 2223, 41 L.Ed. 2d 1 (1974).

NOTE—This decision illustrates the difficulties in which a company can find itself because of changing labor laws. Initially, men were employed on the night shift because state law prohibited females from working on that shift. A higher base rate was necessary for night shift inspectors because men would not work for the rate paid to women inspectors on the day shift. Developments in labor law invalidated the law prohibiting women from working on night shifts. The more recent Equal Pay Act required equal wages for men and women doing the same work. Since the employer did not equalize the base rates of inspectors on the day and night shifts, the employer was found to have violated the Act. The treating of the higher base rate as a red circle rate did not bring the employer into compliance with the Act; the law required the raising of lower base rates so that all inspectors were paid the highest rate applicable for the equal work.

LEGAL GEMS—Age Discrimination In Employment Act

1. The Age Discrimination In Employment Act of 1967, 29 U.S.C.A. §§ 621–634, is designed to promote the employment of older workers based on ability rather than age.

OTHER LAWS GOVERNING LABOR RELATIONS

2. The Act applies to companies with twenty or more employees in an industry affecting commerce. It also applies to employment agencies and labor organizations.

3. The Act, as amended, prohibits age discrimination in employment for most persons between 40 and 70 years of age in:

    (a) hiring,

    (b) discharge,

    (c) compensation, and

    (d) other terms, conditions, or privileges of employment.

4. The Act does not apply where:

    (a) age is a bona fide occupational qualification reasonably necessary to the normal operations of a business,

    (b) the different treatment is based on reasonable factors other than age.

    e.g. A seniority system or employee benefit plan which is not a subterfuge to evade the Act,

    (c) an employee is discharged for good cause.

5. The Act was amended in 1978 to prohibit:

    (a) private employers from requiring employees to retire before age 70, and

    (b) the federal government from requiring its employees to retire at any specified age.

6. To remedy violations of the Act a written charge must be filed within 180 days after the discrimination. The aggrieved person must then wait 60 days before filing suit.

7. The Act was administered by the Secretary of Labor, who could make investigations, issue rules and regulations for administration of the law, and enforce its provisions by legal proceedings when voluntary compliance could not be obtained. Since July 1, 1979 the Act has been administered by the EEOC.

LEGAL GEMS—Walsh-Healey Public Contracts Act

1. The Walsh-Healey Public Contracts Act, 41 U.S.C.A. §§ 35–45, sets basic labor standards for work performed pursuant to a contract with the United States government.

2. The Act applies to contractors and subcontractors where the contract exceeds $10,000.00 in value for materials, supplies, articles, equipment, or naval vessels.

3. Under the Act the Secretary of Labor is authorized to determine the prevailing minimum wages for similar work in the locality in

LABOR LAW—EMPLOYMENT DISCRIMINATION

which the contract work is to be performed. The contractor must pay such wage rates to his employees.

4. Overtime at the rate of one and one-half times the hourly rate must be paid for all work in excess of eight hours per day or forty hours per week, whichever number of overtime hours is greater. The overtime must be based on all work performed by the employee, whether on the government contract or on other work.

NOTE—This is a change from the overtime provisions of the Fair Labor Standard Act which only requires payment of overtime for more than forty hours of work in a week.

5. A contractor who violates the Act must make up the underpayment to employees involved. In addition, violations may be punished by cancellation of the government contract with any additional cost charged to the original contractor, and the withholding of government contracts from the offending firm for three years.

6. The Act is administered by the Secretary of Labor.

LEGAL GEMS—Davis-Bacon Act

1. The Davis-Bacon Act, 40 U.S.C.A. §§ 276a–276a–5, provides that laborers and mechanics engaged in public construction be paid wages and fringe benefits comparable to those for similar jobs in the locality.

2. The Act applies whenever the government contract exceeds $2,000.00.

3. The prevailing wage scale is determined by the Secretary of Labor, and it is incorporated into the contract as minimum rates of pay.

NOTE—As a practical matter, that rate is determined by the collective bargaining agreements which the various building trade unions have negotiated in the area. Thus, a nonunion employer has no advantage in bidding for federal contracts over a unionized contractor.

4. Each contracting federal agency has the duty of enforcing the provisions of the Act. The Department of Labor has the duty to see that there is a coordinated and consistent enforcement by the responsible federal agencies.

LEGAL GEMS—Service Contract Act

1. The Service Contract Act, 41 U.S.C.A. §§ 351–358, was enacted to ensure adequate standards for service employees working under a service contract with the federal government in excess of $2,500.00.

   e.g. Contracts for services subject to the Act include laundry and drycleaning, maintenance, guard services, and persons engaged in any trade or craft.

OTHER LAWS GOVERNING LABOR RELATIONS

2. The Act requires the contractor or subcontractor to include a statement of the minimum wages to be paid to service employees as well as their fringe benefits in the contract with the government.

    (a) Where the contractor is bound by a collective bargaining agreement, those wages and fringe benefits are used.

    (b) If there is no collective bargaining agreement, the Secretary of Labor determines the prevailing wages and fringe benefits for such employees in the locality and those rates of pay are incorporated into the contract between the employer and the government.

3. The Act also requires contractors to provide safe and helpful working conditions in a sanitary, hazard free work place for employees.

4. The Act is administered by the Department of Labor which has authority to investigate and prosecute violations of the Act.

LEGAL GEMS—Executive Order No. 11246—Office of Federal Contract Compliance

1. Executive Order No. 11246, 3 C.F.R. 339, was issued by President Johnson on September 24, 1965. As amended, this Order prohibits discrimination by government contractors and subcontractors on the basis of race, color, religion, sex, or national origin. Regulations implementing the Order are contained in Revised Order No. 4, 41 C.F.R. 60–60.

2. Executive Order No. 11246 provided for the creation of the Office of Federal Contract Compliance (OFCC) within the Department of Labor to administer its provisions and to ensure that no federal contracts were awarded to companies practicing discrimination in employment.

3. The Order applies to all employers doing work under a government contract except where the face amount is less than $10,000.00 per year or the work is performed outside the United States.

4. The principal provisions of the Order are as follows:

    (a) A standard clause must be included in government contracts under which the employer agrees not to discriminate among employees because of race, color, religion, sex or national origin.

    (b) Each nonconstruction contractor with fifty employees or more must maintain a written affirmative action compliance program for each of its establishments with a time table for the achievement of full, equal employment opportunity. Similar affirmative action plans are required for contractors in the construction industry.

    (c) Help wanted advertising must identify the contractor as an equal opportunity employer.

LABOR LAW—EMPLOYMENT DISCRIMINATION

(d) Each union with which the employer has a contract must be notified of the employer's obligations under the Executive Order.

(e) The employer must furnish required information, file compliance reports and permit access to its books for the purpose of ascertaining compliance.

5. The employer must include the same provisions in every non-exempt subcontract and purchase order, and agree to take such action as may be dictated by the contracting agency to bring about compliance by subcontractors and vendors.

6. In the construction industry, the OFCC assists local contractors, unions, minority group representatives, civic leaders and others in preparing areawide agreements for achieving equal job opportunity. In addition, it provides technical assistance to communities seeking to develop such agreements. In localities which do not have established guidelines for achieving equal job opportunity, bidders on federally assisted construction work must submit affirmative action plans setting specific goals and time tables for hiring and training minority group members.

NOTE—The OFCC has an agreement with the Equal Employment Opportunity Commission (EEOC), whereby compliance reviews are coordinated between the two agencies and information on contractors is exchanged. Generally, the OFCC handles the broad, company-wide compliance reviews while the EEOC handles complaints of discrimination filed by individuals.

7. If a complaint of discriminatory practice is filed, the OFCC attempts to resolve the matter through conciliation, involving the contracting agency and the party making the allegation.

8. If conciliation fails, public hearings are then held by the contracting agency or by the OFCC. The OFCC may also recommend that the Civil Rights Division of the Justice Department or the Equal Opportunity Employment Commission handle certain cases. See CASE 83, below.

9. The failure of the contractor to comply with Executive Order No. 11246 may result in suspension or cancellation of the government contract. Further, the contractor or subcontractor may also be debarred from future contract work for the federal government until the employer has satisfied the OFCC that he has established and will carry out the employment policies in compliance with the Order.

CASE 83—*seniority system carrying forward effects of former, discriminatory system found unlawful*

An employer maintained "lines of progression" for jobs in its paper mill. Jobs within each line were functionally related so that experience in one job served as training for the next. Prior to the Civil Rights Act of 1964, certain lines of progression were reserved for white employees and other lines for Negroes. The Papermakers Union represented all employees, but it had different locals for white and Negro employees. Generally, the jobs reserved for white employees paid higher wages and carried greater responsibility than jobs reserved for Negroes. Promotion within each line was determined by job seniority in the slot below it in the line of progression. The seniority system also worked to give white employees preference on recalls. When the Civil Rights Act was passed the company and the two union locals agreed to merge the lines of progression in each department by pay rates. In all jobs except one, this meant taking the Negro lines to the bottom of white lines. Negro employees could thereby advance to jobs formerly restricted to white employees. However, they were not able to bid for the better jobs in the white lines because they lacked job seniority in the slot below the vacancy. The OFCC concluded that this new seniority system was unlawful because it perpetuated the discriminatory effects of the old system. The OFCC proposed a seniority system which would permit Negroes to bid on all job vacancies in the new, combined lines of progression and informed the employer that it would receive no more government contracts unless the seniority system proposed by the OFCC were adopted. After bargaining to an impasse with the local unions, the company put the OFCC seniority system into effect unilaterally. The white employees then voted to strike. The United States government filed suit for an injunction to prevent the strike, and for a declaratory judgment to ascertain the lawful seniority system to be used. The government asked that the job seniority system be declared illegal and that mill seniority, that is the total time employed at the mill, be used for all purposes. The employer and the union contended that after the merger of the white and Negro lines of progression, there was a racially neutral system of job seniority. The fact that the new system preferred whites in filling vacancies was not unlawful racial discrimination. Is a racially neutral job seniority system valid where it tends to perpetuate the effects of the former, discriminatory seniority system?

Ans. No. There are three theories which can be applied in the present case: (a) the "freedom now" theory under which Negroes could displace white incumbents who would not hold their present jobs *but for* the discrimination, (b) the "status quo" theory under which merely ending the discriminatory practice is sufficient regardless of the continued effects of past discrimination, and (c) the "rightful place" theory under which the future awarding of vacant jobs must not be based on a prior, discriminatory seniority system, but incumbent employees could not be bumped from their present position. It has been held that "reliance on a standard, neutral on its face, is no defense under the Act when the effect of the standard is to lock the victims of racial prejudice into an inferior position." The employer and union contend that the status quo theory satisfies their legal obligations. However, the job seniority system is not essential to the safe and efficient operation of the employer's mill. Thus, there is no business necessity for it, and it would adversely affect future bidding by Negroes. This system would tend to perpetuate past discrimination and should not be adopted. It is not necessary to use the "freedom now" or "but for" theory under the circumstances of this case. Some experience is required to fill the higher paid jobs. The rightful place theory is the most appropriate theory to apply. As applied to the present case, the selection of an employee to fill a vacant job must be based on total seniority at the employer's mill where both white and Negro employees hired under the discriminatory seniority system bid for the job. However, where time in another job is reasonably required to fill a vacancy, such job experience may be required. Thus, the employer need not promote an employee based on mill seniority alone, but can deny a promotion to an employee who lacks the ability or qualifications to perform the job properly. The Court concluded that the job seniority system which carried forward the discriminatory system without any business necessity was unlawful. The Court directed the institution of the seniority system permitting Negroes who were hired under the old discriminatory system to use mill seniority. This protects the victims of past discrimination, and permits job seniority to be used where such persons are not affected.

See Local 189, United Papermakers and Paperworkers Union and Crown Zellerbach Corp. v. United States, 416 F.2d 980 (5th Cir. 1969), cert. denied 397 U.S. 919, 90 S.Ct. 926, 25 L.Ed.2d 108 (1970).

NOTE—The Court also granted other relief to end discriminatory practices including the merger of the white and Negro locals.

LEGAL GEMS—Occupational Safety and Health Act

1. The Occupational Safety and Health Act of 1970, 29 U.S.C.A. §§ 651–678, was enacted "to assure so far as possible every working man and woman in the Nation safe and healthful working conditions and to preserve our human resources."

2. The Act applies to every employer engaged in a business affecting commerce, except employers covered by other federal safety and health laws, such as the Federal Coal Mine Health and Safety Act and the Atomic Energy Act.

3. The Act created the Occupational Safety and Health Administration (OSHA) within the Department of Labor. OSHA has primary responsibility for administering the provisions of the Act, as well as the safety and health provisions of some other Acts.

4. The procedure followed under 29 U.S.C.A. § 657 is as follows:

    (a) The Labor Department, either on its own initiative or based on a request from others, may inspect the premises of an employer to ascertain whether there is compliance with safety and health standards. The Act authorizes inspections "without delay and at reasonable times".

    (b) A "walk-around" inspection of the premises of an employer is conducted, during which a union or other employee representa-

OTHER LAWS GOVERNING LABOR RELATIONS

tive and a management representative are entitled to accompany the OSHA representative.

(c) If the investigator believes that there are violations, a written citation is issued "with reasonable promptness" setting forth with particularity the violation charged.

(d) Citations must be promptly posted near the place of each violation and fix a reasonable time for abatement.

(e) When a citation is issued, the employer is separately notified of the proposed penalty. The employer has fifteen working days to contest either the citation or the penalty.

(f) If a citation is contested there is a hearing before an administrative law judge of the Occupational Safety and Health Review Commission (OSHRC) and testimony is taken under oath.

(g) The decision of the administrative law judge may be appealed by the employer, the employee representative or OSHA to the three-member OSHRC.

(h) The OSHRC decision may be appealed to an appropriate United States Court of Appeals within sixty days. Final review may be sought in the United States Supreme Court.

NOTE—The findings of the OSHRC will be upheld by the Court if they are supported by substantial evidence on the record as a whole. If no appeal is pending after sixty days, the Clerk of the Court of Appeals may enter a decree enforcing the order.

5. If a danger is discovered during the "walk-around" which could reasonably be expected to cause death or serious physical harm before it could be eliminated through normal enforcement procedures, injunctive relief may be sought to remove the imminent danger, including a shutdown of the plant, if necessary.

6. The citation may propose a monetary penalty even for initial violations.

    (a) A $1,000 penalty may be imposed for each violation, whether classified as serious or non-serious.

    (b) A willful or repeated violation subjects the employer to a fine of up to $10,000 for each violation.

    (c) The failure to correct a violation within the time prescribed subjects the employer to a penalty of up to $1,000 for each day the violation continues.

7. Periodic reports are required from employers on work-related deaths, injuries, and illnesses, other than minor injuries requiring only first aid treatment.

8. Discrimination against an employee for filing a complaint or exercising any right under the Act is prohibited. Such a charge must

be filed within thirty days of the alleged discrimination. If the charge has probable merit, the Secretary of Labor will file suit in the United States District Court against the charged party. Remedies include reinstatement with back pay.

9. The Act also established a National Institute of Occupational Safety and Health (NIOSH) within the Department of Health, Education, and Welfare. NIOSH has research and educational responsibilities, as well as authority to develop and recommend occupational safety and health standards.

LEGAL GEMS—Consumer Credit Protection Act

1. The Consumer Credit Protection Act of 1968, as amended, 15 U.S. C.A. §§ 1671–1677, reflects congressional concern over the unscrupulous and unfair use of wage garnishments by creditors. The Act was enacted to protect employees from "predatory extensions of credit."

2. Under the Act a limit is placed on the earnings of an employee which may be garnisheed in either a federal or state court. That limit may vary depending on the circumstances. See 15 U.S.C.A. § 1673.

3. The Act prohibits the discharge of an employee because of a garnishment for any one indebtedness. "One indebtedness" refers to a single debt regardless of the number of levies made or creditors seeking satisfaction.

4. The Act provides only criminal penalties for a willful violation. However, the employee has an implied, private civil remedy for a discharge made unlawful by the statute. See Stewart v. Travelers Corp., 503 F.2d 108 (9th Cir. 1974).

5. The Secretary of Labor is charged with enforcement of the Act.

TABLE OF CASES

References are to Pages

Adair v. United States, 16
Adams Dairy, Inc., NLRB v., 76
Aero Corp. v. NLRB, 69
Alabama v. United States, 205
Albemarle Paper Co. v. Moody, 189, 190
Alexander v. Gardner-Denver Co., 200
Allied Chem. Workers v. Pittsburgh Plate Glass Co., 25
Allis-Chalmers Mfg. Co., NLRB v., 113
Amalgamated Ass'n of Street, Elec. Ry. and Motor Coach Employees v. Lockridge, 168
Amalgamated Lithographers of America, NLRB v., 147
American Broadcasting Cos. v. Writers Guild, 117
American Cable Systems, Inc., NLRB v., 68
American Federation of Television & Radio Artists (Great Western Broadcasting Corp. d/b/a KXTV), 142
American Federation of Television & Radio Artists (Hearst Corp.), 140
American League of Professional Baseball Clubs, 26
American Nat. Ins. Co., NLRB v., 61
American Newspaper Publishers Ass'n v. NLRB, 122
American Potash & Chem. Corp., 178, 179
American Seating Co., 175
American Shipbuilding Co. v. NLRB, 57
Anderson Federation of Teachers v. School City of Anderson, 103
Arlan's Dept. Store, 51
Avco Corp. v. Aero Lodge No. 735, Int'l Ass'n of Machinists and Aerospace Workers, 22

Babcock & Wilcox Co., NLRB v., 43
Baptist Hospital, NLRB v., 41
Barton Brands, Ltd., 109
Beacon Castle Square Bldg. Corp. v. NLRB, 136
Bell Aerospace Co., Div. of Textron, Inc., NLRB v., 186
Bernel Foam Prods. Co., 67

Black-Clawson Co. v. Intern of Machinists, 78
Blue Flash Express, Inc., 35
Board of Trustees of Keene State College v. Sweeney, 202
Boeing Co., NLRB v., 113
Boire v. Greyhound Corp., 180
Booster Lodge 405, I. A. M. v. NLRB, 111
Bowe v. Colgate-Palmolive Co., 193
Boys Markets, Inc. v. Retail Clerk's Union, Local 770, p. 22
Brooks v. NLRB, 70
Brown, NLRB v., 57
Brown, United States v., 165
Bryan v. Pittsburgh Plate Glass Co., 203
Budd Mfg. Co., Edward G. v. NLRB, 49
Burns Int'l Security Services, Inc., NLRB v., 91
Burnup & Sims, Inc., NLRB v., 39

C & C Plywood Corp., NLRB v., 84
C & S Industries, 95
Calhoun v. Harvey, 163
Carey v. Westinghouse, 85
Carolina Supplies and Cement Co., 26
Carpenters Dist. Council of Denver & Vicinity, AFL–CIO (Rocky Mountain Prestress, Inc.), 120
Case Co., J. I. v. NLRB, 71
Cheney California Lumber Co. v. NLRB (Lumber & Sawmill Workers Local 2647), 120
Christiansburg Garment Co. v. EEOC, 190
City of (see name of city)
Collyer Insulated Wire, 95
Commonwealth v. ———— (see opposing party)
Connell Constr. Co. v. Plumbers and Steamfitters, Local 100, p. 23
Construction, Bldg. Material and Miscellaneous Drivers Local Union No. 83, Int'l Bhd. of Teamsters (Marshall and Haas), 145
Container Corp., 175
Corning Glass Works v. Brennan, 208
Cumberland Shoe Corp., 68, 69

Smith's Review of Labor Law 2d Ed.

TABLE OF CASES
References are to Pages

Cal-Tex Optical Co., 34
Denver Bldg. & Constr. Trades Council, NLRB v., 137
Detroy v. American Guild of Variety Artists, 164
Dixie Ohio Express Co., 85
Dorchy v. Kansas, 128
Dothard v. Rawlinson, 192
Douds v. Metropolitan Federation of Architects, Engineers, Chemists & Technicians, 139
Douglas Corp., McDonnell v. Green, 202
Dubo Mfg. Co., 94
Dunlop v. Bachowski, 162
Duplex Printing Press Co. v. Deering, 18

Eastex, Inc. v. NLRB, 44
EEOC v. Cleveland Mills Co., 199
EEOC v. Huttig Sash & Door Co., 199
EEOC v. Liberty Mutual Ins. Co., 204
EEOC v. Pacific Press Pub Ass'n, 204
EEOC v. Tufts Institution of Learning, 204
Electronic Reproduction Service Corp., 95
Elk Lumber Co., 38
Emporium Capwell Co. v. Western Addition Community Organization, 79
Erie Resistor Co., NLRB v., 55
Espinoza v. Farah Mfg. Co., 196
Essex Int'l, Inc., 43
Evans v. Sheraton Park Hotel, 190
Excelsior Underwear, Inc., 181
Exchange Parts Co., NLRB v., 36

Falsetti v. Local 2026, United Mine Workers of America, 166
Farmer v. United Bhd. of Carpenters, Local 25, p. 166
Farmers' Cooperative Congress, 45
Fibreboard Paper Prods. Corp. v. NLRB, 78
Fleetwood Trailer Co., NLRB v., 50
Florida Power & Light Co. v. International Bhd. of Elec. Workers Local 641, p. 117
Ford Motor Co. v. Huffman, 154
Franks Bros. Co. v. NLRB, 72
Fruit and Vegetable Packers, Local 760, NLRB v., 142
Furnco Constr. Corp. v. Waters, 202, 205

G & S Metal Prods. Co., 37
Gamble Enterprises, Inc., NLRB v., 123
Garza v. Texas Educational Foundation, Inc., 204
Gateway Coal Co. v. United Mine Workers, 53

General American Transp. Corp., 95
General Elec. Co. v. Gilbert, 194, 195
General Elec. Co. v. NLRB, 60
General Elec. Co., NLRB v., 64
General Knit of California, Inc., 183
General Motors Corp., 76
Gissel Packing Co., NLRB v., 68
Globe Machine and Stamping Co., 176
Golden State Bottling Co. v. NLRB, 89
Golub Corp., NLRB v., 34
Grand Lodge of Machinists v. King, 162
Granite State Joint Bd., Textile Workers Local 1029, NLRB v., 111
Great Dane Trailers, Inc., NLRB v., 54
Griggs v. Duke Power Co., 197
GTE Lenkurt, Inc., 43
Guernsey-Muskingum Elec. Co-op, NLRB v., 37
Gulf King Shrimp Co. v. Wirtz, 205
Gustafson v. Fred Wolferman, 206

Hayes Int'l Corp., United States v., 204
Hazelwood School Dist. v. United States, 205
Hershey Chocolate Corp., 175
Highway Truck Drivers and Helpers Local 107 v. Cohen, 164
Holdeman v. Sheldon, 164
Hollywood Ceramics Co., 183
Honaker, Charles E., 65
Houston Bldg. and Constr. Trades Council (Claude Everett Constr.), 131
Howard Johnson Co. v. Hotel & Restaurant Employees Detroit Local Joint Bd., 93
Hudgens v. NLRB, 129
Humphrey v. Moore, 157
Hunt, Commonwealth v., 15
Hutcheson, United States v., 21

Independent Metal Workers Union, Local 1 and Local 2, Hughes Tool Co., 108
Industrial Union of Marine and Shipbuilding Workers of America, AFL-CIO, NLRB v., 114
Insurance Agents' Int'l Union, AFL-CIO, 30
Insurance Agents Int'l Union, NLRB v., 60, 121
International Ass'n of Machinists v. Street, 168
International Ass'n of Machinists (Jones Constr. Co.), 151
International Bhd. of Teamsters, Chauffeurs, Warehousemen, and Helpers of America, Local 695, AFL v. Vogt, Inc., 128

TABLE OF CASES
References are to Pages

International Harvester Co., 96
International Hod Carriers, Bldg. and Common Laborers Union, Local 840, AFL–CIO (Blinne Constr. Co.), 133
International Ladies Garment Workers Union v. NLRB, 48
International Ladies' Garment Workers Union v. Quality Mfg. Co., 40
International Longshoremen's & Warehousemen's Union, CIO, Local 6, (Sunset Line & Twine Co.), 106
International Longshoremen's & Warehousemen's Union, Local 50, NLRB v., 152
International Molders' and Allied Workers Union, Local No. 125, AFL–CIO (Blackhawk Tanning Co.), 115
International Rice Milling Co., NLRB v., 135
International Typographical Union, AFL–CIO v. NLRB, 116
International Union of Elec., Radio and Machine Workers, AFL–CIO, Local 485 (Automotive Plating Corp.), 107
International Union of Operating Engineers, Local 513 (Long Constr. Co.), 119
International Union, UAW v. NLRB, 75
Isis Plumbing and Heating Co., 31

Jacobs Mfg. Co., NLRB v., 84
Jenkins v. William Schluderberg-T. J. Kurtle Co., 153
Johnson v. University of Pittsburgh, 204
Jones & Laughlin Steel Corp., NLRB v., 26
Jubilee Mfg. Co., 45

Katz, NLRB v., 66
Kohler Co., 52

Laidlaw Corp. v. NLRB, 51
Lane v. NLRB, 57
Leedom v. Kyne, 180
Leisner v. New York Tel. Co., 204
Linden Lumber Div., Summer & Co. v. NLRB, 70
Lithographers and Photoengravers Int'l Union (Holiday Press), 105
Local 12, Rubber Workers v. NLRB, 110
Local 68, Wood, Wire & Metal Lathers Union, 152
Local 174, Teamsters, Chauffeurs, Warehousemen & Helpers of America v. Lucas Flour Co., 88

Local 182, Int'l Bhd. of Teamsters, Chauffeurs, Warehousemen and Helpers of America (Woodward Motors), NLRB v., 125
Local 189, Amalgamated Meat Cutters v. Jewel Tea Co., 21, 23
Local 189, United Papermakers and Paperworkers Union and Crown Zellerbach Corp. v. United States, 214
Local 357, International Bhd. of Teamsters, Chauffeurs, Warehousemen & Helpers of America v. NLRB, 118
Local 456, Int'l Bhd. of Teamsters (J. R. Stevenson Corp.), 123
Local 761, Int'l Union of Electrical, Radio and Machine Workers, AFL–CIO v. NLRB, 138
Local 983, United Bhd. of Carpenters and Joiners of America, AFL–CIO, 31
Local 1229, IBEW (Jefferson Standard Broadcasting Co.), NLRB v., 39
Local 4186, United Steelworkers of America, AFL–CIO (McGraw Edison Co.), 115
Local 12419, International Union of Dist. 50 (National Grinding Wheel Co.), 111
Local 14055, United Steelworkers of America, AFL–CIO (Dow Chem. Co.), 143
Loewe v. Lawlor, 16
Love v. Pullman Co., 198

Mackay Radio & Telegraph Co., NLRB v., 54
Magnavox Co., NLRB v., 42
Mallinckrodt Chem. Works, 178
Mar-Jac Poultry Co., 72
Mastro Plastics Corp. v. NLRB, 55
Meat & Highway Drivers, Local 710 v. NLRB, 149
Metropolitan Life Ins. Co., 178
Metropolitan Life Ins. Co. v. NLRB, 177
Metropolitan Life Ins. Co., NLRB v., 178
Miami Newspaper Pressmen's Local 46 (Knight Newspapers, Inc.), 140
Midwest Pipe and Supply Co., 47
Miranda Fuel Co., Inc., NLRB v., 109
Mitchell v. International Ass'n of Machinists, 167
Monticello Charm Tred Mills, Inc., 173
Morrison Cafeterias Consolidated, Inc., 75

Nashville Gas Co. v. Satty, 195
National League of Cities v. Usery, 97

TABLE OF CASES
References are to Pages

National Woodwork Mfrs. Ass'n v. NLRB, 147
New York, City of v. De Lury, 103
New York Local 11, National Ass'n of Broadcast Employees and Technicians, AFL–CIO (NBC), 122
Newman v. Piggie Park Enterprises, 190
NLRB v. ——— (see opposing party)

Oatis v. Crown Zellerbach Corp., 190, 203
Occidental Life Ins. Co. v. EEOC, 199
Ozark Trailers, Inc., 75

Pacific Intermountain Express Co., 176
Peerless Plywood Co., 180
Phelps Dodge Corp. v. NLRB, 50
Phillips v. Martin Marietta Corp., 194
Pipefitters Local Union No. 562 v. United States, 169
Plasterers' Local 79, NLRB v., 150
Port Drum Co., 107
Porter Co., H. K. v. NLRB, 73
Post Pub. Co., NLRB v., 46
Price v. NLRB, 115
Pride v. Community School Bd., 204
Progressive Mine Workers v. NLRB, 119
Pullis, Commonwealth v., 14

Quaker City Life Ins. Co., 177

Radio Officers' Union v. NLRB, 118
Radio & Television Broadcast Engineers Union, Local 1212, IBEW (CBS), NLRB v., 151
Reid v. Day & Zimmerman, 206
Republic Aviation Corp. v. NLRB, 42
Retail Clerks Int'l Ass'n, Local 324 (Barber Bros. Corp.), 132
Retail Clerks Int'l Ass'n, Local Union No. 899 (State-Mart, Inc.), 131
Robinson Chevrolet, Roy, 95
Royal Plating & Polishing Co., NLRB v., 75, 76

Sailor's Union of the Pacific (Moore Dry Dock Co.), 139
Salzhandler v. Caputo, 160
Savair Mfg. Co., NLRB v., 182
Scofield v. NLRB, 113
Sears, Roebuck & Co. v. San Diego County Dist. Counsel of Carpenters, 43
Senter v. General Motors Corp., 205
Servette, Inc., NLRB v., 141
Shea Chem. Corp., 47
Shopping Kart Food Market, 183
Siemons Mailing Service, 26

Smitley, d/b/a Crown Cafeteria v. NLRB, 131
Spielberg Mfg. Co., 94
Steele v. Louisville & Nashville Railroad Co., 155
Stewart v. Travelers Corp., 216
Stoddard-Quirk Mfg. Co., 44
Struksnes Constr. Co., 35
Teamsters Local 200 v. NLRB, 55
Teamsters Local 327 (Coca-Cola Bottling Works of Nashville), 105
Texas & New Orleans Railroad Co. v. Brotherhood of Railway Clerks, 18
Textile Workers Union v. Darlington Mfg. Co., 58
Textile Workers Union v. Lincoln Mills of Alabama, 85
Thermo-Rite Mfg. Co., NLRB v., 25
Thornhill v. Alabama, 128
Trans World Airlines, Inc. v. Hardison, 195
Tri-County Medical Center, Inc., 44
Truck Drivers Local 568 v. NLRB, 110
Truitt Mfg. Co. v. NLRB, 65

Union de Tronquistas de Puerto Rico, Local 901, International Brotherhood of Teamsters (Lock Joint Pipe & Co.), 119
United Bhd. of Carpenters and Joiners of America, AFL–CIO, Local No. 639 (American Modulars Corp.), 145
United Federation of Postal Clerks v. Blount, 100
United Furniture Workers (Colonial Hardwood Flooring Co.), 105
United Furniture Workers of America, CIO, 31
United Mine Workers of America v. Patton, 136
United Mine Workers of America v. Pennington, 20
United Mine Workers of America and United Mine Workers of America, District 2 (Solar Fuel Co.), 107
United Mine Workers of America, Dist. 12 (Truax-Traer Coal Co.), 125
United Packinghouse Workers Union v. NLRB, 44
United States v. ——— (see opposing party)
United States Gypsum Co., 174
United Steelworkers of America v. American Mfg. Co., 86
United Steelworkers of America v. Enterprise Wheel & Car Corp., 87
United Steelworkers of America v. NLRB (Carrier Corp.), 138

TABLE OF CASES
References are to Pages

United Steelworkers of America v. Warrior & Gulf Navigation Co., 87
Universal Camera Corp. v. NLRB, 30

Vaca v. Sipes, 154, 158
Vegelahn v. Guntner, 15

Wallace v. Debron Corp., 197
Weingarten, Inc., J., NLRB v., 40
Weltronic Co. v. NLRB, 76
West Coast Gasket Co., NLRB v., 35

Westinghouse Elec. Corp., 74
Wiley & Sons, Inc., John v. Livingston, 90, 91
Wirtz v. Hotel, Motel and Club Employees Union, Local 6, p. 161
Wood, Wire and Metal Lathers Int'l Union (Acoustical Contractors Ass'n), 150
Wooster Div. of Borg-Warner Corp., NLRB v., 77
Wyman-Gordon Co., NLRB v., 185

*

TABLE OF FEDERAL STATUTES

(See also Table of Statutory References and Index)

Age Discrimination in Employment Act, 208
Civil Rights Act, 188
Clayton Act, 16
Consumer Credit Protection Act, 216
Davis-Bacon Act, 210
Equal Pay Act, 207
Executive Order No. 11246—Office of Federal Contract Compliance, 211
Fair Labor Standards Act, 205
Federal Service Labor Management and Employee Relations Law, 98
Labor-Management Relations Act of 1947 (Taft-Hartley Act), 27
Labor-Management Reporting and Disclosure Act of 1959 (Landrum-Griffin Act), 28, 158
Landrum-Griffin Act, 28, 158
Lloyd-LaFollette Act of 1912, p. 98
National Labor Relations Act of 1935 (Wagner Act), 24
Norris-LaGuardia Act of 1932, p. 19
Occupational Safety and Health Act, 214
Railway Labor Act of 1926, p. 18
Service Contract Act, 210
Sherman Act, 16
Title VII, Civil Rights Act, 188
Walsh-Healey Public Contracts Act, 209

*

TABLE OF STATUTORY REFERENCES

(See also Table of Federal Statutes and Index)

NATIONAL LABOR RELATIONS ACT

(As Amended)

N.L.R.B. Sec.	This Work Page
7	32
8(a)	102
8(a)(1)	32, 33, 34, 36, 39, 40, 44, 57, 129
8(a)(2)	32, 45, 47
8(a)(3)	32, 48, 49, 56, 58
8(a)(4)	32, 48
8(a)(5)	32, 59, 69, 70, 119
8(b)	60, 102
8(b)(1)(A)	48, 104, 105, 109, 110, 113, 135
8(b)(1)(B)	104, 115
8(b)(2)	49, 104, 117
8(b)(3)	104, 119, 124
8(b)(4)	104, 126, 127, 133
8(b)(4)(i)	140
8(b)(4)(ii)(A)	126
8(b)(4)(ii)(B)	126, 134, 144, 145

NATIONAL LABOR RELATIONS ACT

(As Amended)

N.L.R.B. Sec.	This Work Page
8(b)(4)(ii)(D)	149, 150
8(b)(5)	104, 121
8(b)(6)	104, 122
8(b)(7)	104, 125, 127, 130, 131, 132
8(b)(7)(C)	132, 145
8(c)	105
8(d)	51, 72, 83, 119, 124
8(e)	28, 133, 146, 147, 148
8(g)	104, 123, 124
9(a)	59, 78
9(b)(1)	176
10(b)	46
10(k)	149, 150
203(d)	94
301	85, 156
303	136

INDEX

References are to Pages

AGE DISCRIMINATION IN EMPLOYMENT ACT
Other laws governing labor relations, 208

ALLY DOCTRINE
Picketing and boycotts, 139

AMENDMENT OF CERTIFICATION
Representation proceedings, 177

ANALYSIS OF A LABOR LAW PROBLEM, 5
Development of labor legislation, 5
Employer unfair labor practices, 6
Federal labor legislation, 5
Union unfair labor practices, 6

ANTITRUST ACTS USED AGAINST LABOR
Clayton Act, 17
Sherman Act, 16

APPROPRIATE BARGAINING UNIT
Representation proceedings, 170, 175

AREA STANDARDS PICKETING
Picketing and boycotts, 130

ASSISTANCE
Employer unfair labor practices, 45

BACK PAY
Remedies, 31

BENEFITS
Rights of employees, 33

BOYCOTTS
Picketing and boycotts, 125

CHARGES UNDER NATIONAL LABOR RELATIONS ACT
Unfair labor practice charges, 2

CHART I
Types of charges under the N.L.R.A., Unfair Labor practice charges, 2

CHART II
Types of petitions which may be filed under the N.L.R.A., 4

CHART III
Permissible employer conduct before an N.L.R.B. election, 171

CHART IV
Impermissible employer conduct before an N.L.R.B. election, 172

CHARTS
Chart, I, p. 2
Chart II, p. 4
Chart III, p. 171
Chart IV, p. 172

CIVIL RIGHTS ACT
Attorney fees, 190
Class actions, 203
Damages, 190
EEOC, 189
General types of discrimination prohibited, 190
Introduction, 188
Only job-related test permissible for employees, 196
Plaintiff has burden of proof, 200
Preliminary injunction relief, 203
Procedure for instituting suit, 198
Reporting requirements, 205
Specific discriminatory acts prohibited, 192
Unlawful employment practices, 190

CLAYTON ACT
Definition and analysis, 17

COLLECTIVE BARGAINING
Good faith bargaining, 78
No duty to bargain with sub-group of employees who are represented by union, 79
Rights of individual employees, 78

COLLECTIVE BARGAINING AGREEMENT
Analysis, 80
Arbitration, 82
Bargaining required when jobs are eliminated, 84
Court favors arbitration of disputes, 86

Smith's Review of Labor Law 2d Ed.

INDEX
References are to Pages

COLLECTIVE BARGAINING AGREEMENT—Cont'd
Court may compel arbitration of grievance, 86
Discipline and discharge, 81
Discrimination, 81
Dues checkoff, 81
Duration of contract, 82
Duties during contract period of the agreement, 83
Enforcement of a collective bargaining agreement, 85
Grievance procedure, 82
Holidays, 81
Introduction, 80
Management rights, 81
N.L.R.A. and arbitration proceedings, 94
No strike or lockout, 82
Obligations of successor employers, 88
Other pay provisions, 82
Pension and insurance programs, 82
Probationary employees, 81
Rates and classifications, 81
Recognition, 81
Reopening, 82
Seniority, 81
Separability, 82
Successorship, 81
Typical clauses, 80
Union shop, 81
Vacation, 82
Wage reopening clause, limits employer's duty to bargain, 84
Work schedule, 81
Working conditions, 81
Wrapup clause, 82

COMMUNICATIONS AMONG EMPLOYEES
Employer unfair labor practices, 41
Working time, 42

COMPUTATION OF BACK PAY
Remedies, 31

CONSUMER CREDIT PROTECTION ACT
Other laws governing labor relations, 216

CONTRACT BAR
Representation proceedings, 175

CRAFT UNIT
Representation proceedings, 178

DAVIS–BACON ACT
Other laws governing labor relations, 210

DEFINITIONS
See also Terminology Used in Labor Relations, 7–13
Ally doctrine, 139
Amendment of certification, 177
Appropriate bargaining unit, 170, 175
Area standards picketing, 130
Assistance, 45
Back pay, 31
Boycott, 125
Certification of representative, 172
Clayton Act, 17
Collective bargaining, 78
Contract bar, 175
Craft unit, 178
Decertification, 172
Domination, 45
Economic striker, 50
Featherbedding, 122
Good faith bargaining, 59
Hiring hall, 117
Hot cargo, 146
Judicial review, 179
Jurisdictional disputes, 149
Labor-Management Relations Act of 1947, p. 27
Landrum-Griffin Act, 28
Lockout, 56
National Labor Relations Board, 30
No distribution rules, 41
No solicitation rules, 41
Norris-LaGuardia Act, 19
Peerless Plywood Rule, 180
Picketing, 125
Questions concerning representation, 175
Representation, 170
  Employer petition, 172
Runaway shop, 56
Secondary boycott, 125
Sherman Act, 16
Successorship, 88
Taft-Hartley Act, 27
Tree fruits doctrine, 142
Twenty-Four Hour Rule, 180
Unfair labor practice striker, 50
Unit clarification, 177
Withdrawal of union shop authority, 173
Working time, 42

DEVELOPMENT OF LABOR LEGISLATION
Antitrust Acts used against labor, 16
Common law decisions unfavorable to labor, 14
Injunction proper for breach of no strike clause where grievance subject to arbitration, 21
Introduction, 14

228

INDEX
References are to Pages

DEVELOPMENT OF LABOR LEGISLATION—Cont'd
Labor-Management Relations Act of 1947, p. 27
Labor-Management Reporting and Disclosure Act of 1959, p. 28
Landrum-Griffin Act, 14
National Labor Relations Act of 1935, p. 24
Norris-LaGuardia Act, 14, 19
Railway Labor Act, 18
Strike not a criminal conspiracy, antitrust acts interpreted, 21
Taft-Hartley Act, 14
Union agreement restraining competition without furthering federal labor policy, subject to antitrust laws, 22
Wagner Act, 14

DISCHARGE FOR CONCERTED ACTIVITIES
Concerted activity for mutual aid, 37
Discharge without anti-union motivation, held unlawful, 39
Discussion among employees of appointment of inexperienced foreman is protected activity, 37
Employee entitled to union representation and investigative interview, 40
Employer unfair labor practices, 36
Introduction and analysis, 36
Not all concerted activity protected, 38

DISCHARGES CAUSED BY UNION
Union unfair labor practices, 117

DISCRIMINATION BASED ON RACE, COLOR, RELIGION, SEX, OR NATIONAL ORIGIN
Employer unfair labor practices, 44

DISCRIMINATION FOR UNION ACTIVITIES
Discharge for union activities unlawful, 49
Employer unfair labor practices, 48

DOMINATION
Employer unfair labor practices, 45

DUE PROCESS CLAUSE
Picketing and boycotts, 125

ECONOMIC STRIKER
Rights of strikers, 50

EMPLOYER UNFAIR LABOR PRACTICES
Analysis of a labor law problem, 6
Communication among employees, 41

EMPLOYER UNFAIR LABOR PRACTICES—Cont'd
Competing unions, employer recognition prohibited, 47
Definition and analysis, 32
Discharge for concerted activities, 36
  For union activities, unlawful, 49
  Without anti-union motivation, held unlawful, 39
Discrimination, based on race, color, religion, sex, or national origin, 44
  For union activities, 48
  Regarding the hiring of employees unlawful, 49
Domination or assistance of union, 45
Employee entitled to union representation and investigative interview, 40
Introduction, 32
No solicitation and no distribution rules, 41
Prohibitions of union activities in the plant, the rules and exceptions, 44
Recognition of minority union violates Section 8(a)(2), good faith no defense, 47
Remedies for domination or assistance, 46
Rights, of employees, 33
  Of strikers, 50
Temporary or permanent plant closing, 56

EMPLOYER'S BARGAINING OBLIGATION
Board cannot require parties to agree to a specific contract clause, 72
Duration of bargaining order, 71
Good faith bargaining, 70
Individual employee privileges subservient to collective interests under Act's scheme of collective bargaining, 71

EQUAL EMPLOYMENT OPPORTUNITY ACT
Civil Rights Act, 188

EEOC
Analysis, 189
Jurisdiction, 189

EQUAL PAY ACT
Other laws governing labor relations, 207

FAIR LABOR STANDARDS ACT
Other laws governing labor relations, 205

INDEX
References are to Pages

FEATHERBEDDING
Analysis, 122
Definition, 122
Full payment for minor services, is not featherbedding, 123
Payment for work not performed, 122

FINES
Union unfair labor practices, 112

FIRST AMENDMENT
Picketing and boycotts, 125

FOURTEENTH AMENDMENT
Picketing and boycotts, 125

FUTILITY OF UNIONIZATION
Rights of employees, 33

GOOD FAITH BARGAINING
Analysis, 59
Bad faith bargaining shown by course of conduct, 62
Collective bargaining, 78
Concept, 59
Employer's bargaining obligation, 70
Insisting on clause giving employer great control over employment terms, not unlawful per se, 61
Introduction, 59
Obligations arising during collective bargaining, 64
Obtaining bargaining rights, 66
Partial closing, 75
Subjects for bargaining, 73

HIRING HALL
Union unfair labor practices, 117

HOT CARGO
Picketing and boycotts, 146

INITIATION FEES
Union unfair labor practices, 121

INTERROGATION
Rights of employees, 33

JUDICIAL REVIEW OF REPRESENTATION CASES
Representation proceedings, 179

JURISDICTIONAL DISPUTES
Picketing and boycotts, 149

LABELS
RC, 172
RD, 172
RM, 172
UD, 173

LABOR LAW
Analaysis of a labor law problem, 5
Introduction, 1

LABOR–MANAGEMENT REPORTING AND DISCLOSURE ACT OF 1959
Other rights of employees, 158

LABOR RELATIONS UNDER STATE LAWS
Public sector bargaining, 100

LANDRUM–GRIFFIN ACT
Definition and analysis, 28
Labor-Management Reporting and Disclosure Act of 1959, p. 28
Other rights of employees, 153

LLOYD–LaFOLLETTE ACT
Public sector bargaining, 98

LOCKOUT
Temporary or permanent plant closing, 56

NATIONAL LABOR RELATIONS ACT
Chart I, p. 2

NATIONAL LABOR RELATIONS ACT OF 1935
Definition and analysis, 24
Wagner Act constitutional under Interstate Commerce Clause, 25

NATIONAL LABOR RELATIONS BOARD
Conduct secret ballot elections, 30
Definition and analysis, 30
Functions, 30
Prevent and remedy unfair labor practices, 30

NATIONAL LABOR RELATIONS BOARD AND ARBITRATION PROCEEDINGS
Arbitration award binding on parties, 96
Collective bargaining agreement, 94

NATIONAL LABOR RELATIONS BOARD ELECTION PROCEDURE
Representation proceedings, 172

NO DISTRIBUTION RULES
Employer unfair labor practices, 41

NO SOLICITATION RULES
Employer unfair labor practices, 41

NO STRIKE CLAUSE
Rights of strikers, 51

INDEX
References are to Pages

NORRIS–LaGUARDIA ACT
Definition and analysis, 19
Development of labor legislation, 19

OBLIGATIONS ARISING DURING COLLECTIVE BARGAINING
Employer not required to show financial records if ability to pay not at issue, 64
Employer required to show financial records if ability to pay at issue, 64
Test, 64
Unilateral change in employment terms of employer during negotiations, held unlawful, 66

OBLIGATIONS OF SUCCESSOR EMPLOYERS
Duty to arbitrate may survive merger and bind successor, 89
Successor has duty to recognize union if majority of work force unchanged, 90
Successor has no duty to recognize union if work force substantially changed, 92
Successorship, 88

OBTAINING BARGAINING RIGHTS
Employer's right to insist on N.L.R.B. election under the Act, 69
Good faith bargaining, 66
Without an election after substantial employer violations, 67

OCCUPATIONAL SAFETY AND HEALTH ACT
Other laws governing labor relations, 214

OTHER LAWS GOVERNING LABOR RELATIONS
Age Discrimination in Employment Act, 208
Civil Rights Act, 188
　Equal Employment Opportunity Act, 188
Class actions, 203
Consumer Credit Protection Act, 216
Davis-Bacon Act, 210
EEOC, 189
Equal Pay Act, 207
Executive Order No. 11246, Office of Federal Contract Compliance, 211
Fair Labor Standards Act, 205
Introduction, 187
Occupational Safety and Health Act, 214
Seniority system carrying forward effects of former discriminatory system found unlawful, 213

OTHER LAWS GOVERNING LABOR RELATIONS—Cont'd
Service Contract Act, 210
Unequal base rates for the same work on different shifts unlawful, 208
Walsh-Healey Public Contracts Act, 209

OTHER RIGHTS OF EMPLOYEES
Bargaining agent must represent all employees fairly, 155
Employees may sue union under Section 301 for a violation of duty under contract, 156
Employee's right to sue on his own behalf, 153
Expenditure of union funds for political purpose limited, 168
Introduction, 153
Landrum-Griffin Act, 153
Member may not sue for Title IV violation, 163
No absolute duty to exhaust internal union remedies prior to suit, 163
No federal pre-emption of employee's right to sue union for arbitrary and capricious conduct under contract, 157
Responsibility of union officers, 164
Rights of union members under state law, 165
Rights under Landrum-Griffin Act, 158
State court jurisdiction preempted by federal labor law, 167
Union officers may be summarily removed from office, 162

PARTIAL CLOSING
Subjects for bargaining, 76

PEERLESS PLYWOOD RULE
Representation proceedings, 180

PICKETING AND BOYCOTTS
Ally doctrine, 139
Analysis of jurisdictional disputes, 149
Area standards picketing, 130
Board must consider all relevant factors in resolving jurisdictional disputes, 151
Broad statute prohibiting all picketing unconstitutional, 128
Circumstances where recognition picketing is prohibited, 129
Constitutionality of state laws regulating picketing, 127
Defenses to charge of unlawful secondary activity analyzed, 143
Definitions, 125
Due process clause, 125

INDEX
References are to Pages

PICKETING AND BOYCOTTS—Cont'd
Failure to file petition within thirty days is not excused by filing an unfair labor practice charge, 132
First Amendment, 125
Fourteenth Amendment, 125
Freedom of press, 127
Freedom of speech, 127
Hot cargo clauses unlawful, 146
Introduction, 125
Jurisdictional disputes, 149
Legal restrictions on secondary boycotts, 133
No absolute right to picket, 128
Other elements of secondary boycott, 140
Peaceful publicity picketing which specifies struck product permitted at business of a neutral employer, 142
Picketing of neutral employer permitted when primary employer is working there, 138
Picketing prohibited at gate reserved for neutral employers, 137
Primary boycott, 125
Prohibited activity, 126
Publicity picketing permitted even if the ultimate object is recognition, 131
Request to neutral employers not to handle certain goods is lawful, 141
Right to picket on private property and shopping mall explained, 128
Secondary boycott, 125
Situs of dispute, 138

Strike against general contractor to force him to stop doing business with subcontractor is secondary boycott, 136
Subcontracting, 148
Tree fruits doctrine, 142
Union may recapture lost work, 148

PROCEDURE AND REMEDIES
Back pay, 31
Computation of back pay, 31
Introduction, 29
Procedure before N.L.R.B. in unfair labor practice cases, 29
The board and its remedies, 30

PUBLIC SECTOR BARGAINING
Analysis, 97
Collective bargaining agreements for state employees, 101
In the federal government, 98
Introduction, 97
Labor relations under state laws, 100
Lloyd-LaFollette Act, 98

PUBLIC SECTOR BARGAINING—C't'd
Representation elections in the states, 101
State labor relations, unfair labor practices, 102

QUESTIONS CONCERNING REPRESENTATION
Representation proceedings, 175

RAILWAY LABOR ACT
Definition and analysis, 18

RECOGNITION PICKETING
Picketing and boycotts, 129

REMEDIES FOR DOMINATION OR ASSISTANCE
Definition and analysis, 46

REMEDIES FOR UNION UNFAIR LABOR PRACTICES
Union unfair labor practices, 119

REPRESENTATION PROCEEDINGS
Agency has discretion to make rules either through adjudication or rule-making procedures, 186
Amendment of certification, 177
Appropriate bargaining unit, 170, 175
Certification of representative, 172
Chart III, p. 171
Chart IV, p. 172
Company-wide units, extent of organization considered, 177
Contract bar, 175
Craft unit, 178
Decertification, 172
Failure to follow A.P.A. rulemaking requirements invalidates rule, 184
False election campaign statements may cause election to be set aside, 183
Influencing employees by unfair means invalidates election, 182
Introduction, 170
Involuntary recognition, 170
Judicial review of representation cases, 179
N.L.R.B. election procedure, 172
Original court review when board violates statute, 179
Peerless Plywood Rule, 180
Questions concerning representation, 175
Representation-employer petition, 172
Rulemaking authority of the N.L.R.B., 183
Section 552(a)(1) of the A.P.A., 184
Section 553 of the A.P.A., 184
Setting aside an election, 180

INDEX
References are to Pages

REPRESENTATION PROCEEDINGS—Cont'd
Severance of a craft unit, factors considered, 178
Showing of interest, 174
Thirty percent rule, 174
Twenty-Four Hour Rule, 180
Unit clarification, 177
Voluntary recognition by employer, 170
Withdrawal of union shop authority, 173

RESPONSIBILITY OF UNION OFFICERS
Other rights of employees, 164

RESTRAINT OR COERCION OF EMPLOYEES
Union unfair labor practices, 105

RESTRAINT OR COERCION OF EMPLOYER BY UNION
Union unfair labor practices, 115

RIGHTS OF EMPLOYEES
Benefits, 33
Futility of unionization, 33
Interrogation, 33
Pool of employees, 36
Section 8(a)(1), prohibits benefits to influence union activity, 36
Violations, 33
Surveillance, 33
Unlawful statements, 34
Unlawful statements which are isolated, 35

RIGHTS OF STRIKERS
Economic striker, 50
Employer unfair labor practices, 50
Limitation on strikes in contract and act not applicable to unfair labor practice strikes, 55
No strike clause, 51
Replacement of economic striker, may not discriminate against union supporters, 54
Unfair labor practice striker, 50
Withholding of benefits to striking employees to which they were entitled, held unlawful, 53

RIGHTS OF UNION MEMBERS UNDER STATE LAW
Other rights of employees, 165

RULEMAKING AUTHORITY OF THE NATIONAL LABOR RELATIONS BOARD
Representation proceedings, 183

RUNAWAY SHOP
Temporary or permanent plant closing, 56

SECONDARY BOYCOTTS
Picketing and boycotts, 133

SECRET BALLOT ELECTIONS
National Labor Relations Board, 30

SERVICE CONTRACT ACT
Other laws governing labor relations, 210

SETTING ASIDE AN ELECTION
Representation Proceedings, 180

SHERMAN ACT
Definition and analysis, 16

SHOWING OF INTEREST
Representation proceedings, 174

STRIKES AGAINST HEALTH CARE INSTITUTIONS
Union unfair labor practices, 123

SUBCONTRACTING
Picketing and boycotts, 148

SUBJECTS FOR BARGAINING
Analysis, 73
Mandatory or compulsory subject, 73
No strike clause, 73
Non-bargainable subject, 73
Party may not insist permissive bargaining subjects be included in contract, 77
Permissive subject, 73
Rules for partial closing of a business, 76
Subcontracting as a mandatory subject of bargaining, 77

SUCCESSORSHIP
Obligations of successor employers, 88

SURVEILLANCE
Rights of employees, 33

SUSPENSION
Union unfair labor practices, 112

TAFT–HARTLEY ACT
Definition and analysis, 27

TEMPORARY OR PERMANENT PLANT CLOSING
Analysis, 56
Discriminatory closing of entire business lawful, 58
Employer may lock out employees after impasse, 56
Lockout, 56
Partial closing, 56
Runaway shop, 56

INDEX
References are to Pages

TERMINOLOGY USED IN LABOR RELATIONS
Administrative law judge, 7
Affirmative order, 7
AFL–CIO, 7
Authorization card, 7, 174
Bargaining unit, 7, 176
Bid, 7
Boycott, 7, 125
Cease and Desist Order, 8, 29–31
Certification, 8, 172
Charge, 2, 8
Checkoff, 8, 81
Closed shop, 8, 27
Collective bargaining, 8, 78
Collective bargaining agreement, 8, 80
Contract bar, 8, 175
Craft, 8, 178
Dovetail seniority, 9, 156
Economic strike, 9, 50
Endtail seniority, 9
Equal Employment Opportunity Commission, 9, 188
Featherbedding, 9, 122
Globe election, 9, 176
Hearing officer, 9, 173
Hiring hall, 9, 177
Hot cargo, 9, 146
Impasse, 9, 64
Independent union, 13
Insulated period, 9, 175
International union, 12
Jurisdictional dispute, 10, 149
Local union, 13
Lockout, 10, 56
Maintenance of membership, 10, 49
Mass picketing, 10, 127–128
Most favored nation clause, 10
National Labor Relations Board, 5, 10
Peerless Plywood Rule, 10, 180
Petition, 10, 172
Picketing, 10–11, 125
Primary activity, 11, 133
Primary boycott, 11
Primary employer, 11, 133
Protected activity, 11
Question concerning representation, 11, 175
Red circle rate, 11
Runaway shop, 11, 56
Scab, 11
Schism, 11, 175
Secondary activity, 11, 133
Secondary boycott, 11, 125
Secondary employer, 12, 133
Seniority, 12, 81
Steelworker's trilogy, 12, 86

TERMINOLOGY USED IN LABOR RELATIONS—Cont'd
Strike, 12, 50
Sympathy strike, 12
Twenty-Four Hour Rule 12, 180
Unfair labor practice strike, 12, 50
Unilateral action, 12, 74
Union, 12
Union security, 13, 81
Union shop, 13, 81
Unprotected activity, 13, 32–35
Whipsaw strike, 13
Wildcat strike, 13
Yellow dog contract, 13, 20

TITLE VII
Civil Rights Act, 188

TREE FRUITS DOCTRINE
Picketing and boycotts, 142

TWENTY–FOUR HOUR RULE
Representation proceedings, 180

UNFAIR LABOR PRACTICE STRIKER
Rights of strikers, 50

UNION UNFAIR LABOR PRACTICES
Analysis of a labor law problem, 6
Discharges caused by unions, 117
Discriminatory or excessive union initiation fees, 121
Duty to represent all employees in bargaining unit fairly, 108
Exclusive hiring hall requires employer to hire all employees through a hall, 117
Failure to process grievance in good faith violates Section 8(b)(1)(A), p. 109
Featherbedding, 121
Fines, 112
Introduction, 104
N.L.R.B. lacks authority to determine reasonableness of otherwise valid union discipline, 113
Remedies for union unfair labor practices, 119
Restraint or coercion of employees, 105
Restraint or coercion of employer by union, 115
Strikes against health care institutions, 123
Supervisor-members subject to discipline by union for crossing picket line, 116
Suspension, 112

INDEX
References are to Pages

UNION UNFAIR LABOR PRACTICES —Cont'd
Union may expel member to protect itself, 114
Union may fine members for crossing picket line, 112
    May not limit employee's right to utilize board's processes, 114
    Responsible for picket line misconduct, 106
Union's duty to bargain, 119
    To bargaining unit employees, differing views of court and board, 108
    To represent employees in the bargaining unit, 107
Union's right to govern its internal affairs, 110
Unlawful conduct during negotiations does not mean that union bargained in bad faith, 120

UNION'S DUTY TO BARGAIN
Union unfair labor practices, 119

UNION'S DUTY TO REPRESENT EMPLOYEES IN BARGAINING UNIT
Union unfair labor practices, 107

UNION'S RIGHT TO GOVERN ITS INTERNAL AFFAIRS
Union unfair labor practices, 110

UNIT CLARIFICATION
Representation proceedings, 177

VOCABULARY
See pages 7–13 for alphabetical listing of Terminology Used in Labor Relations

WAGNER ACT
National Labor Relations Act of 1935, p. 24

WALSH–HEALEY PUBLIC CONTRACTS ACT
Other laws governing labor relations, 209

WORKING TIME
Communications among employees, 42

†

235